Projected Shadows

Projected Shadows presents a new collection of essays exploring films from a psychoanalytic perspective, focusing specifically on the representation of loss in European cinema. This theme is discussed in its many aspects, including: loss of hope and innocence, of youth, of consciousness, of freedom and loss through death. Many other themes familiar to psychoanalytic discourse are explored in the process, such as:

- Establishment and resolution of Oedipal conflicts
- Representation of pathological characters on the screen
- Use of unconscious defence mechanisms
- The interplay of dreams, reality and fantasy

Projected Shadows aims to deepen the ongoing constructive dialogue between psychoanalysis and film. Andrea Sabbadini has assembled a remarkable number of internationally renowned contributors, both academic film scholars and psychoanalysts from a variety of cultural backgrounds, who use an array of contemporary methodologies to apply psychoanalytic thinking to film.

This original collection will appeal to anyone passionate about film, as well as professionals, academics and students interested in the relationship between psychoanalysis and the arts.

Andrea Sabbadini is a Fellow of the Institute of Psychoanalysis and honorary senior lecturer at University College London. He has published extensively in psychoanalytic journals, and edited books including *Even Paranoids Have Enemies* (Routledge, 1998) and *The Couch and the Silver Screen; Psychoanalytic Reflections on European Cinema* (Brunner-Routledge, 2003).

THE NEW LIBRARY OF PSYCHOANALYSIS
General Editor   Dana Birksted-Breen

The New Library of Psychoanalysis was launched in 1987 in association with the Institute of Psychoanalysis, London. It took over from the International Psychoanalytical Library which published many of the early translations of the works of Freud and the writings of most of the leading British and Continental psychoanalysts.

The purpose of the New Library of Psychoanalysis is to facilitate a greater and more widespread appreciation of psychoanalysis and to provide a forum for increasing mutual understanding between psychoanalysts and those working in other disciplines such as the social sciences, medicine, philosophy, history, linguistics, literature and the arts. It aims to represent different trends both in British psychoanalysis and in psychoanalysis generally. The New Library of Psychoanalysis is well placed to make available to the English-speaking world psychoanalytic writings from other European countries and to increase the interchange of ideas between British and American psychoanalysts.

The Institute, together with the British Psychoanalytical Society, runs a low-fee psychoanalytic clinic, organizes lectures and scientific events concerned with psychoanalysis and publishes the *International Journal of Psychoanalysis*. It also runs the only UK training course in psychoanalysis which leads to membership of the International Psychoanalytical Association – the body which preserves internationally agreed standards of training, of professional entry, and of professional ethics and practice for psychoanalysis as initiated and developed by Sigmund Freud. Distinguished members of the Institute have included Michael Balint, Wilfred Bion, Ronald Fairbairn, Anna Freud, Ernest Jones, Melanie Klein, John Rickman and Donald Winnicott.

Previous General Editors include David Tuckett, Elizabeth Spillius and Susan Budd. Previous and current Members of the Advisory Board include Christopher Bollas, Ronald Britton, Catalina Bronstein, Donald Campbell, Sara Flanders, Stephen Grosz, John Keene, Eglé Laufer, Juliet Mitchell, Michael Parsons, Rosine Jozef Perelberg, Richard Rusbridger, David Taylor and Mary Target.

ALSO IN THIS SERIES

Impasse and Interpretation Herbert Rosenfeld
Psychoanalysis and Discourse Patrick Mahony
The Suppressed Madness of Sane Men Marion Milner
The Riddle of Freud Estelle Roith
Thinking, Feeling, and Being Ignacio Matte-Blanco
The Theatre of the Dream Salomon Resnik
Melanie Klein Today: Volume 1, Mainly Theory Edited by Elizabeth Bott Spillius
Melanie Klein Today: Volume 2, Mainly Practice Edited by Elizabeth Bott Spillius
Psychic Equilibrium and Psychic Change: Selected Papers of Betty Joseph Edited by Michael Feldman and Elizabeth Bott Spillius
About Children and Children-No-Longer: Collected Papers 1942–80 Paula Heimann. Edited by Margret Tonnesmann
The Freud–Klein Controversies 1941–45 Edited by Pearl King and Riccardo Steiner
Dream, Phantasy and Art Hanna Segal
Psychic Experience and Problems of Technique Harold Stewart
Clinical Lectures on Klein and Bion Edited by Robin Anderson
From Fetus to Child Alessandra Piontelli
A Psychoanalytic Theory of Infantile Experience: Conceptual and Clinical Reflections E. Gaddini. Edited by Adam Limentani
The Dream Discourse Today Edited and introduced by Sara Flanders
The Gender Conundrum: Contemporary Psychoanalytic Perspectives on Feminitity and Masculinity Edited and introduced by Dana Breen
Psychic Retreats John Steiner
The Taming of Solitude: Separation Anxiety in Psychoanalysis Jean-Michel Quinodoz
Unconscious Logic: An Introduction to Matte-Blanco's Bi-logic and its Uses Eric Rayner
Understanding Mental Objects Meir Perlow
Life, Sex and Death: Selected Writings of William Gillespie Edited and introduced by Michael Sinason
What Do Psychoanalysts Want? The Problem of Aims in Psychoanalytic Therapy Joseph Sandler and Anna Ursula Dreher
Michael Balint: Object Relations, Pure and Applied Harold Stewart
Hope: A Shield in the Economy of Borderline States Anna Potamianou
Psychoanalysis, Literature and War: Papers 1972–1995 Hanna Segal
Emotional Vertigo: Between Anxiety and Pleasure Danielle Quinodoz
Early Freud and Late Freud Ilse Grubrich-Simitis
A History of Child Psychoanalysis Claudine and Pierre Geissmann
Belief and Imagination: Explorations in Psychoanalysis Ronald Britton

A Mind of One's Own: A Kleinian View of Self and Object
    Robert A. Caper
Psychoanalytic Understanding of Violence and Suicide Edited by Rosine Jozef
    Perelberg
On Bearing Unbearable States of Mind Ruth Riesenberg-Malcolm
Psychoanalysis on the Move: The Work of Joseph Sandler Edited by Peter Fonagy,
    Arnold M. Cooper and Robert S. Wallerstein
The Dead Mother: The Work of André Green Edited by Gregorio Kohon
The Fabric of Affect in the Psychoanalytic Discourse André Green
The Bi-Personal Field: Experiences of Child Analysis Antonino Ferro
*The Dove that Returns, the Dove that Vanishes: Paradox and Creativity in
    Psychoanalysis* Michael Parsons
*Ordinary People, Extra-ordinary Protections: A Post-Kleinian Approach to the
    Treatment of Primitive Mental States* Judith Mitrani
The Violence of Interpretation: From Pictogram to Statement
    Piera Aulagnier
The Importance of Fathers: A Psychoanalytic Re-Evaluation Judith Trowell and
    Alicia Etchegoyen
Dreams That Turn Over a Page: Paradoxical Dreams in Psychoanalysis Jean-Michel
    Quinodoz
The Couch and the Silver Screen: Psychoanalytic Reflections on European Cinema
    Edited and introduced by Andrea Sabbadini
In Pursuit of Psychic Change: The Betty Joseph Workshop Edited by Edith
    Hargreaves and Arturo Varchevker
*The Quiet Revolution in American Psychoanalysis: Selected Papers of Arnold M.
    Cooper* Arnold M. Cooper. Edited and introduced by Elizabeth L.
    Auchincloss
*Seeds of Illness and Seeds of Recovery: The Genesis of Suffering and the Role of
    Psychoanalysis* Antonino Ferro
The Work of Psychic Figurability: Mental States Without Representation César
    Botella and Sára Botella
*Key Ideas for a Contemporary Psychoanalysis: Misrecognition and Recognition of the
    Unconscious* André Green
*The Telescoping of Generations: Listening to the Narcissistic Links Between
    Generations* Haydée Faimberg
Glacial Times: A Journey Through the World of Madness Salomon Resnik
This Art of Psychoanalysis: Dreaming Undreamt Dreams and Interrupted Cries
    Thomas H. Ogden
Psychoanalysis as Therapy and Storytelling Antonino Ferro
Psychoanalysis and Religion in the 21st Century: Competitors or Collaborators?
    Edited by David M. Black
Recovery of the Lost Good Object Eric Brenman
The Many Voices of Psychoanalysis Roger Kennedy

Feeling the Words: Neuropsychoanalytic Understanding of Memory and the Unconscious Mauro Mancia

Projected Shadows: Psychoanalytic Reflections on the Representation of Loss in European Cinema Edited by Andrea Sabbadini

TITLES IN THE NEW LIBRARY OF PSYCHOANALYSIS
TEACHING SERIES

Reading Freud: A Chronological Exploration of Freud's Writings Jean-Michel Quinodoz

THE NEW LIBRARY OF PSYCHOANALYSIS

General Editor: Dana Birksted-Breen

Projected Shadows

Psychoanalytic Reflections on the
Representation of Loss in European Cinema

Edited by Andrea Sabbadini

Routledge
Taylor & Francis Group
LONDON AND NEW YORK

First published 2007
by Routledge
27 Church Road, Hove, East Sussex BN3 2FA

Simultaneously published in the USA and Canada
by Routledge
270 Madison Avenue, New York, NY 10016

Routledge is an imprint of the Taylor & Francis Group, an informa business

© 2007 selection and editorial matter, Andrea Sabbadini;
individual chapters, the contributors

Typeset in Bembo by RefineCatch Limited, Bungay, Suffolk
Printed and bound in Great Britain by TJ International Ltd, Padstow, Cornwall
Cover design by Sandra Heath

All rights reserved. No part of this book may be reprinted or
reproduced or utilized in any form or by any electronic,
mechanical, or other means, now known or hereafter
invented, including photocopying and recording, or in any
information storage or retrieval system, without permission in
writing from the publishers.

This publication has been produced with paper manufactured to
strict environmental standards and with pulp derived from
sustainable forests.

British Library Cataloguing in Publication Data
A catalogue record for this book is available from the British Library

Library of Congress Cataloging-in-Publication Data
Projected shadows : psychoanalytic reflections on the representation of loss in European
cinema / edited by Andrea Sabbadini.
  p. cm. — (The new library of psychoanalysis)
Includes bibliographical references and index.
ISBN-13: 978-0-415-42816-3 (hardback)
ISBN-10: 0-415-42816-5 (hardback)
ISBN-13: 978-0-415-42817-0 (pbk.)
ISBN-10: 0-415-42817-3 (pbk.)
1. Loss (Psychology) in motion pictures.   I. Sabbadini, Andrea.
PN1995.9.L59P76 2007
791.43′653—dc22
                                                                    2006038585

ISBN 978–0–415–42816–3 (hbk)
ISBN 978–0–415–42817–0 (pbk)

Contents

Contributors	xi
Foreword GLEN O. GABBARD	xv
Acknowledgements	xxi
Introduction ANDREA SABBADINI	1
1 The night of melancholia and the daylight of mourning: Anne Fontaine's *Comment j'ai tué mon père* T. JEFFERSON KLINE	6
2 Quest for a lost mother: Alina Marazzi's *Un'ora sola ti vorrei* PIETRO ROBERTO GOISIS	21
3 Is there light at the end of the tunnel? Keren Yedaya's *Or (Mon Tresor)* SHIMSHON WIGODER AND EMANUEL BERMAN	35
4 The anorexic paradox: Matteo Garrone's *First Love* MARIA VITTORIA COSTANTINI AND PAOLA GOLINELLI	46
5 Reparation and the empathic other: Christian Petzold's *Wolfsburg* RALF ZWIEBEL	56
6 The talking cure from Freud to Almodóvar: *Hable con ella* ANDREA SABBADINI	65

Contents

7   Intergenerational transmission: the Holocaust in Central European
    cinema   73
    CATHERINE PORTUGES

8   Cut and laced: traumatism and fetishism in Luis Buñuel's
    Un Chien Andalou   92
    ANDREW WEBBER

9   Two short films by Jan Svankmajer: *Jabberwocky* and *Punch and Judy*   102
    HELEN TAYLOR ROBINSON

10 Compilation film as 'deferred action': Vincent Monnikendam's
    Mother Dao, the Turtle-like   109
    LAURA MULVEY

11 Moving beyond the constraints of the mortal self: universal images
    of narcissism in Jan Troell's *The Flight of the Eagle*   119
    LISSA WEINSTEIN

12 Tricycles, bicycles, life cycles: psychoanalytic perspectives on
    childhood loss and transgenerational parenting in Sylvain Chômet's
    Belleville Rendez-Vous   132
    ALEXANDER STEIN

13 Loss, mourning and desire in midlife: François Ozon's *Under the
    Sand* and *Swimming Pool*   145
    DIANA DIAMOND

14 Three sisters: sibling knots in Bergman's *Cries and Whispers*   160
    ANDREA SABBADINI

15 Time regained: the complex magic of reverse motion   168
    IAN CHRISTIE

    Films index   183

    Index   185

Contributors

Emanuel Berman Ph.D. is a Professor of Psychology at the University of Haifa, and a Training Analyst at the Israel Psychoanalytic Institute. He edited *Essential Papers on Literature and Psychoanalysis* (NYU Press, 1993) and authored *Impossible Training: A Relational View of Psychoanalytic Education* (Analytic Press, 2004). He is the editor of Hebrew translations of Freud, Ferenczi, Balint, Winnicott, Mannoni, Hanna Segal and Ogden. His work appeared in Gabbard's *Psychoanalysis and Film* (Karnac, 2001) and in Sabbadini's *The Couch and the Silver Screen* (Brunner-Routledge, 2003).

Ian Christie is a film historian, writer and broadcaster, and Professor of Film and Media History at Birkbeck College, University of London. He has published extensively on Russian cinema, Powell and Pressburger and Scorsese, as well as on the relationship between film and the visual arts – which was the subject of his Slade Professorship lectures at Cambridge in 2006 and of his contribution to the Victoria & Albert Museum's exhibition, *Modernism: Designing a New World*, also in 2006.

Maria Vittoria Costantini is a psychiatrist and psychoanalyst of the Società Psicoanalitica Italiana (SPI), and Professor of Psychoanalytic Diagnostics at the Institute of Psychology of the University of Padua. She is concerned with theoretical and clinical issues on loss, separation and working through, and with applied psychoanalysis, with a special interest in cinema.

Diana Diamond is Associate Professor in the Doctoral Program in Clinical Psychology at the City University of New York, and Adjunct Assistant Professor of Psychiatry at the New York Presbyterian Hospital-Weill Cornell Medical Center. She has co-authored *Affect and Attachment in the Family* (Basic Books, 1994), *Borderline Patients: Extending the Limits of Treatability* (Basic Books, 2000) and other books, and has published articles on attachment theory, borderline personality disorder, trauma studies and film and psychoanalysis. She is on the editorial board of *Psychoanalytic Inquiry*, co-editor of a volume produced by *Psychoanalytic Inquiry* (Analytic Press, 1998) on film and psychoanalysis (*Projections of Psychic Reality: A Centennial of Psychoanalysis and Film*) and of a four volume monograph series on *Attachment Research and Psychoanalysis* (Analytic Press, 1999, 2000, 2003, 2007). She is a psychoanalytic candidate at the New York University Postdoctoral Program in Psychoanalysis, in private practice in New York.

Glen O. Gabbard is Brown Foundation Chair of Psychoanalysis and Professor of Psychiatry at Baylor College of Medicine in Houston, Texas. He is also Joint Editor-in-Chief of the *International Journal of Psychoanalysis*. He is the author or editor of 20 books, including *Psychiatry and the Cinema* and *Film and Psychoanalysis*. He was the first Film Review Editor of the *International Journal of Psychoanalysis*. He has won many awards, including the Mary Sigourney Award in 2000 for outstanding contributions to psychoanalysis.

Pietro Roberto Goisis is a psychiatrist and a full member of the SPI (Società Psicoanalitica Italiana) and of the IPA. He is responsible for the 'Film and Psychoanalysis' section of the SPI website and has been the chairman of several events on cinema and psychoanalysis. He is the author of a number of educational videos and has already presented his work (on two families of Italian film directors) at *epff2*.

Paola Golinelli, the Italian Consultant of *epff*, is a full member of the SPI (Società Italiana di Psicoanalisi) and Foreign Secretary of its Board. She is also a member of the Croatian Sponsoring Committee, having been engaged since 1994 in the programme of developing psychoanalysis in that country. She is interested in the creative process and in the interrelation between psychoanalysis and the arts, with a special interest in cinema, painting and poetry.

T. Jefferson Kline is Professor of French at Boston University. His publications include *Andre Malraux and the Metamorphosis of Death* (Columbia University Press, 1973), *Bertolucci's Dream Loom: A Psychoanalytic Study of Cinema* (University of Massachusetts Press, 1987), *Screening the Text: Intertextuality in New Wave French Film* (Johns Hopkins University Press, 1992), *Bernardo Bertolucci Interviews* (co-edited with Bruce Sklarew and Fabien Gerard) (University of Mississippi Press, 2000), and articles on the French novel, French theatre and European cinema. Kline is now at work on *The Cinema and its Doubles*, a project intended to explore cinema's 'co-optation' of rival aesthetic, cultural and psychological domains. He currently serves on the editorial board of *Studies in French Cinema* (UK).

Laura Mulvey is professor of Film and Media Studies at Birkbeck College,

University of London, and the author of *Visual and Other Pleasures* (Macmillan, 1989), *Fetishism and Curiosity* (British Film Institute, 1996) and *Citizen Kane* (British Film Institute, 1996). She has co-directed six films with Peter Wollen, including *Riddles of the Sphinx* (BFI, 1978) and *Frida Kahlo and Tina Modotti* (Arts Council, 1980) and, with artist/film-maker Mark Lewis, *Disgraced Monuments* (Channel 4, 1994). She has just completed *Death 24 x a Second: Stillness and the Moving Image* (Reaktion Books, 2006).

Catherine Portuges is Director, Interdepartmental Program in Film Studies; Professor & Graduate Program Director, Comparative Literature at the University of Massachusetts Amherst. She has published many papers and film reviews, is the author of *Screen Memories: the Hungarian Cinema of Márta Mészáros* (Indiana University Press, 1993) and co-editor of *Cinema in Transition, Gendered Subjects: the Dynamics of Feminist Pedagogy* (Temple University Press, 1999). A leading scholar of contemporary European cinema, with specialties in post-communist Eastern Europe and French film cultures, she is the founder and curator of the Massachusetts Multicultural Film Festival.

Andrea Sabbadini, the Chairman of *epff* and of the *Screening Conditions* series of films at the ICA, is a Fellow of the Institute of Psychoanalysis, honorary senior lecturer at University College London, and the book review editor of *The International Journal of Psychoanalysis*. He has published extensively in psychoanalytic journals and edited *Time in Psychoanalysis* (Feltrinelli, 1979), *Even Paranoids Have Enemies* (Routledge, 1998) and *The Couch and the Silver Screen: Psychoanalytic Reflections on European Cinema* (Brunner-Routledge, 2003).

Alexander Stein's pre-psychoanalytic career as a concert pianist continues to inform his listening and writing. He has authored numerous articles exploring the interrelationships between music and psychoanalysis, in addition to book reviews and psychoanalytic film essays. 'Music, Mourning, and Consolation', published in the *Journal of the American Psychoanalytic Assocation* (52/3), was a 2004 recipient of the prestigious Gradiva Award. He is on the editorial board of *The Psychoanalytic Review*, and is a reader for the Film Essay Section of the *International Journal of Psychoanalysis*. He is also a frequent presenter at international psychoanalytic and multidisciplinary conferences and symposia. He is a faculty member of The Institute for Expressive Analysis (IEA), member and training analyst of The National Psychological Association for Psychoanalysis (NPAP) in New York, and is in private practice.

Helen Taylor Robinson is a Fellow of the Institute of Psychoanalysis in full-time private practice, a child analyst and a contributor to previous *epff1* and *epff2* on Samuel Beckett's 'Film', with Juliet Stevenson and Ian Christie; on Michael Apted (on the relationship of fiction to documentary), and on the animated films of Ruth Lingford. She lectures and publishes on psychoanalysis and the arts and most recently spoke with Ian Christie, Ruth Lingford and Simon Pummell at the 'Animating the Unconscious' Symposium at the NFT.

Andrew Webber is Reader in Modern German and Comparative Culture in the University of Cambridge and a Fellow of Churchill College. He is the author of *The Doppelgänger* (OUP, 1996) and of *The European Avant-garde 1900–1940* (Polity, 2004) as well as of many essays on early and more recent film, especially its relationship to psychoanalysis. His current research project, supported by a Major Research Fellowship from the Leverhulme Trust, concerns the cultural topography of twentieth-century Berlin.

Lissa Weinstein is an Assistant Professor in the Doctoral Program in Clinical Psychology at the City University of New York. She is a graduate of the New York Psychoanalytic Institute and is currently on the faculty of the Columbia Center for Psychoanalytic Research and Training. Along with Arnold Wilson, she was the winner of the Heinz Hartmann Award for outstanding publication in the theory or practice of psychoanalysis by a recent graduate. She is the author of *Reading David: A Mother and Son's Journey through the Labyrinth of Dyslexia* (Penguin, 2003), which won the Margot Marek Prize from the International Dyslexia Association. She has published articles on the relevance of the work of Lev Vygotsky to psychoanalysis, Freud's theory of language and representation, as well as clinical papers on child psychoanalysis and film.

Shimshon Wigoder received his Ph.D. in clinical psychology at CSPP, Berkeley. In his training and work in San Francisco he specialized in psychotherapy with adults, adolescents, couples and families of diverse ethnic backgrounds. In Tel Aviv he maintains a private practice, teaches in the school of psychotherapy at Bar Ilan University, and is one of the founders and a candidate at the Tel-Aviv Institute of Contemporary Psychoanalysis. He published papers in the fields of psychoanalysis and literature and wrote the introduction to the Hebrew translation of Thomas Ogden's *The Primitive Edge of Experience* (Jason Aronson, 1989).

Ralf Zwiebel is a psychoanalyst and professor of psychoanalytical psychology at the University of Kassel and training analyst of the German Psychoanalytic Association (DPV) at the Alexander Mitscherlich-Institut in Kassel. He has been working on clinical issues of psychoanalysis, mainly countertransference; on inner working models of the analyst, including the reflecting function; on psychoanalytic education (especially at the university); on the relationships between psychoanalysis and Eastern philosophy (especially Zen Buddhism); and on film and psychoanalysis (with papers on Hitchcock and Kieslowski).

Foreword

Glen O. Gabbard

In an era when psychoanalysis as a clinical practice is beleaguered, psychoanalytic interdisciplinary studies appear to be thriving. The dialogue between psychoanalysis and cinema studies seems particularly alive with intellectual excitement. This superb new collection of essays, largely drawn from the third European Psychoanalytic Film Festival in November 2005, reflects that rich and productive interchange. A brief glance at the contributors reveals roughly equal numbers of academic film scholars and psychoanalysts. This new volume is further evidence that the relationship between the two disciplines is truly collaborative and not a sadomasochistic enterprise where one discipline is subjugated by the other. Andrea Sabbadini, the volume editor, has chosen to make the representation of loss the overarching theme of the essays. Indeed, the central organizing structure is the representation of traumatic losses. The cinema has always provided a unique opportunity to rework traumatic losses as one encounters them at a safe distance on the silver screen. A great many films depend on the recreation of infantile trauma and anxieties in the audience to compel re-viewings of the film over time. And how many love stories capitalize on the fact that the audience relives their own lost loves each time they sit through the breakup of a relationship on the screen?

Sabbadini also raises the possibility that there is something intrinsic in films regarding loss — in fact, he suggests that films themselves are forms of mourning and of recovering lost objects. Films are there for us when we need them. We have our favourite actors preserved on celluloid exactly as they were at the time we first viewed the film. They do not age. They do not die. They do not let us down. We return to the films again and again, knowing that we can recover these objects from our youth that have begun to fade with the passage of time. As we contemplate how the characters looked years ago, we remember how we ourselves looked, and we mourn the youth that has escaped us.

The contributions in this volume, however, transcend the elaboration of how loss is represented in the European cinema. The essays in this book offer an array of the contemporary methodologies used to apply psychoanalytic thinking to film (Gabbard 1997). No one approach is superior to others, and the very nature of film, with its shifting montages and its elusive visual effects, lends itself to multiple narratives and meanings. The playwright Tom Stoppard (1999: 8) once noted that, 'The question, "what does it mean?", has no correct answer. Every narrative has at least a capacity to suggest a meta-narrative'. Hence a number of approaches are useful, and several are illustrated in the essays contained herein.

The analysis of spectatorship centres on how the perspective of the camera creates a 'gaze' on the events of the film's narrative. Derived from the perspectives of Lacan and Derrida, the focus is on 'deep structures' at work in films and how meaning is generated in the cinema. Christian Metz (1982), one of the most articulate elaborators of this approach, notes that the experience of sitting in a darkened movie theatre is closely linked to the primal scene. He compares it to a theatrical production by noting that in film, the voyeurism is unauthorized, making it more forbidden. In live theatre, on the other hand, consent of the object being observed is intrinsic to the drama on stage.

Laura Mulvey (1975, 1989), a distinguished contributor to this volume, has been highly influential in her semiotic theories of the gaze. She wrote of the anxiety produced in the male viewer when watching a film. Borrowing Lacan's notion of 'lack', she suggested that the woman's body is fetishized in film because it produces anxiety in male audience members. For them, in Mulvey's view, the female body represents castration. Hence specific assumptions in the spectator interact with the visual aspects of the film to illuminate meanings.

This point of view has allowed psychoanalytic film criticism to go beyond the analysis of specific characters in the narrative as though they were patients on the couch. It offers a visual element that brings together cinema scholars and psychoanalysts. In the discussion of the Israeli film, *Or*, in Chapter 3, for example, Wigoder and Berman comment on the shower scene characterized by a motionless camera. The film refuses to manipulate the viewer by zooming in or concealing aspects of Or's body. As the authors note, the filmmaker challenges the viewer to take more responsibility. Moreover, the gaze of the camera more closely approximates that of the voyeur who is confined to one location and sees what is available from that location without the help of a cinematographer. At the end of the film, Or looks directly at the camera, implicating the audience in the phenomenon of teenage prostitution by the voyeuristic interest inherent in watching the film.

In his brilliant essay on *Un Chien Andalou*, Andrew Webber uses this semiotic methodology to understand the classic prologue in which the eye is cut by a razor blade. In this difficult-to-watch scene, the audience is punished for its voyeurism. The castration of the male viewer is graphically depicted in an upwardly displaced form, rather than allowing the female figure to serve as a fetish that defends against the castration anxieties of the audience. Buñuel forces the viewer to confront his fears rather than deny them.

In Sabbadini's chapter on *Talk to Her*, he notes that Almodóvar has always drawn the spectator into reconsidering standard assumptions about the nature of perversity. Almodóvar makes much of the male gaze, even within the film, by the motif of two devoted men watching over comatose women who don't know they are being watched. Moreover, the director has some fun with the trope of the female body as fetish. The scene in which Benigno watches a seven-minute silent film satirizes the male viewer's castration anxiety. The protagonist is shrunk to the size of Tom Thumb, and the camera follows him as he walks over the nude body of the sleeping woman. He scales the breasts as though they are mountains, and the camera lingers as he confronts the gaping maw between the sleeping woman's legs. The audience then watches him disappear into the vagina of the sleeping woman. Here Almodóvar suggests that more than castration anxiety is at work in the male viewer. Perhaps male audience members also struggle with a wish/fear of disappearing into the female character's womb, just as Benigno would like to crawl inside his comatose patient.

An entirely different methodological approach is featured in the discussion of Ozon's two films by Diana Diamond. She examines *Under the Sand* and *Swimming Pool* as examples of midlife transitions in the female protagonist. In this regard, she suggests that a universal developmental crisis is being depicted in the film and vicariously experienced by the audience. The intimate linkage of erotic fantasies of the Charlotte Rampling characters to the vicissitudes of ageing is beautifully depicted.

While the analysis of a character in the film as though he/she is a patient on the couch has fallen out of favour to some extent, some authors continue to use this approach effectively to discover meanings in a film. Lissa Weinstein does an admirable job in Chapter 11 of examining *The Flight of the Eagle*, Jan Troell's account of an ill-fated expedition to the North Pole in a hydrogen gas balloon. Weinstein's analysis of Andrée's narcissism allows the viewer to more fully grasp the motives inherent in the ill-fated attempt to land at the North Pole in his balloon. Perhaps the fact that Andrée was a real, live character rather than a fictional creation makes the application of our clinical understanding of narcissism particularly useful in this film. In this regard, Weinstein approaches the character in much the same way a psychobiographer would.

In his essay on Christian Petzold's film *Wolfsburg*, Ralf Zwiebel introduces a novel methodology. He suggests that we should consider a film a 'quasi-person'. We must ask of the film, 'Who is he?' and 'What is the meaning for the analyst watching the film?' Borrowing from the ideas of Gerhard Schneider, he advocates a decoding of the film's unconscious message by the analyst. He argues that repeated viewings are necessary to establish the relationship with the film in the same way that an analyst might establish a relationship with an analysand. Clearly, the meanings grasped in a single viewing would fall into a different category for Zwiebel.

Another novel approach to methodology is introduced by Laura Mulvey in her essay on compilation films. She borrows the Freudian concept of *Nachtraglichkeit*, involving the revision of past events through the lens of the contemporary perspective. Freud and many French analysts after him have spent a good deal of time processing the way that we all apply new meanings to old memories and experiences. Sometimes referred to as *après-coup* (Faimberg 2005), this concept underscores the fact that the retrospective understanding of past phenomena is invariably altered by the course of one's life experience and the perspective of a new developmental phase.

Using the Dutch film *Mother Dao, the Turtle-like* as an example, Mulvey illustrates how filmed events recorded in the past may be interspersed with more contemporary clips that provide a different perspective on the past events. She suggests that the temporality of film provides a bridge between this psychoanalytic phenomenon and the cinematic art form. She suggests that cinema has a unique ability to bear witness to the past and then carry the message forward.

Ian Christie ends the volume with another psychoanalytic reflection on the use of time in film. He notes the fascination we all have with reverse motion in the cinema. He cites numerous examples of how the audience's fantasy of restoring things to the way they used to be is fulfilled by this cinematic technique. I would add that the audience can vicariously experience doing and undoing as they contemplate their regrets or their wish to undo what is impossible to change. Christie's emphasis on the capacity to reverse time may also touch on a fundamental theme in the cinema – namely, escapism. Movies have always allowed us to harbour the illusion that truth is not as it is, but as we wish it to be.

As a whole, this volume is a state-of-the-art account of where we are today with the study of cinema through a psychoanalytic lens. Sabbadini has brought together a group of gifted authors who show that methodologies continue to evolve, while at the same time we can still mine the ore of the time-honoured traditions.

References

Faimberg, H. (2005) *The Telescoping of Generations*. London: Routledge.
Gabbard, G.O. (1997) Guest editorial: The psychoanalyst at the movies, *International Journal of Psycho-Analysis*, 78(3): 429–34.
Metz, C. (1982) *The Imaginary Signifier: Psychoanalysis and the Cinema*, trans. C. Britton et al. Bloomington, IN: Indiana University Press.

Mulvey, L. (1975) Visual pleasure and narrative cinema, *Screen*, 16: 6–18.
Mulvey, L. (1989) *Visual and Other Pleasures*. Bloominton, IN: Indiana University Press.
Stoppard, T. (1999) Pragmatic theatre, *New York Review of Books*, 23 September: 8–10.

Acknowledgements

Photographs appear by courtesy of the following individuals and organizations: Ciné B (*Comment j'ai tué mon père*); Alina Marazzi (*Un'ora sola ti vorrei*); Marc Rosenbaum (*Or*); Matteo Garrone and Fandango (*Primo amore*); Zweites Deutches Fernsehen (*Wolfsburg*); El Deseo S.A./Pathé (*Hable con ella*); Magyar Filmunio and Hungarian National Film Archives, Budapest (*Valalhól Europában; Apa; Sorstálanság*); Kino Video (*Un Chien Andalou*); Krátky Film Praha (*Zvahlav aneb Saticky Slameného Huberta; Rakvickarna*); Nederlandse Programma Stichting (*Moeder Dao, de schildpadg elijkende*); Adnorsk (*Ingenjör Andreées luftärd*); Sony Pictures Entertainment, Inc. (*Belleville Rendez-Vous*); Winstar Cinema (*Sous le sable*); Universal Cinemas (*Swimming Pool*); Svenska Filminstitutet (*Viskningar och rop*); British Film Institute Video Publishing (*Le Sang d'un poète; Le testament d'Orphée*); Kino Video/Mosfilm (*Idi I smotri*); Artificial Eye Video (*5 × 2*); Tartan Video (*Irréversible*).

I would also like to thank the Institute of Psychoanalysis for permission to reprint Chapter 12.

Stein, A. (2006) Tricycles, bicycles, life cycles: Psychoanalytic perspectives on childhood loss and transgenerational parenting in Les triplettes de Belleville (2003) [Film essay]. *International Journal of Psychoanalysis*, 87:1125–34. © Institute of Psychoanalysis, London, UK.

INTRODUCTION
Andrea Sabbadini

> Great lords, wise men ne'er sit and wail their loss,
> But cheerly seek how to redress their harms.
> William Shakespeare, *King Henry VI – Part Three*, 5, iv, 1–2

Much has been happening in the last few years in the interdisciplinary field of psychoanalytic film studies. With increasing frequency, psychoanalytic and academic institutions around the world have been organizing festivals, screenings followed by encounters between filmmakers and therapists, and conferences on analytic approaches to film criticism. Furthermore, there now exists a growing literature, and many dedicated websites and online discussion groups, on various aspects of the relationship between psychoanalysis and cinema.

The aim of *Projected Shadows: Psychoanalytic Reflections on the Representation of Loss in European Cinema* is to further deepen this ongoing, constructive dialogue between these two disciplines. This volume includes fifteen new essays written by internationally renowned psychoanalysts or film scholars from a variety of cultural backgrounds and ideological orientations, who propose here analytically-informed arguments and illustrate them with reflections on characters and scenes from recent European films.

All the chapters in the book are concerned with the representation of *loss*, explored in its many different aspects and meanings. As John Bowlby emphasized in his seminal text on the subject, 'there is a tendency to underestimate how intensely distressing and disabling loss usually is and for how long the distress, and often the disablement, commonly lasts' (1980: 8). While by no means attempting to cover exhaustively what is a vast theoretical and clinical field, the chapters nevertheless intend to articulate a coherent

Introduction

discourse on this theme and on others closely related to it. From the moment of birth when we lose the comfort of intrauterine life, to our last breath, losses of all kinds, and our efforts to gradually come to terms with them through mourning, constitute important points of reference in our existences. Each new loss is also a reminder of our own ultimate fragility, and a challenge to our unconscious fantasy of immortality. Such experiences, with all their painful or even traumatic connotations, can however also provide a stimulus to recovery, to learning and to creative growth, whenever a successful negotiation of ambivalent feelings can be accomplished. Shadows and lights complement each other.

What emerges from the chapters relates experiences of individual and collective loss, and their psychological implications, as they manifest themselves in the narratives of the films being discussed by our authors, and in the psychoanalytic interpretations they offer. Consistently with a developmental approach to our understanding of psychological events, losses and their emotional consequences – the 'shadows' of the book's title – are here reflected upon in the wider context of the passing of time, experienced as loss of what we used to have earlier, regardless of what may also have been gained through growing older.

Some of the essays collected here deal with the death of significant others. In the opening chapter, Kline, reflecting on Anne Fontaine's *Comment j'ai tué mon père*, considers the loss of the father in the context of the deliberately induced sense of uncanny, whereby we are led to believe in the actual reality of what may only be the protagonist's conflictual wishful thinking. Goisis, focusing on Alina Marazzi's documentary, analyses the loss by suicide of the young filmmaker's mother in the emotionally powerful biographical reconstruction of her life and mental illness (Chapter 2). Loss of both parents is explored by Stein in the context of a work of animated cinema about an orphaned boy raised by his grandmother to become a cycling champion (Chapter 12), while Sabbadini, revisiting Ingmar Bergman's *Cries and Whispers*, looks at the impact of losing a sister: two embittered women are unable to express grief for their sibling's death, while her servant, more in touch with her inner world, can experience true empathy (Chapter 14). Zwiebel, in his comments on Christian Petzold's *Wolfsburg*, describes the loss of a child's life following a road accident, where the man responsible for it runs away from his crime but not his guilt, and indulges in a 'perversion of reparation' by falling in love with the child's mother (Chapter 5).

Not all losses, however, involve the deaths of those close to us. Our lives can also be profoundly affected by losses of less tangible, if not always less painful, kinds. For instance, in the Israeli film *Or* reviewed by Wigoder and Berman, an adolescent girl, herself torn between contrasting drives and desires, tragically loses all hope as she fails to rescue her mother from prostitution and depression (Chapter 3); the loss of innocence is represented in two surrealistic

2

animation shorts, discussed by Taylor Robinson, that exemplify the conflictual coexistence of unrestrained id drives, the need to contain them, and the danger of destroying them through excessive controlling measures (Chapter 9). Webber refers to Vermeer's painting of *The Lacemaker* to emphasize the loss of clarity of vision, symbolically represented by lace – a blocking visual structure, but made of holes – in the context of Buñuel's fetishistic classic *Un Chien Andalou* (Chapter 8).

In her discussion of two films by François Ozon, Diamond dwells on the loss of youth: fantasy and reality, past and present, even life and death, are confounded, engaging the spectators with the anxieties and enchantments of midlife (Chapter 13). Costantini and Golinelli, reflecting on Matteo Garrone's *First Love*, comment on a woman's progressive loss, to the point of anorexic self-starvation, of body weight as her fear of being abandoned colludes with her lover's perverse needs (Chapter 4). The loss of consciousness in two young women in a state of coma is the theme of Pedro Almodóvar's *Hable con ella*, a title that, for Sabbadini, recalls Anna O's definition of psychoanalysis itself as 'the talking cure' (Chapter 6), while Weinstein reflects on the inevitability of the loss of narcissistic grandiosity in the protagonist of a Swedish documentary who has to confront the dire consequences of embarking on a manically unrealistic flight in a balloon over the North Pole (Chapter 11).

The loss of just about everything which is human is the theme of a number of recent Central European films on the Holocaust reviewed and discussed here by Portuges (Chapter 7). The loss of freedom and spontaneity in Indonesians working under their Dutch colonizers and their machines (including the movie camera itself!) – as portrayed in *Mother Dao*, a contemporary compilation of old documentaries – is the starting point for Mulvey's chapter. It focuses on the transformations of meaning when the same film material – a cultural artefact in its own right as well as a somewhat impermanent record of other cultural events – is placed in a different context (Chapter 10).

Something that emerges from this and other chapters in the book is also the close and profoundly complex relationship that both cinema and psychoanalysis have with time: for instance, in its relation to movement and to memory, or in the context of the phenomenon of *Nachtraglichkeit*, or in its paradoxical presence as timelessness in the unconscious. The inversion of time direction in films is the subject of the last chapter in the book, where Christie reviews and comments on the multiple uses of this technical potentiality of cinema throughout its history. I would add that the cinematic illusion to make time run backwards may conflict with our rational appreciation of the laws of causality, but is consistent with our unconscious wish-fulfilling fantasy to go back to a blissful *Aurea Aetas* preceding all suffering and all losses. It is almost as if cinema, having demonstrated throughout the book its power to represent all sorts of losses, would then also perform a final conjuror's trick and leave us with the illusion that none of it was really true as it could also be so easily undone . . .

In the real world of our everyday life, however, we know that losses of all kinds do occur all the time and that in order to psychologically survive we have somehow to come to terms with them. For instance, we are familiar from our psychoanalytic work, or even from our personal experience, with those many individuals with a characterological difficulty in reaching decisions. This condition, that may take the form of a combination of obsessionality and emotional paralysis, is often found to derive from a pathological incapacity to accept and mourn losses, in so far as the choice of one option inevitably involves the renunciation of another, at least whenever a compromise solution is not available. We are reminded here of the philosophical dilemma of 'The donkey of Buridano': placed equidistantly between two identical bales of hay, it starved to death because it could not decide which to choose – or, rather, which to give up.

In commenting about the mourning process of internalization and identification with what we have lost, Freud offered us the famous image of *the shadow of the object falling upon the ego* (1917: 249). Could we not understand this to be also a description of what cinema does to us spectators? Given the ubiquity and pervasive quality of these experiences, I would like to suggest that *all* films represent some sort of loss and, indeed, are themselves (among many other things, of course) forms of mourning and of recovering lost objects.

Film historians teach us that cinema (as well as, incidentally, psychoanalysis) was born in 1895, when the Lumière brothers showed their first films in public. However, the *idea* of cinema goes back more than two millennia, when Plato (360 BC) used the 'simile of the cave' to described how chained prisoners, unable to move or turn their heads back, would mistakenly believe that the wooden and stone statues carried in front of a fire behind them, and whose shadows were thus projected on the cave wall facing them, were real people and not simulacra. 'And so in every way', Plato concluded, 'they would believe that the shadows of the objects we mentioned were the whole truth' (*The Republic*: 241).

Similarly, the very nature of film is illusory, and for that reason emblematic. It rests on the deception of making us perceive that what is in front of our eyes is 'real', while in fact it only consists of lights and shadows; of showing us in the present (at the time of the screening) something that has occurred in the past (at the time of the shooting); of presenting us as three-dimensional 'moving' images what is but a sequence of 'stills', projected on a flat screen at the constant frequency of 24 frames per second.[2] Mostly because of the limitations of our optical apparatus, we fall for this deception every time. A blessing in disguise, I believe, because without it we would be deprived of all that cinema has to offer us . . .

Introduction

If, as I have emphasized, considerations centered around the representation of traumatic losses provide the central organizing structure to *Projected Shadows*, it is also true that many other themes familiar to psychoanalytic discourse are observed and discussed in these articles from the original perspective of their presence in European cinema. Problems in the establishment or in the resolution of Oedipal conflicts, the display of fundamental affective ambivalence in all relationships, the exploration of pathological characters, the use of unconscious defence mechanisms to protect ourselves from unacceptable realities, the disturbing presence of uncanny phenomena in our everyday life such as dreams or unclear boundaries between reality and fantasy . . . It is cinema's intrinsically ambiguous nature, as well as the contents of some of its best products such as those analysed in the chapters of the present volume, that has the power to stimulate creative thinking and strike emotional chords in all of us. Psychoanalysis has much to learn from films, and much to contribute to their interpretation and understanding.

Notes

1 Most of the chapters are revised and expanded versions of lectures originally presented at the Third European Psychoanalytic Film Festival (*epff3*) which took place in London in November 2005. The contributions to the first *epff* were published in Sabbadini (2003), while some of the essays presented at *epff2* are included in a monographic issue of *Psychoanalytic Inquiry*, edited by Harriet Kimble Wrye, Diana Diamond and Andrea Sabbadini, to come out in 2007.
2 New technologies, and in particular the digital revolution, have profound implications for our perception and experience of cinema. For a thorough exploration of these issues, see Mulvey (2006).

References

Bowlby, J. (1980) *Attachment and Loss, Vol. III: Loss: Sadness and Depression*. Harmondsworth: Penguin, 1981.
Freud, S. (1917) Mourning and melancholia, in *Standard Edition, Vol. XIV*. London: Hogarth Press, 1957, pp. 243–58.
Mulvey, L. (2006) *Death 24x a Second: Stillness and the Moving Image*. London: Reaktion Books.
Plato (360 BC) The simile of the cave, in *The Republic*, trans. and introduced by Desmond Lee. Harmondsworth: Penguin Classics, 1955, Part 7, para 7, pp. 240–8.
Sabbadini, A. (ed.) (2003) *The Couch and the Silver Screen: Psychoanalytic Reflections on European Cinema*. Hove: Brunner-Routledge.

1

THE NIGHT OF MELANCHOLIA AND THE DAYLIGHT OF MOURNING
Anne Fontaine's
Comment j'ai tué mon père

T. Jefferson Kline

> The dread of something after death – the undiscovered country from whose bourn no traveller returns – puzzles the will.
>
> *Hamlet*, III, 1

Comment j'ai tué mon père (*How I Killed My Father*) (France, 2001)
Director: Anne Fontaine
Distributor: A-Film Distribution

Moments into Anne Fontaine's *Comment j'ai tué mon père* Jean-Luc Borde (Charles Berling), a successful gerontologist, enters the living room of his sumptuous Versailles mansion, and distractedly opens his mail. A voiceover – apparently 'reading' the letter he holds – intones, 'We regret to inform you of the death of your father which occurred last month in Africa. He was unable to return to France as he had hoped'. As he finishes the letter, Jean-Luc sinks dejectedly onto the arm of a sofa and glances out the window at his wife, Isabelle (Natacha Régnier), reclining in a deckchair, then lapses into a kind of trance which is accompanied by lush but eerie chamber music. Fontaine effects a transition from Jean-Luc's vacant expression to a gala soirée which his wife Isa has organized to celebrate an award given to her husband in recognition of his civic service, by the Mayor of Versailles. In the middle of his speech thanking the Town of Versailles for this honour, Jean-Luc realizes that the letter announcing his father's death is apparently either a sadistic joke or a terrible mistake, for there, standing before him, is his father, Maurice (Michel Bouquet).

Rather than rush to greet his father with happy effusion, Jean-Luc simply asks emotionlessly, 'How long have you been in Versailles [and] what are you doing here?' Maurice happily answers the first question and ignores the second. His purpose will only gradually, and painfully, become apparent. Indeed, the film follows Maurice as he moves through the next few days as a guest of his son, wandering about the town, visiting Jean-Luc's clinic, getting to know Isabelle and Jean-Luc's brother, Patrick (Stephane Guillon) and causing a rapidly escalating degree of discomfort for his son. What Jean-Luc's father discovers is that his son is emotionally dead, his marriage to Isa overshadowed by Jean-Luc's false diagnosis of Isa that claims medically to eliminate the possibility of their having children. Maurice's presence also provokes Jean-Luc's brother Patrick to break free of his deadening enslavement to Jean-Luc, and Jean-Luc's mistress to end his manipulations of her. So angered is Jean-Luc by his father's intrusiveness in his life that he assaults him after dinner one night, throws him to the ground and chokes him to death.

Or does he? Leaving his father's lifeless body on the lawn, Jean-Luc retreats to the lavatory where he stares bewildered at his image in the mirror. Suddenly a knock on the door jolts him out of his reverie and he hears his father's voice pleading, 'Open the door! Don't leave me in this hole!' Jean-Luc opens the door to find his father 'undead'. The scene fades out as Jean-Luc, standing directly behind Maurice, begins gently to stroke his father's right temple. Fontaine cuts from this scene back to Jean-Luc sitting on the couch in his living room, where we had left him at the beginning of the film, still holding the letter announcing his father's death, still staring out of the window at Isa, reclining in a deckchair.

Certainly, Anne Fontaine is not the first director to choose to introduce into her film a character who is entirely the product of another's imagination. *The Swimming Pool* (Ozon 2004; see Chapter 13), *A Beautiful Mind* (Howard 2001) and *Fight Club* (Fincher 1999) have used this narrative 'trick' with enormous effectiveness. Both of these latter two films catch us off guard at the end and cause us to re-evaluate what we have seen as the hallucinations of a schizophrenic (split personality). Like Ozon's film, what makes Fontaine's film different, and very much worth our attention, is the fact that we are not dealing with a delusion, but a fantasy – what Anne Fontaine terms 'a blend of dreams and memory'.[1] The more we look at Fontaine's film, the more we realize that the letter Jean-Luc is reading produces a long fantasy involving his dead father – indeed a fantasy that is the product of mourning and melancholia. This interpretation seems to have entirely escaped most critics of this film, including such 'stars' as Roger Ebert, Tom Dawson, Elvis Mitchel and Ty Burr, who either bemoan the film's flatness or, sensing that something is going on, resort to such labels as 'a Freudian self-help pamphlet'.[2]

What is remarkable, then, in Fontaine's narrative structure is not the *fact* of dissociation per se, but *the process of mourning* in which Jean-Luc engages and *the interpretation* that this process elicits. The factors that determine the 'irreality' of the diegesis of this film are subtle, but multiple. Not only does the film use a return to 'the present' (Jean-Luc sitting, reading the same letter, dressed in the same clothes, with Isa in the same position, also wearing the same clothes as in the opening scene), but it punctuates every one of its scenes with the same portrait of Jean-Luc, with the same faraway look in his eyes as he had at the fading of this first scene, accompanied by the same darkly emotive chamber music. It is thus that Fontaine situates the point of view of the entire film in Jean-Luc's 'imagined perception' of the events. Frequently we will view a scene and then discover that Jean-Luc has magically materialized at a window or doorway or shadowy corner looking on.[3] In other cases, Fontaine abandons the semblance of reality (e.g. his brother Patrick's comic monologues presumably delivered in a comedy club in Versailles) for a dream-like fantasy (e.g. all of Patrick's monologues after the first two are delivered in a dreamy tone against a blue backdrop, without any of the audience responses we expect in a nightclub).

From his first appearance Maurice presents his status as existentially ambiguous. He makes no answer when Jean-Luc says, 'I thought you were dead!' but confirms that he has been able to make this visit '*à mes risques et périls*'. When his son guesses, 'Are you retired now?', he cleverly equivocates, 'Oh, not entirely, would you believe?' When asked if he'd like to try Jean-Luc's gerontological experiments, Maurice replies artfully, 'Oh no, I don't want to delay the call . . . Perhaps it will surprise you but I don't think about death any more.' While at the restaurant, faced with another 'guess' at his condition ('You're in very good shape'), Maurice allows that 'the machine has had a few classical breakdowns' – we might read 'death' here! And finally, in a highly ambiguous exchange with Jean-Luc purportedly about Africa, Maurice exclaims, Orpheus-like, 'There are even people who are returning!' And, to Jean-Luc's incredulous reply, 'Don't tell me you're one of them!', Maurice intones with a sphinx-like smile, 'Listen, I wouldn't have believed it, but it seems as though it IS possible.'

Maurice manages, moreover, to find his way into the lives of every one of Jean-Luc's intimates (wife, brother, mistress) in ways that defy rational geography or explanation. Even his old white Dauphine makes an appearance in a purely associative way after Jean-Luc's own car has crashed and Jean-Luc is remembering a moment when his father's car had broken down in Spain.

In a film that is presumably about his father's effect on his life, it is astonishing that there is not a single flashback. Everything in the film has an eerily produced sense of present tense with no reference to any clock or calendar to situate present time. We can only conclude that this is a fantasy constructed like a dream, but clearly situated in the mind of a man awake. Like a dream, it

The night of melancholia

seems to compress a large amount of imagery into a very brief period of time. What is this fantasy – how would it be different from psychotic delusion and what implications does it have for our reading of this film?

Susan Isaacs (1943) has noted that phantasy is a common means of externalizing psychic contents and that fantasy often works (as it seems to here) in sudden unintentional representations that intrude on the ego. In this sudden break in continuity, there occurs an incongruous shift from present conscious concerns signalling that the ego has renounced its own self-government and becomes a spectator of psychic images, often representations of libidinal destructive instincts. Inasmuch as, like dreams, the content of phantasy arises from the unconscious, it is less dependent on words than on plastic images. Often, Isaacs notes, the phantasy is produced as a kind of call for help. These images do not form the basis for the ego's continuing interactions with its surroundings (as would be the case in a psychotic delusion in which a fictional person would be understood to enter the subject's real situation) but rather represent a kind of 'time-out' from the real during which the ego may 'work through' previously unconscious material (p. 112).

To understand quite suddenly, as Fontaine's viewer is forced to do, that all that we have imagined to be reality is but fantasy, is to necessitate a retrospective re-evaluation and interpretation of everything we have heretofore believed to be simply 'how things are'. And as our viewers' minds move backwards through the material represented to us (presumably by Jean-Luc Borde), we find ourselves exactly replicating the work of at least three other important states: that of the mourner confronting his loss, that of the dreamer confronting the manifest content of his dream, and that of the analyst faced with material produced by the analysand. Let us examine each of these three psychological moments.

Mourning, as Freud (1917: 243–5) notes in 'Mourning and Melancholia',

> is regularly the reaction to the loss of a loved person [and] although mourning involves grave departures from the normal attitude to life, it never occurs to us to regard it as a pathological condition . . . Profound mourning involves loss of interest in the outside world and the turning away from any activity that is not connected with thoughts of him . . . and can be so intense that a turning away from reality takes place and a clinging to the object through the medium of a hallucinatory wishful psychosis. Normally respect for reality gains the day . . . bit by bit, at a great expense of cathectic energy, but in the meantime the existence of the lost object is psychically prolonged . . . Each single one of the memories and expectations in which the libido is bound to the object is brought up and hypercathected, and detachment of the ego is accomplished in respect of it.

As Alicia Ricciardi has noted, there are numerous connections between mourning and psychoanalysis, first of all because 'for Freud, analysis will always be an act of mourning, for without its focus on the subject's lost history, psychoanalysis would lose its *raison d'être*'. Thus, the '*Trauerarbeit*, like psychoanalysis, is a transformative activity that occurs over a long period. And like analysis, the work of mourning assumes a productive value' (2003: 19, 21, 22).

Although Freud himself was careful to separate *Trauerarbeit* from his work on dreams, it is significant that the first word of his essay on mourning is, in fact, the word 'Dreams' (1917: 243). Thus, despite his attempt to keep them separate, I would like to suggest that the two activities, the *Trauerarbeit* and the *Traumarbeit* may be to some degree unconsciously conflated, despite Freud's argument that the former was more concerned with reality testing and the latter with primary process and associations. Yet, as Ricciardi notes, 'The work of mourning mimics the labor of analysis in the sense that the very rhythms of the subject's withdrawal from the object and of the analysand's uncovering of repressed material are similarly defined by a *pars destruens* that resolves otherwise obscure psychic components into their discrete elements and that represents the necessary conditions of any further reshaping of the psyche' (2003: 26–7). Indeed, such might be the very latent sense of Freud's essay, for the more mourning and analysis progress, the more indistinguishable become the subject's distortions of reality and the very reality he seeks to recover 'bit by bit'.

Such would certainly be the sense of the second reading necessitated by the structure of Anne Fontaine's film, for the conclusion of the film jolts us into the realization that what we have been watching is not a distressing reality to which Jean-Luc begrudgingly submits, but a self-punishing fantasy which he unconsciously creates. Now we are forced to attempt to parse out two Jean-Lucs: the one whose unconscious produces the images we see vs the Jean-Luc represented as a fantasy.

What becomes gradually and painfully apparent in our re-reading of the film is the massively deadening nature of this fantasized self. In Fontaine's presentation of Jean-Luc's father's imagined return, the director mobilizes two dominant allusions to 'explain' this deadness: Hamlet and Pygmalion. As he begins to make his speech accepting the honour that the Mayor of Versailles has just bestowed upon him, Jean-Luc suddenly catches sight of what we may now call 'the ghost of his father' standing in the crowd before him. The apparition of his father's ghost leads Hamlet, as we remember, to his confrontation with a series of terrible truths about his incestuous and murderous feelings about his mother and father, that culminate in his conclusion that life is but 'the heartache and the thousand natural shocks that flesh is heir to'.[4] Indeed, Hamlet asks 'who would fardels bear, to grunt and sweat under a weary life, but for the dread of something after death' (*Hamlet*, III, 1). As if on cue, Jean-Luc, faced with his father's ghost, loses the thread of his acceptance speech and finds himself intoning, '*Mais tout le monde sait que la vie est tout de même un fardeau . . .*' (But everyone knows that life is a burden, all the same . . .), and his voice trails off into perplexed silence. '*Fardeau*' is an exact 'replica' of Hamlet's word '*fardels*' and this allusive lapsus unveils a side of this very successful physician we had not expected to see: the melancholic.

From here on out, we witness a fantasy that puts into play an image of Jean-Luc that is, as R.D. Laing (1965: 40–1) would put it, 'life without feeling alive', or 'cathecting his ego-as-object with mortido' (p. 112). Elsewhere Laing refers to this state as 'petrification . . . the dread of being turned from a live person into a stone' which often results in 'the "magical" act whereby one may attempt to turn someone else into stone . . . since the very act of experiencing the other as a person is felt as virtually suicidal' (pp. 46–7).[5] As we come to realize, Jean-Luc is not only unable to express any feeling for others, he is massively dedicated to transforming everyone around him from living beings to statues – an uncanny reversal of Pygmalion's 'birthing' of Galatea from her stone statue, but one very much in keeping with Ovid's more general tendency in *The Metamorphoses* toward prosopopoeia, a rhetorical figure that J. Hillis Miller (1990: 4) labels 'the trope of mourning'.[6]

In their first scene alone together, Jean-Luc's wife Isa mechanically takes a smorgasbord of pills before going to bed, all presumably prescribed by her doctor-husband to help her sleep. Later we are to learn that Jean-Luc has also medically proscribed having any children, thereby depriving her of her life's fondest wish and, along the way, turned their relationship into what Isa will angrily denounce as '*une vitrine*' (window dressing) and allowed her only to 'greet the guests, open the door, smile, put flowers on the table'. And this accusation is accompanied by her realization that he is 'a dried up man, all shrunk to nothing, which speaks, but nothing comes out. There's no flesh and blood there'. To which Jean-Luc confesses helplessly, '*Tout ça* [the idea of raising and loving children] *ça m'effrayait. Prendre en charge, élever, s'inquiéter, punir . . . Pour tout ça je suis inapte*'.[7] And in yet another confession of the lonely sterility of his life, he has earlier confessed to Maurice that, 'the truth is that nine out of ten times we screw alone [*tout seul*]'.

Every shot of Jean-Luc up until this accusation fully corroborates Isa's fury: he treats his patients with undisguised disdain, as (largely unsuccessful) experiments. His brother Patrick is only good enough to chauffeur him from party to party or else 'only stand and wait', a condition against which Patrick, like Isa, revolts – in his case by wrecking their expensive car and walking off into the night. Jean-Luc's associate and mistress, Myriem (Amira Casar), exists only as a puppet whom he can undress on demand and move about like a chess piece when it suits him. When Maurice, the father, first meets Myriem, he immediately guesses that Jean-Luc '*l'a formée en quelque sorte*'. And when Myriem seems to be too alive, Jean-Luc resorts to a prostitute to fulfil his

Myriem (Amira Casar) and Maurice (Michel Bouquet)

sexual needs. So many Galateas whom Jean-Luc is desperately trying to turn back into stone!

When we enquire as to the etiology of this 'deadness' in Jean-Luc, we find that it seems to result not only from his father's abandonment years previously, but from some much more remote and troubled past moment. Of course this moment might be the traumatic departure of his father when he was still but a child, but some children successfully mourn their departed parents and subsequently, as Freud puts it, 'regain the capacity to adopt a new object of love' (1917: 244). Indeed, when Jean-Luc gets around to asking his father why he had left, he listens to Maurice's explanation with a vaguely consensual interest and even asks, sympathetically, 'So, what was it you couldn't tolerate?' And when his father answers, 'I no longer knew who I was, I felt like I was part of another system', Jean-Luc wonders almost tenderly, 'And did it work? Can one really forget?' This is hardly a subject which produces a violent conflict between them.

No, what seeps through this repeated and not entirely convincing reproach is another, more disturbing, one: that on one occasion Maurice gave up and talked of killing himself. 'I can remember,' Jean-Luc bitterly tells his father, 'a man who could suddenly jump up during dinner and say, "I'm going to put a bullet in my brain".' And on another occasion Jean-Luc tells Maurice that he has 'the look you had when we were on a trip to Spain in the Dauphine. You had lost your wallet and all your money and papers and you stood by the side

12

of the road moaning, "We're screwed, we're done for!" '. These two incidents seem to be the nexus of Jean-Luc's problematic connection with his father. Such nexial moments would have inspired a fearful rage that his father might kill himself – an outcome that would suggest Jean-Luc's deeper connections with Hamlet – who experiences, in Jones' words, 'the guilty Oedipal complex of patricidal phantasies' (1949: 69). Jean-Luc's Hamlettian melancholia feels like an unbearable burden or fardel, for these long-buried murderous phantasies include not only his father, but also his unborn children: he thus evokes the Laius figure of the Oedipus legend who, as Laura Mulvey (1989: 198) notes, 'represents something that returns like a ghostly apparition when his son curses his own sons'.

We are familiar with Freud's assessment of melancholia:

> There is no difficulty in reconstructing this process. As object-choice, an attachment of the libido to a particular person had at one time existed; then, owing to a . . . disappointment coming from this loved person, the object-relationship was shattered. The result was not a normal one of withdrawal of the libido from this object and a displacement on to a new one, but . . . a withdrawing into the ego . . . where it served to establish an *identification* of the ego with the abandoned object. Thus the shadow of the object fell upon the ego, and the latter could henceforth be judged by a special agency, as though it were an object, the forsaken object . . . If the love for the object thus takes refuge in narcissistic identification, then the hate comes into operation on this substitutive object, abusing it, debasing it, making it suffer and deriving sadistic satisfaction from its suffering . . . a self-tormenting in melancholia that signifies that sadism and hate of the original object have been turned round upon the subject's own self.
>
> (1917: 248, 249, 251, my italic)

Christopher Bollas (1987), who borrows Freud's phrase 'the shadow of the object' as title to his study of melancholia, calls the mental representations that the child incorporates into his unconscious arrangement of this 'loving-hate', *the unthought known* (pp. 3–4).[8] But it is Abraham and Torok (1994) who perhaps best delineate this state as an incorporation of the love-hated object. Indeed, it is precisely in their oppositional pairing of the terms 'incorporation' and 'introjection' that we might best understand the dynamics at work in Anne Fontaine's film. In the first place, Abraham and Torok argue,

> incorporation is invariably distinct from introjection (a gradual process) because it is instantaneous and magical and implies the loss of an object before the freeing of the desires concerning that object: the object of [intense feeling] being absent, incorporation obeys the pleasure principle and functions by way of processes similar to hallucinatory fulfillments . . .

Incorporation is an eminently illegal act. It must hide from view and from the ego. Secrecy is imperative for survival ... Installed in the place of the lost object, the incorporated object continues to recall the fact that something else was lost: the desires quelled by repression ... Like a commemorative monument, the incorporated object betokens the place, the date and the circumstances in which the desires were banished from introjection; they stand like *secret tombs* in the life of the ego ... and in this way the ego keeps alive that which causes its greatest suffering and is condemned to suffer the illness of mourning [or melancholia].

(1994: 113–17)

Incorporation constitutes a '*refusal to mourn*' in that it is 'the refusal to reclaim as our own the part of ourselves that we placed in what we lost'; a reclamation and a realization that would 'effectively transform us'. It reveals 'a gap in the psyche that points to something missing where introjection should have occurred' (Abraham and Torok 1994: 127).

It seems quite clear that Jean-Luc's entire self-portrait (remember, he is the 'author' of this entire fantasy) is a self-punishing revelation of his own deadness and his petrifying treatment of Isa, Myriem, Patrick and even his father('s ghost). The trauma of his father's threat to kill himself – possibly doubly traumatic both because of its hugely deflating performance by the father and because it risks revealing the son's own mortal Oedipal designs – is the cryptophoric writing that unconsciously scripts Jean-Luc's every move. It is cryptophoric both because it entombs him in its design and because it is an encrypted text which he is unable consciously to decipher, but must blindly obey. Since the departed father remains Jean-Luc's ego-ideal, this suicidal-patricidal urge becomes the dirty secret that needs to be kept, a sense of shame that needs to be covered up in an endless repetition of acts that offer Jean-Luc's body as a whipping post for his father's disappearance. In a way, Jean-Luc might be said to be wearing his incorporated father's death-mask as his own.[9]

Were this all that we could see of Jean-Luc's fantasy, we would no doubt find this film to be as dead as its subject, as devoid of development as *Memento* (Christopher Nolan 2000) and just as fatally condemned to the uncertainty of what is real and what is merely a replica (or simulacrum) of the real. As such it would constitute a refusal to mourn and a shunning of the potential consequences of mourning. Anne Fontaine's narrative purpose, however, turns out to be quite remarkably different. For if the self-portrait offered up by Jean-Luc turns out to be relentlessly 'petrified' and a self-punishing entombment, the portrait of the father's returned ghost has a very different 'agenda'. For, as Abraham and Torok (1994) note (paraphrasing Freud's theory of the return of the repressed), 'sometimes in the dead of night, when libidinal fulfillments have their way, the ghost of the crypt comes back to haunt the

The night of melancholia

Maurice, Jean-Luc (Charles Berling) and Isabelle (Natacha Régnier)

cemetery guard, giving him strange and incomprehensible signals, making him perform bizarre acts, or subjecting him to unexpected sensations' (p. 130). Anne Fontaine says of her protagonist, 'He isn't part of his life and flesh . . . It's as if, at times, you were a ventriloquist's dummy controlled by your father or your mother. You never know why but, all of a sudden, you feel your father or mother's expression on your face, overriding your own, as if there were someone inside of you'.[10]

Dominick LaCapra (2000: 179) emphasizes this ghost-like figure as a reminder that 'something of the past always remains, if only as a haunting presence or a revenant'. What is indeed surprising in Fontaine's arrangement is that this 'revenant' who elicits from Jean-Luc bizarre acts and unexpected sensations is also bodied forth as the character of Maurice in his fantasy. If Jean-Luc, as son, must continue almost to the end of this story to wear the mask of the entombed memory of his departed father's deflating desire of self-annihilation, the Maurice of Jean-Luc's present fantasy is revealed to be a wholly different figure – not merely the Oedipal father, but rather a figure that Julia Kristeva would call ' "the imaginary father" ' who ensures the subject's entrance into the universe of signs and creation' (1989: 23). Unlike the image Jean-Luc himself wears as a mask, the Maurice we as spectators are allowed to see is vital, beneficent, paternally caring, loving and concerned, able to elicit the best from his 'other son', Patrick.

To wit: Patrick does a series of monologues at his nightclub which are

15

masochistically 'funny' and the invisible audience apparently enjoys them. But gradually, through repetition of these monologues, the audience disappears completely and we are clearly in an emptied-out space of pure fantasy. In some of these more obviously oneiric scenes, Patrick wistfully reproaches his father for abandoning him, but the last of the series involves Patrick replaying his first monologue and receiving warm congratulations from his father. Maurice asks him about his prospects and Patrick confesses that he has thought of marriage and a co-ownership of a video store in the south of France, but doesn't dare leave his brother. Maurice plays paternity to the hilt here, questioning whether Jean-Luc really needs Patrick and telling his younger son, 'You know, the years rush by. You can't get stuck in messy situations. If you've got a serious opportunity, take it!' What is curious about this second scene is how subversive it appears toward Jean-Luc in Jean-Luc's own fantasy. What seems to be happening here is a huge battle going on between the incorporated image of the long-departed father and a newly rediscovered one in which the positive pieces of this incorporated object no longer fit the old dead image.

The most directly problematic sequence of this type occurs when Jean-Toussaint Dialo (Hubert Koundée) arrives from Africa to sing Maurice's praises. He tells Jean-Luc, 'It was your father who got me started. He changed my life. He encouraged me. He was always there for me.' The reports of Maurice's role in Africa reveal his courage, devotion, dedication and effectiveness.[11] One part of Jean-Luc (the incorporated dead object comprised of his father's impotent and suicidal words) openly disdains this possibility and sarcastically voices his suspicions that the appearance of this Dialo is but a con-game to win his (financial) support. But the overriding image of Jean-Luc's fantasized father presents a loving, capable and vital parent, a much happier type of introjection.

Now, the battle rages. How can Jean-Luc maintain the incorporated image in the face of increasing 'evidence' of his father's deeply sensitive paternal devotion? What is going on? Anne Fontaine seems intuitively to have put into play a battle between what Abraham and Torok (1994) term 'incorporation' and 'introjection' as two radically different responses to object loss, the former as an unchanging fantasy, the latter as an evolving process (p. 125). If introjection represents a gradual inclusion of the positive and growthful parts of the parental object in the ego and the consequent broadening of the ego by an extension to the external world of original autoerotic interests, incorporation simply denies that a loss ever occurred. Of course, Abraham and Torok remind us, 'even incorporation has introjection as its nostalgic vocation' (p. 129). This formulation allows us to comprehend the character of Maurice in this film as a recovery of memories that begin to reintroduce the lost object into the ego in a form that can be positively assimilated as a life force able to counteract the incorporated tomb-like image that Jean-Luc has up until now worn as a mask.

If, as Freud argues, the work of successful mourning involves substituting a new object for its lost predecessor (1917: 244–5), in Anne Fontaine's (Jean-Luc's) version, this new object seems to be constructed out of long-repressed memories of the positive aspects of the object hidden behind a deadening incorporated imago produced by an early trauma of patricidal urges, revealed as omnipotent thoughts. In other words, in Jean-Luc's fantasy the vital character of Maurice struggles thoughout to dethrone his entombed double which has been masquerading as Jean-Luc.

Ironically, this new Maurice includes in his arsenal of qualities the ability to love – to love precisely that person whom the dead father in Jean-Luc has long forbidden him to love: Isa, his wife. This proscription is emblematized by Jean-Luc's prohibition of childen – a circumstance that might risk resuscitating and unmasking the dead father. But clearly Maurice feels no inhibitions about loving this estranged woman. He dines with her, walks her home at night from work and, in a surprisingly long scene, they do a close dance that could only be interpreted as involving a couple in love. The irony here is that such a fantasy brings up a host of old Oedipal feelings that risk sending our Hamlet-Oedipus deeper into a murderous melancholy. This conflict is played out in the brilliant final scene of Jean-Luc's fantasy, in which he throws his father to the ground and strangles him 'to death'.

Everything in this film prepares us for this violent eventuality, notably Jean-Luc's unremitting hostility to Maurice – a hostility doubly motivated by the son's belief in the father's betrayal, but also by the father's renewal of feelings of Oedipal rivalry. Yet clearly to kill his father-figure connotes a potential impasse for Jean-Luc: whereas killing the incorporated father would liberate Jean-Luc from the throes of melancholy by an extension to the external world of the ego's long-repressed erotic interests; killing Maurice, the figure of the newly introjected father, risks a return of the deadening repression to which Jean-Luc can ill afford to succumb. Much more quietly, however, Fontaine has also laid the groundwork for the successful 'resolution' of this impasse. LaCapra (2000: 183) writes:

> In converting absence to loss, one assumes that there was (or at least could be) some original unity, whose wholeness, security or identity others have ruined, polluted or contaminated and thus made 'us' lose. To regain it, one must somehow get rid of or eliminate those others – or perhaps the sinful other in oneself.

Fontaine gives us the scene in which Jean-Luc readmits Maurice back into the space in which he is examining himself (for the first time in the film) in a mirror. The father and son join not *forces* but *faces*, and Jean-Luc's gesture of tenderness goes a long way toward welcoming this newly introjected imago. Jean-Luc will presumably now be able to don Maurice's vital, caring and paternal expression. LaCapra writes, 'specific phantoms or ghosts that possess the self . . . can be laid to rest through mourning only when they are specified and named as historically lost others' (2000: 187). By abjuring the unnamed paternal incorporation in favour of his now named father, Jean-Luc moves toward an active or generative position.[12] Anne Fontaine suggests that 'father and son live out the deep-rooted relationship that binds them beyond death itself . . . The film's denouement marks the birth of a being who had been living alongside himself until that point . . . We realize that Jean-Luc will never be the same man again. He can move towards a new life at last. For the first time probably, the father has fulfilled his task as a father'.[13]

But we must not forget that this is a French film! Anne Fontaine does not allow us an unambiguously or unambivalently happy vision of a 'reinvestment in life that allows one to begin again, allowing distance, change, resumption of social life, ethical responsibility and renewal' (LaCapra 2000: 189). We are left to wonder and, in the first few viewings of this film at least, to painfully rework the materials of our past and our fantasy into a new interpretation of what it means to act out one's melancholy and what it means to work through one's mourning, and whether both acting out (melancholy) and working through (mourning) can be accomplished concurrently – indeed are not always accomplished concurrently in a state that Jacques Derrida has characterized as 'mid-mourning'.[14]

Because the necessity of re-reading the past is inevitably common to both mourning and film, Anne Fontaine invites us, nay *provokes* us to understand the deeper connections between film and mourning as psychological events requiring us, first by retrospection and then by interpretation, to re-evaluate 'bit by bit' the terms and figures of our own fantasies and dreams. This is especially marked in a film such as this one, where as a character in the film's diegesis, Jean-Luc observes a 'fictional' figure – a mirroring of the way we, as spectators, watch the fictional Jean-Luc. Such a doubling of character and spectator positions cannot fail to evoke other connections between the transferential work of analysis and the experience of film viewing. Along the way, the work of this film implicitly argues for an extension of Freud's theory of *Trauerarbeit* into the realm of *Traumarbeit* – to help us to see the way in which the dreamwork and mourning can resuscitate elements of our repressed incorporated others into positive introjections. Fontaine would thus confirm Erik Santner's contention that 'film turns out to be remarkably well suited to be the site of the symbolic procedures of funerary ritual because film is an inherently *elegiac* medium' (1990: 69, my italic). Both cinema and psychoanalysis would thus, in Derrida's words, be 'phantom sciences', spectral discourses that constantly renegotiate the question of loss (cited in Ricciardi 2003: 38). We might never confuse the one with the other, but thanks to Anne Fontaine's film we may understand how each endlessly reflects (in both senses of the word) and reinterprets the work of the other.

Notes

1 New Yorker Films Publicity Packet: interview, p. 5.
2 Dennis Lim, 'Shock Waves', *The Village Voice*, 21/8/02. See also Ty Burr, *The Boston Globe*, 19/12/03; Tom Dawson, *The BBC*, 19/6/02; Elvis Mitchell, *The New York Times*, 23/8/02; and Roger Ebert, *The Chicago Sun Times*, 22/1/02.
3 This may be the first of a series of references to *Hamlet* which will be explored in more detail below. For a discussion of the prominent role played by spying and deception in Shakespeare's play and the Hamlet saga, see Ernest Jones, *Hamlet and Oedipus* (1949, pp.148–49).
4 Jones was the first to insist on Hamlet's incestuous and parricidal feelings as constituting the barrier to any action (1949: 92–100).
5 Jones notes in his study of Hamlet that 'psychoneurosis means a state of mind where the person is unduly, and often painfully driven or thwarted by the "unconscious" part of his mind, that buried part that was once the infant's mind and still lives on side by side with the adult . . . and signifies *internal* mental conflict' (1949: 69).
6 Miller (1990: 4) notes that 'the story of Pygmalion dramatizes the process by which an anthropomorphism takes place [and thus] makes the story of Pygmalion a prosopopoeia of prosopopoeia'.
7 We recall that in the opening sequence of the film, one of Jean-Luc's patients confesses, 'I have a 2-year-old child. I've calculated that when he's 20, I'll be an old man. I won't have any exit prestige or authority in his eyes. I can't be affectionate with him. I feel like he's a stranger. Almost a threat'. In retrospect this sounds like a projection from Jean-Luc onto his client.
8 Bollas adds, 'If the love-object is an insufficient selfobject, then the child must form some kind of alternate selfobject that is most likely to be composed of projected self states, such as isolation, despair, helplessness, frustration and rage' (1987: 127).
9 Jones (1949) notes that for Hamlet, to kill Claudius is to kill himself and thus his moral fatae is bound up with his uncle's (p. 88). Jones further notes the presence of the themes of masks and self-deception in *Hamlet* (pp. 149–50).
10 Anne Fontaine, interview, *New Yorker Films* press kit, p. 1.
11 Here again we see a parallel with Jones' discussion of Hamlet, for Shakespeare effects a *decomposition* of the father into various attributes, some good, the others bad (1949: 122, 131). We might ultimately wonder if the entire discourse on Africa in this film is not an allegory of death that would suggest that Maurice had long ago committed suicide and that the letter of the film's opening and closing scenes represents a level of Jean-Luc that simply refuses to believe his father committed suicide years before and engages in a recuperative fantasy: 'Perhaps my father is still alive and has continued all these years to be an important doctor in Africa.'
12 Eric Santner notes a similar tendency in German cinema which he describes as follows: 'The thanatotic element is a homeopathic procedure using controlled introduction of a negative element (symbolic or real poison) to heal a system infected by a similar poisonous substance' (1990: 20). Elsewhere he adds, 'In these mythological performances of "consolatory figuration" the cutting a subsequent shaping of an organic material – its transformation . . . into a medium of art – empowers the mourner to survive his loss. In both cases the mourner inherits the power and title of singer and poet' (p. 23). Julia Kristeva extends this thought to a more general sense of the connections between art and psychoanalysis when she writes, 'Aesthetic and literary creation . . . constitute a very faithful semiological representation of the subject's battle with symbolic collapse. Such a literary representation . . . diverges from the psychoanalytic course, which aims at dissolving the

symptom. Nevertheless the literary representation possesses a real and imaginary effectiveness that comes closer to catharsis than to elaboration; it is a therapeutic device used in all societies throughout the ages. Psychoanalysts ... should pay greater attention to these sublimatory solutions' (1989: 24–5).
13 Anne Fontaine, interview, pp. 2, 4.
14 Ricciardi notes that Derrida situates 'mid-mourning' between the step-forward (*fort*) that goes nowhere, and the step backward that always comes back as a revenant, as raising the possibility for psychoanalysis to articulate a politics and ethics of mourning. Unlike the *Arbeit* of mourning, mid-mourning does not pretend to achieve a successful 'dismissal' of the lost object, but instead adopts an inconclusive psychic rhythm of oscillation between introjection and incorporation (Ricciardi 2003: 36).

References

Abraham, N. and Torok, M. (1994) *The Shell and the Kernel: Renewals of Psychoanalysis*, trans. Nicholas T. Rand. Chicago: University of Chicago Press.
Bollas, C. (1987) *The Shadow of the Object*. New York: Columbia University Press.
Freud, S. (1917) Mourning and Melancholia, in *The Standard Edition of the Complete Psychological Works of Sigmund Freud, XIV*. London: Hogarth Press, 1957.
Isaacs, S. (1943) The nature and function of phantasy, in M. Klein and J. Riviere (eds) *Developments in Psychoanalysis*. London: Hogarth Press, 1952.
Jones, E. (1949) *Hamlet and Oedipus*. New York: W.W. Norton, 1976.
Kristeva, J. (1989) *Black Sun: Depression and Melancholia*, trans. Leon Roudiez. New York: Columbia University Press.
LaCapra, D. (2000) Reflections on trauma, absence and loss, in P. Brooks and A. Woloch (eds) *Whose Freud? The Place of Psychoanalysis in Contemporary Culture*. New Haven, CT: Yale University Press.
Laing, R.D. (1965) *The Divided Self*. Baltimore, MD: Penguin Books.
Miller, J.H. (1990) *Versions of Pygmalion*. Cambridge, MA: Harvard University Press.
Mulvey, L. (1989) The Oedipus myth, in *Visual and Other Pleasures*. Bloomington, IN: Indiana University Press.
Ricciardi, A. (2003) *The Ends of Mourning: Psychoanalysis, Literature, Film*. Stanford, CA: Stanford University Press.
Santner, E. (1990) *Stranded Objects: Mourning, Memory and Film in Postwar Germany*. Ithaca, NY: Cornell University Press.

2

QUEST FOR A LOST MOTHER
Alina Marazzi's
Un'ora sola ti vorrei[1]

Pietro Roberto Goisis

Un'ora sola ti vorrei (*For One More Hour with You*) (Italy, 2002)
Director: Alina Marazzi
Distributor: Dolmen Home Video

Alina Marazzi, the director of *Un'ora sola ti vorrei* (*For One More Hour with You*) who had already produced documentaries and acted as assistant director in a number of films, belongs to a Milanese family involved with books and publishing. Her grandfather, who died in 2003, was Ulrico Hoepli, proprietor of the publishing house of the same name and of the bookshop in the city centre in Milan which had been founded by his great-uncle. As well as being an able businessman in his own field, Ulrico had various passions, the most interesting and important of which, for the purpose of our story, was his love of the cinema. In the 1920s, through a business exchange, he apparently obtained one of the first cine-cameras. He then got hold of a Pathe Baby, with which he recorded the almost complete story of his family from 1926 until around 1980 on over 60 reels (all silent, of course, 8 and 16mm films).

In 1938 his second child was born, his daughter Luisella (known as Liseli). A beautiful and charming girl and woman, she was however sad and afflicted with problems. She married Antonio Marazzi and in 1964 gave birth to her second child, her daughter Alina. In the meantime Liseli's emotional difficulties increased, leading to her first admission to a psychiatric clinic in 1966. This period in care was followed by others, both in Italy and abroad, in psychiatric and/or psychoanalytic treatment – or attempts at treatment. In 1972 Liseli tragically took her own life.

At that time her daughter Alina was 7 years old. We do not know how she reacted to her mother's death – she herself does not remember anything about it. She chose to follow her profession, first as a director of documentaries, then in films as assistant director. She certainly did not forget her own history and her own loss, but one might say that she learned to live with her loss, using the typical defence mechanisms available to children and later to adults. Here are her own words from the interview which appeared on Cine@forum:[2]

> I wasn't able to mention her, nor to think of the fact that she had decided to end it all the way she did. When I was a child, nothing at all. If anyone asked me, 'where's your mother?', I stood there tongue-tied, in total block, belly-ache, tremendous embarrassment, etc. That continued till I was about 20. I was unable to find the words. When I was about 18 I talked with a friend of hers, Sonia. I read her letters and discovered her as a person from them. Then when I was 27 I got to know the letters and diaries that my father had kept: the impact was even stronger. That was my first step on a journey that I had always known was necessary and that I would have to solve.

In the meantime her grandfather's reels had remained carefully stored (or, better: hibernating) in a cupboard at his home in Milan. No one had bothered with them, maybe they had even been forgotten. But in 1995 Alina felt the time had come. She went to see her grandfather, asked his permission, and began watching the films, some of which were marked with a letter 'L' for Liseli, and copying them on an amateur video (minidv). Her words again:

> You certainly don't sit down and plan time. The right time had come, and in a surprisingly creative way. I had already used video as a means of communication and work. I knew about cine films, but not that they could be so rich in quality. The approach was very timid, I was afraid to look my mother in the face. And indeed, the effects of those first contacts with her eyes and with her as a child were devastating.

I think that her courage in watching the films was fundamental, and it then led her grandfather to ask her if she had found anything there that he had been unable to see. That was the beginning of a path which, from a private and intimate dimension and experience, gradually and overpoweringly became public as it became a film and reached us, its spectators. While her original intent had been to make something that would be useful to herself and her family, later, thanks also to the crucial cooperation with her friend and film editor Ilaria Fraioli, she conceived and developed the project of sharing the work with others.

Alina Marazzi reconstructs these passages in her intense self-presentation, 'How did I make this film?' on the film's internet website:[3]

The gesture of feeding the old film into the projector and looking at the pictures on the screen immediately took on a magic significance for me: as I showed those films, which had been left in their boxes for 30 years without anyone showing any interest in them, I experienced the heart-rending paradox of living at the time when those pictures were taken. By that I mean that, as I watched my mother learn to walk, or my grandmother dance in a field, or my uncle dive into the sea, I was at the same time spectator and participant. Their faces appeared on the screen, smiled and then disappeared in a merciless game of seduction with me. People appeared to me in flesh and blood but did not allow me to touch or embrace them. I penetrated the magic of the cinema, which allows us to call up that which is not and to make it present. In my case that 'power' was emotionally charged, not only because it called up the past, but my own past, which I had not known until that moment . . . I discovered that my mother's life, which I knew nothing about, had been documented right from the day of her birth, and those traces of her existence had been kept and 'catalogued' in that cupboard. It was a great thrill to discover, and look right into, the eyes in that face, and indeed it is an emotion that is renewed, always in a different way, every time I look at the film that I made from those short films. At the beginning I was hungry for pictures, I wanted to understand and discover things that I did not know about the life of my mother and my family. Each frame was a treasure brought to light and I hoped that, as I looked at those pictures, other images would float to the surface from the depths of my memory. That didn't happen, but I did learn to recognise the expressions and the look of that woman, and to recognise similarities to myself. It was a new experience for me, because until then I had never been able to see a reflection of myself in any female face. This reflection was the beginning of a path that led me to tie up the thread of my past, as regards my mother, but also my grandmother and my origins in general. In the film the two women, my mother and grandmother, can often be seen exchanging looks, and at the same time my own gaze is always present, I think it's something that the spectators notice, even though they don't know me. I had missed that maternal look in my life, but I found it again the moment I set my eyes on those pictures, on those past lives. And so this dialogue and interweaving of glances accompanied me as I got to know about my mother and then enabled me to transform this process into something more articulated and complex that started off from me, but gradually assumed an identity of its own . . .

My first encounter with the film was in December 2002, during a session with one of my patients, a very cultured and sensitive journalist. She told me about this film and about the director who made it, I don't remember why or in what context. Then, for some unknown reason, I wrote down the title and the name on a loose sheet of paper on the table near my armchair. Psychoanalysts know how their patients often become a source of inspiration or a stimulus for reading, films, songs, concerts, shows, holidays or other things. In such a context my reaction did not seem to be strange or peculiar; what I did not expect was that, after that quick note, I would enter an emotional dimension that still accompanies me and which, among other things, has led me now to write a contribution to this book.

Starting from that note, in today's internet culture, I typed the title into a search engine; the system immediately replied, indicating a site, and this marked the beginning of accurate, surprised and curious surfing. I enrolled in a special mailing list and received periodic news about the various public showings of the film, until a place and date that suited me finally turned up. That evening, in the back room of a quiet pub in Milan, I at last had the chance to see the film; I had dragged my wife along too, feeling that it certainly wouldn't be a waste of time. The only seats left were on a bench near the front. We made our way to our seats with a little embarrassment, waited and sat through a short presentation, looked around, curious to see the director, then the lights went out and the show began.

A magic hour! An hour that I would have liked never to end.

Un'ora sola ti vorrei

Liseli

The conversation with the director, the editor and the audience opened new doors to evocation, suggestion and curiosity. This led to a rapid contact with the director, an exchange of emails, the kind confirmation of her willingness to collaborate, and the organization of a film show on the final evening of the scientific year 2002/3 at the 'Cesare Musatti' Centre of Psychoanalysis in Milan. It was an intense evening, warm and exciting for all those taking part in it. For me it was the continuation of a journey, side by side with this film, which never seems to end.

I agree with Silvia Ballestra (*L'Unità*, 23 February 2003) when she says that in this case calling it a film is an understatement, because the term imposes strict limits. *Un'ora sola ti vorrei* is literature, it is memory, it is truth, it is existence. But it is also a film, next to which I shall now continue to travel, exploring some of its aspects.

Synopsis

The film begins with some background noises (someone opening the lid of a gramophone) and with the image of a record turning after a hand has moved the pickup arm and the stylus. A woman's voice is speaking, a mother greeting her children by means of this strange gift, an old 45-rpm recorded for fun in the entrance hall of the Central Station in Milan, on the way back from a trip abroad. There are pictures of a pretty young woman (Liseli), serene and rather melancholy, and of a child eating (Alina herself). At the end of the record a wish is discreetly whispered in the form of a song. Then a mother's voice (Liseli, but it is the director's voice) starts to read a hypothetical letter written to her daughter Alina, to try to explain and tell something of her own story 30 years after her death. At this point the pictures (from her grandfather's films) and the words (from the mother's letter) begin to overlap and form a story. The first sequences take us into a family of Lombardy's upper middle class, who originally came from a small town in Switzerland. Elegant weddings, parties, extraordinary trips, happy holidays by the sea and in the mountains, visits to the country, fields, children playing, grown-ups joking. As the private affairs of this family are narrated, the screen is filled with beauty. In particular, Liseli herself is extraordinarily beautiful, as a child, then when she got engaged and married Antonio; when she became the mother of Martino and Alina and went to live with her young children in the United States. This whole part of the film also becomes a rich documentation of a social environment, through all those happy family rituals. But then, as announced by the voice of the narrator, something snaps, there is a kind of eclipse and illness takes over. Now Liseli is in a clinic for nervous diseases and her medical records indicate a depressive disorder. We follow the attempted treatment, we no longer see her beautiful face as before, perhaps it already shows signs of illness, but we hear the intense and passionate words that she writes to her children, to her dearest friend, to her husband, we even look through the pages of her diaries. Then simply, without rhetoric, we come to the end of the story, the mystery of death. A suicide that we are aware of, but which is not seen. It is there, but it is not shown. Then a heart-rending, desperate appeal in the words of a popular song: *'Un'ora sola ti vorrei!'* – for one more hour with you! As Antonello Catacchio has pointed out (*Il Manifesto*, 4 August 2002), it is impossible not to agree with François Truffaut who advised us not to underrate pop songs because, in their own way, they tell the truth.

The meaning of the film

Alina Marazzi tried to explain the reasons for making this film both to others and to herself. I shall try to integrate her explanations with a few more personal observations.

I think we have to start by imagining a little girl who has grown up without being able to count on the relationship with her own mother and on the processes of identification with a female figure, with her face and expressions. We can also surmise that, just as children do when they find themselves in traumatic, painful situations (bereavements, losses and separations), she may have wondered if she herself might in some way have been unable to prevent her mother's tragic end, or even if she had been responsible for it. When she grew up, by some strange trick of fate (destiny, unconscious perception, transmission across generations?), this girl decided to work with pictures and discovered that the history of her family and of her mother was recorded on films that her grandfather had made and kept. I think any one of us would have felt a strong desire to go and look for this past and get to know something about it. The thought comes to me that in a sense everything was there already, just waiting for someone to pick it up, but at the same time it also had to be cultivated, nourished, protected and be grown with love.

For Alina everything begins with the search for her mother's face, a face that was unknown, that had been avoided and hidden. The story unwinds following the theme of nostalgia, which in this case is understood in the broadest sense, so that it perhaps becomes the central theme of the film.

Alongside this theme, to make it even more incisive, I believe there is another meaning which we can describe as a search for the truth. Even the spectators will be aware that the scenes filmed by Alina's grandfather were not 'real movie' scenes (if we admit that these can even exist in the presence of a TV- or movie-camera), but rather scenes that he had set up, in a kind of self-representation that was never done by chance and was certainly not neutral. In this sense, the representation is even slightly false: 'There was no serenity, outside that which the images wanted to show' (Alberto Crespi, *L'Unità*, 1 August 2002). So Alina Marazzi's work also becomes a process of revealing a series of masks and veils that, I believe, heavily conditioned her mother's life. The well-being that is shown in the films was also fake, artificial, intentionally shown and not a true representation of Liseli's inner world; perhaps also an impediment to the free expression of her true feelings.

In conclusion, we may say that, again using Alina's words, the overall meaning of the film, perhaps its very existence, is that of being a beautiful gift that she made to herself, to her mother, to all children and to all parents. In a sense, she told herself the story of her own mother and of herself. And in doing it, as Fabio Ferzetti wrote (*Il Messaggero*, 29 July 2002), she gave a lesson of courage, firmness and trust in herself and in the cinema: 'In the end I don't know how I managed to make this film, perhaps I only followed my desire to spend some time with my mother. Just an hour. But that's already a lot.'

The images

As we know, the images we find in this film were already there, even though shot by someone else. How did she choose them for an hour-long show, starting off from such a lot of 'already shot' material? I believe that what Alina Marazzi used was the magic of the cinema, its very essence: calling up that which is not, and making it present. It is a magic that is renewed in this film each time I see it and I believe it is metaphorically represented by the choice of the shots in which her great-uncle does conjuring tricks.

Firstly, the images are a kind of journey through the twentieth century, if only for the existence itself of the pictures and for the way they proceed from black and white to colour. They are a frame, as Elena Rossi writes on *Erewhon*,[4] which becomes almost indispensable in order to understand, situate and narrate the whole story. A kind of social and family documentary, a precise representation of a cross-section, albeit a partial one, of Italian life in those years. We need only think of the shots of post-war Milan at the time of the great economic boom, of the political rally in Piazza Duomo for the 25 April celebrations, of the images filmed in the Hoepli bookshop. Running parallel to these images there is a much more personal dimension, though not for this reason less stimulating for the spectator's processes of identification and involvement. Marriage rituals, parties and ceremonies, holidays and pastimes. Then there are what I would call 'cinematographic images': an uncle who, as a child, plays with magazines such as *Specchio* and *Cinema*; legs walking, feet dancing, faces, mouths, partial glimpses of bodies, or of nature in its various manifestations. Then, between the two forms of expression there is the varied and long sequence of moving images: feet, legs, cars, trains, ships, planes, chaotic traffic, skis, sledges, bicycles, carriages and prams.

The intention, declared at the start, was to tell a story, and this is accomplished in such a way as to make the development of Liseli's whole life captivating. The editing proposes leaps in time and flashbacks, almost refrains, rather similar to the composition of a piece of music. I think that this dimension makes the film fascinating to watch.

Then there are other images taken from shots, or selections specially made by the director: slow motion shots, stills, a record turning, a wood of birch trees, a collection of insects and butterflies, the diaries, letters and postcards written by her mother, hospital files, prescriptions, bills from clinics, newspaper cuttings. I would say that we have now moved on to the next chapter: these are images that speak and convey a message.

Words and writing

Like the pictures, the words too already existed, recorded in diaries and letters. Here too it is quite clear that, in any case, any choice made was not neutral, but determined by a thought and by an idea that supported it, by a reason and a link to the images with which it was associated. The director's work of selection certainly included reading all that her mother had written since the age of 12 and which had then been kept. Certainly she also considered the problem of reserved subject matter – first of all a personal question, since she had access to things that had been written for other eyes. We might say that the pictures were in some way more public, if we can use that term, whereas the written records referred to a much more intimate and reserved dimension.

'Please don't read this diary', wrote Liseli in her diary. We could talk at length about the legitimacy of this intrusion into another person's life (her own mother's . . .). I think that the results that Alina achieved, the quality and universal meaning of her film, can reply to the question of legitimacy.

There is no doubt that thoughts are among the most intimate dimensions of any person. It is the theme of modesty which is raised by her film in the very moment in which, from personal research, it became a product for the public. I consider it an absolutely modest film, despite its rather voyeuristic dimension. I think that perhaps a slight embarrassment may be felt by the spectator who finds himself immersed in places and events that are not his own. Certainly, apart from the private images, there are also names of hospitals and doctors' prescriptions, but they flow past simply, as though to show the sense of inevitability, in a style midway between reportage and documentation. In my opinion the director shows extraordinary sensitivity in leaving us just in the doorway in these passages, avoiding lingering over particular aspects and details which might otherwise have encouraged a climate of morbid curiosity.

The words, which are impossible to report in full when they speak of life and death, love and pain, existence, children and parents, oneself and the world, also fulfil other functions.

They are used in opposition to the images, as a counterpoint to their gilded appearance, revealing a truth that had been concealed for a long time. They are also, and perhaps above all, a way to let her mother speak, to allow her to communicate those thoughts which perhaps no one had ever been able to listen to properly. It is striking how it is Alina herself who reads them in voiceover, reconstructing and narrating her mother's and her own story.

Sounds and music

Another absolutely important dimension of the film is the acoustic one. It is an extraordinary embroidery of sounds which accompanies the images, filling them discreetly with assonance. The first acoustic impact is with the music and the lyrics that give the film its title. It is a song of 100 years ago, sung or hinted at on various occasions and in different ways, from the nostalgic version of the mother on the record at the start of the film to the period repertoire version, or whispered almost like a lullaby by the voice of the narrator Alina, up to the final desperate and liberating invocation.

This work has been possible thanks to the fortunate and positive encounter with Benni Atria, whose collaboration went far beyond the so-called sound montage.[5] This is how the director described the work done on the soundtrack in the interview with Barbara Sorrentini (*Altrocinema*, 2002):[6]

> Some of the musical excerpts I chose have a sentimental value for me, others call to mind the atmosphere of the period. In addition there is a series of noises, sounds and whispered voices which we added as though a trunk were being opened and words, pieces of paper, photographs, films, sounds and children's voices were coming out. There are recordings that I found, also at my grandparents' house, on an old tape where my grandmother is playing the piano while other voices are talking, or phone calls that had been recorded. I felt that all this was somehow relevant to the way we were putting all those memories together.

So, once again memory returns, a kind of collective memory that belongs to each one of us. With nature, exploring in the mountains, lakes or by the sea; with water, which is symbolically present everywhere; with the creaking of a swing and the laughter of children; with a whole series of sounds (camera flashes, biting an apple, trains, bells, songs, waves, choirs, the sound of a projector running, the wind, a German lullaby, a plane, someone blowing out candles, bombs falling, breathing, seagulls, the lift doors, cash registers, a concert of car-horns, bicycle wheels turning, an echo, broken glass, the ticking of a pendulum-clock, the tapping of typewriter keys, a siren), free but never coincidental, right up to music and melodies, and Liseli's theme.

Alina has told us how, at the beginning, viewing the films gave her a paradoxical sensation of being able to contact the people in the films through sight, but without the possibility of feeling them, without body contact. Just as the images enabled her to recover lost relationships, I think that a similar phenomenon also occurred with sound, and that some sounds can perform a kind of vicarious function through evocative mechanisms which, by accessing the dual register of acoustics and memory, allow the recovery of physical perceptions. I refer in particular to the sounds related to water on two particular occasions: the sound of a body coming out of the sea, but above all the splashing of a baby's bath. Where the evocation is also emotional, it is especially moving and harks back to tender care and daily gestures. Or perhaps to the time when a foetus was surrounded by amniotic fluid.

The illness

'Don't worry, I haven't got a bone to pick with psychoanalysts and the like.' That is how Alina Marazzi replied (not by chance using the same words as her mother in the film) to an email I had sent her when organizing the showing of her film at the Psychoanalytic Centre in Milan. In fact, I was worried that the story of her mother might have ill-disposed her towards our profession.

I believe that every psychiatrist or psychoanalyst, faced with a story like hers, asks him or herself some question: What caused her illness? What happened? Why were they unable to cure her, to prevent her meeting such a tragic end?

Let us get back for a moment to the film. I want to begin by debunking a belief and a myth that transpires from some reviews. Some people have suggested the hypothesis of a kind of 'anti-psychiatric' interpretation by the director or have spoken about a 'calvary of pharmacological treatment and forced hospitalization'. It is certainly true that in the end Liseli's story is the report of a failure; but, in my opinion, this is not the tale of somebody who did not receive treatment or who was badly treated. Perhaps Liseli was not sufficiently understood, but certainly every attempt was made to treat and cure her.

In the film, we are rather faced with the verification of the existence of limitations and with the tragic confrontation of the impotence and limits of our own work. Liseli was not put in a straitjacket and confined in a psychiatric institutions of the kind we have seen in *One Flew Over the Cuckoo's Nest* (Milos Forman 1975). Indeed, she was able to have access to the best facilities of the time, both private and public, in Italy and abroad. In her letters she also speaks of the beautiful surroundings of the places she was in and of the various therapies she received, even though she also uses irony and mocking terms about them. She received occupational therapy, rehabilitation, psychotherapy and psychoanalysis. I also believe she came in contact with the best-known and most qualified professionals in the field. I know that she had established an intense relationship with some therapists and felt at ease with them.

Perhaps the social position and renown of her family may have been a disturbing element in the long run, instead of acting in her favour. Certainly, in the classical escalation that accompanies every experience of therapeutic impotence, the therapies gradually become more persistent and incongruous, demonstrating that the initial question about the cause of the illness and the failure of the treatments has not yet found a satisfactory explanation.

It is to be noted how, in the film, the words to be found in the hospital files strongly contrast with Liseli's warmth and emotivity. Her words are also an intense and painful documentation of her illness and of the resulting inner suffering.

I shall now make some observations on her illness, starting from the obvious premise that what we have available here are only pictures and words, and not a clinical relationship with a real person. For example, I have no elements for assessing biological or family factors, nor for making a precise diagnosis (perhaps a primary affective disorder?). Certainly one must not overlook the concomitance with the outbreak of war and the traumatic impact that it had on families and individuals. From an early age Liseli appeared to be a rather rigid, problematic person, discontented and ill at ease, worried that people may not like her. The elements that appear most clearly are the relationships with her parents. A mother described as always too pretty and a bit evasive, whom it was difficult to look straight in the eye, and a father who appears much loved, but whom she could never quite reach because of his often rather cynical and haughty attitude (some traits of his character can also be gleaned from certain scenes and shots in his films). A strict, dictatorial father who, in her words, 'trains' her. It is too little to form a hypothesis, but it is easy to think of the dynamics with an Oedipal background that may have developed along the ridge of maternal inaccessibility and the failure to win her father over: a quite unassailable couple! Rather, there are some questions that remain open. First of all, I wondered why the clinical picture did not follow the evolution towards a form of 'false self' which perhaps would have been more protective and less traumatic. There seem to have been the premises for it in her rather formal relationship with her mother and one of poor authenticity with the surrounding environment. Perhaps Liseli's nature was so little inclined to compromise that she could not tolerate for too long functioning according to the principle of satisfying other people's needs. Clear signals of unease already appeared in her adolescence, with signs of depression and mood swings. One might also hypothesize that the real break, the metaphorical eclipse in the film, came about not so much with her marriage as with her move to the United States. In the film this departure is accompanied by pictures of a ship sailing the seas and by the music of the American anthem played by Jimi Hendrix. There is a double break, both in her departure and in the rather profane rendition of the anthem. It is clear that gratification and false self can exist and develop only in the presence of the internalized external object to be satisfied. After the move to the United States, it seems to me that Liseli's words become more and more affectionate towards her mother, her husband and her children (this is quite compatible with an affective mood disorder), but there is also a considerable difficulty in finding a personal dimension in an environment where she was nobody – a fact entirely new and confusing for her. On the one hand, she hoped that the simpler environment might make things easier for her; on the other, she found that she had to reckon with homesickness and distance. Thanks to distance, Liseli manages to communicate with her mother by letter with feelings of closeness, but unfortunately the physical distance creates further suffering. 'I wish I could be with you to be cuddled.' Besides, she feels a sense of loneliness and abandon that she had never experienced before, even isolated for the first time from her husband, and there is the difficulty of being alone looking after two small children. Perhaps she had fooled herself into believing that love alone was enough to make her feel well and save her from the illness. Across the Atlantic, Liseli seems to have had a clear depressive episode with psychotic symptoms, suffering internal fractures that later proved to be insurmountable: the illness that she mentions with increasing awareness, about which she feels guilty, confusing it with a whim, not believed and not recognized.

It is easy to think that the impotence shown by therapists towards Liseli also depended on an insufficient development of our applied science, still too young at that time to deal with complex people in need of help like her.

The analytical course

I think we can talk about the analytical course of the film from two points of view. On the one hand, as part of the more explicit values of self-treatment that the process of approaching and constructing the film meant for the director (and Alina agrees on this) and which she herself has so clearly described in some of the written texts and interviews already mentioned. A process of self-analysis which enabled her to meet her own mother and to begin and complete the process of dealing with her loss. I believe this process was completed the moment she decided to show the film in public, not only to herself and her own family, and not hiding it again in another box, in another cupboard.

On the other hand, starting from a feeling of overlapping, the analytical work which I felt in viewing the film and in knowing the processes necessary to create it. I think this analogy is responsible for most of the mechanisms of my identification and involvement with the film. I think that *Un'ora sola ti vorrei* must have opened intimate personal files in anyone who has carefully watched it, and that its strength lies in this ability to trigger multiple processes of identification that are different in each one of us. For me, it was the sensation of seeing someone at work using an analytical method in a field other than my own profession. What we are trying to do in psychoanalysis, in my opinion, is to help people get in contact with their own history, their own memories, moods, sensations – memory in the broadest sense. The aim is to transform all that into something truly new: not a replacement, but an integration, a processing, a reworking of one's own interior world and of the objects that inhabit it. I think the director managed to achieve something similar in making her film.

The operation reaches its highest peak when Liseli, with Alina's voice, pronounces the words 'We're expecting a baby', words made intelligeble thanks to lip-reading. I believe that in these words Alina Marazzi found the reply to her unanswered questions, the ones that had led her to make this film. Her mother's ironic happy gaze and the words she spoke are proof of the existence of a project and of a desire: to be wanted. This is the profound and indispensable reason for the life of each one of us. In fact we know that if and when there is a desire, it is there that a person can exist and fully find living space.

Finale

About a year after the film's debut, little Teresa Liseli was born, whose first name is that of her great-grandmother and the second that of her grandmother.

Three years later, the director presented her latest film, *Per sempre* (*For Ever*), a journey into the world of cloistered nuns, in which she touches on themes associated with faith. I was struck by this choice of theme, even though it certainly derives from a previous film in which she was assistant director. I think that, in the quest for her mother, Alina Marazzi started from the perception of something missing, or nostalgia, and not from an absence. It is the faith in the return of someone who is missing that allows us to live and do our work. The notion 'for ever' also introduces another time dimension: 'one more hour' is not enough, as the desire is to remain with one's mother (or with one's daughter . . .) 'for ever'.

Perhaps she has turned full circle and the accounts to be reckoned with the past have really been settled.

Notes

1 A different version of this article was included in De Mari, M., Marchiori, E. and Pavan, L. (eds) (2006) *La mente altrove: Cinema e sofferenza mentale*. Milan: Franco Angeli, pp. 200–15. This article springs from a personal rewriting after meetings with the director, viewing the film, taking part in debates, showing the film in educational environments and scrupulously visiting her website, www.unorasola.it. This site is a kind of transitional space where net travellers and surfers can ideally meet the film, the person who created it and its protagonist, Liseli, at any time of day and night. A bridge, then, between her, the film, Alina and memories.
2 www.psychomedia.it/cine@forum/interviste/marazzi.htm.
3 www.unorasolativorrei.it/filmakers/alina1.html.
4 www.erewhon.ticonuno.it/2003/storie/unorasola/alina.html.
5 www.unorasola.it/filmakers/benniatria.html.
6 www.altrocinema.it/archivi/alinamarazzi.html.

3

IS THERE LIGHT AT THE END OF THE TUNNEL?
Keren Yedaya's *Or (Mon Tresor)*

Shimshon Wigoder and Emanuel Berman

<u>Or (Mon Tresor)</u> (Israel, 2004)
Director: Keren Yedaya
Distributor: Kino International

Keren Yedaya's film, recipient of the Golden Camera Prize and the Critics' Week Grand Prize at the 2004 Cannes Festival, is an Israeli-French co-production, and has two alternative titles. In Israel, where the film was made, it is called *Or*; in France, and several other countries, it was distributed as *Mon Tresor*. We will use the Israeli title, not only because we are Israeli, but because of its deeper significance. 'Or' is the name of the film's protagonist; it is a common Israeli name (which can refer, by the way, to both women and men), and also a Hebrew word meaning 'light'. By choosing the French title *Mon Tresor*, rhyming with Or, the makers of the film found a creative way of distancing their title from the French meaning of 'Or', namely gold; they also refer – with delicate irony, as we will spell out later on – to the place of Or in her mother's life. Still, calling the film *Or* is more consonant with its emphasis on the daughter's own experience, which is radically different from her mother's view of her. Moreover, this title has an even broader meaning, related to one of the film's central questions: is there light at the end of this tunnel? Or perhaps, as a jocular Hebrew version bitterly adds, the light comes from a train rushing towards us.

Or is the story of Ruthie, a Tel Aviv prostitute, played by Ronit Alkabetz (who also played the central female role in Dover Kosashvili's *Late Marriage*, 2001, an earlier award-winning Israeli film). At its emotional core stands her adolescent daughter Or, played by Dana Ivgi (whom we earlier saw in Nir

Bergman's moving *Broken Wings*, 2002). One of the secrets of *Or*'s powerful emotional impact upon its viewers is the degree to which it arouses hope, only to demolish it subsequently. On first viewing, the film appears to be divided into two parts, the first (roughly 55 minutes) more optimistic, if not regarding Ruthie then at least regarding Or's chance to find a different life; and the second (the remaining 45 minutes) more despairing. Most first viewers find the shift unexpected, and therefore shocking and arousing deep disappointment. Only in hindsight, and often only on second or third viewing, does it become clear that the transformation is thoroughly prepared, and does not emerge out of the blue. We come to discover signs throughout the film that foreshadow, or hint at, its eventual outcome. Only then does the film emerge as a unified, integrative work of art. One of the sources of this initial experience of shock is that the film presents two intertwined plots, and on first viewing one plot covers (up to the turning point) the other. The dominant plot, initially, focuses upon the rescue fantasy of Or towards her mother Ruthie (see Berman 1997, 1998a). Or is a lovely, brave and resourceful teenage girl who tries desperately to save her mother from the fate of being a prostitute (there are interesting parallels between *Or* and Ken Loach's *Sweet Sixteen*, 2002). The two of them live together in Tel Aviv; Ruthie is a single parent, and Or's father is never alluded to. We don't know anything of their earlier lives.

Or is a classical parental, or parentified, child. In one of the first scenes of the film, when she comes to collect her mother from the hospital, bringing her food and a sweater, her mother complains, 'I have been waiting for an hour,' like a child in kindergarten awaiting her mum. Or gives Ruthie strict instructions about what medications she should take, clarifying for us both Ruthie's poor state of health (never specifically explained) and her incapacity to look after herself. Or also tells her that she was unable to buy the expensive Vioxx (the knowledgeable viewer may mutter, 'how lucky') and substituted it with a cheaper painkiller – making it clear that they barely survive.

Or does everything possible to try and rescue her mother. She locks Ruthie in the house in order to prevent her from going out into the street, sometimes physically struggling with her to grab the apartment keys. She makes every effort to convince Ruthie to accept the job of a cleaning woman in a middle-class household, where the investment in the family dog, Diva, stands in sharp contrast with Ruthie's and Or's poverty. Or tries to support their household financially by collecting bottles and selling them, at times skipping school for this purpose; the heavy bag of bottles she carries in the film's first scene sets its tone. Or also brings food from the neighbours, and earns money by washing dishes at a restaurant and washing the stairs in their apartment house.

The washing scenes are central in the first part of the film. Or is immaculately clean, and she is always busy cleaning, almost compulsively.[1] She must,

Is there light at the end of the tunnel?

Or (Dana Ivgi)

so we feel, clean up her contaminated mother, get the stains out of their soiled life. In a central early scene, she takes advantage of her shower to also wash the family laundry in the same water. Her nudity in this scene is powerful, innocent and asexual, an aspect of her utter dedication to an ego ideal of purity. It contrasts sharply with another nude scene towards the end of the film.

The shower episode is one of the scenes in which a unique technical strategy of the filmmakers is very influential:[2] the camera never moves. The deliberate decision, discussed by the film's co-screenwriter and editor, Sari Ezouz (2005), to give up all the possibilities of camera movement, including zooming in or out, brings the film back to earlier stages of cinematic history, and gives it a puristic, abstinent, quasi-documentary style. At times, figures go arbitrarily out of the frame, heads are 'cut off'[3] – the camera is still, passive, it does not try to help or to manipulate the viewer. Such manipulation is particularly evident in many commercial films when screen nudity is involved, as conventional filmmaking is often busy with maintaining a balance between showing enough to intrigue and arouse the viewer, while not showing too much (*e.g.* not showing the genitals) in order to protect accepted moral norms or the actors' boundaries. The creators of *Or*, in contrast, seem to tell us, 'you are allowed to see what's there, but we won't make any effort to control how you see it, your experience is up to you'. This message appears to be connected to a subtle goal of the filmmakers: to challenge the viewer to take moral responsibility.[4]

To understand Or's initial position, we must contemplate both conscious and unconscious motivations operating when a child becomes a parent to his or her own parent. First of all, there may be little choice when the parent does not function as a parent, and Ruthie's impulsive, childish and irresponsible sides are clear. The role reversal also seems to occur because of the strong affectionate bond between Ruthie and Or, which makes the option of distancing – not to speak of leaving and abandoning Ruthie – impossible for Or. Instead, Or is a child who parents her parent, in order for the parent to grow up, and turn into a real parent; so that the child can become a child with a parent who looks after her (Searles 1979). But this fantasy need is never gratified in *Or*.

The initial internalization of objects derives from the intensity of the child's need for relatedness and the consequent dilemma posed by parents who are emotionally absent, intrusive or chaotic. A child cannot do without parents, yet living in a world in which parents, constituents of one's entire interpersonal world, are unavailable or arbitrary is unbearably painful. Therefore, according to Fairbairn (1954), the first in a series of internalizations, repressions and splits takes place, based on the necessity for preserving the illusion of the goodness of the parents as real figures in the outside world. The child separates and internalizes the bad aspects of the parents: it is not they who are bad, it is she. The badness is inside her. If she were different, she may fantasize, the parents' love and care would be forthcoming.

Every child needs to feel that their parents understand the world, are just and dependable. If they do not experience them in these ways, they transfer the problem onto themselves. As Fairbairn would describe this dynamic, Or takes upon herself (at first unconsciously) the burden of badness (Greenberg and Mitchell 1983). When children experience the 'badness' as outside, in the real parents, they feel painfully unable to make any impact at all. If the badness is inside them, they preserve the hope of omnipotent control over it.

Another dynamic involved may be Or's survivor's guilt. It is not separation anxiety but rather separation guilt. If I am different and more successful than my mother, whom I love and to whom I am connected, I am abandoning her. When Ruthie loudly protests Or's attempts to reform her ('You don't understand . . . what do you know?'), she may also express her anger at being judged and insulted by her daughter. In this respect, Or's purity may contain the seeds of its demise. To understand this better, we must contemplate Ruthie's motives to remain a prostitute. The economic reasons are not sufficient: Ruthie is emotionally addicted to prostitution.[5] She became addicted to selling herself. She sold something she can never receive back; it's a deal with the devil. She receives only fragments of the price, night after night, but will always remain deprived. So what does she receive? The surprising answer the film seems to offer is: a strange kind of pride, an illusory experience of love. In spite of the awful risks – humiliation, violence, danger to her life – Ruthie keeps going out on the streets. She convinces herself that when she goes out she is a beautiful, desirable woman, strong and wild, radically different from her childish, neglected and weak image when she is at home. One could speak here of dissociation, disavowal, counter-phobic measures or reaction formation.

Looking in the mirror on her way out at night Ruthie is filled with vitality, enjoying what she sees. At the other extreme, when taking orders from a middle-class lady as to how to feed her dog, she is deeply humiliated, and pushed back to the lowest step in the social ladder, in a society from which she is excluded. This is probably the main reason that Or's solution for Ruthie, naively supported by the school counsellor, can never succeed.

Or is very invested in saving her mother. At the same time, Or does everything possible to make her mother see her. But she receives no recognition. She is indeed her mother's valued treasure, but not as a separate object, but rather as a 'subjective object' (Winnicott 1969) coloured by Ruthie's needs. In this respect, being seen as a treasure may be more painful than gratifying. Recognition is sorely missing in Or's world. The school counsellor, Anat, cares about her, but is fully identified with the 'constructive, clean' side of Or – this is why she enthusiastically encourages Or's project of turning Ruthie into a cleaning woman – and is therefore no longer an option when this project collapses. Or starts lying to her, claiming all is fine, and Anat is too easily deceived. Said, the young Arab man who works with Or as a dishwasher in the restaurant, does see her; but he is powerless, he is one of the invisible, unnoticed people who populate Tel Aviv. Or's only effective support comes from Ido, the son of her neighbours (the restaurant owners), who is deeply in love with her, and appears to be attentive, loyal and caring, arousing Or's trust and affection too.

The peak of the first, optimistic, part of the film, is the first sexual night that Or and Ido spend together. They sing and laugh, as Or and Ruthie did in an earlier scene.[6] Their budding sexuality, characterized as warm, pleasurable, playful and mutual, arouses our hope. When Or's girlfriend at school tells her 'you're in love', Or answers 'knock it off', but her huge smile tells a different story.

The collapse starts when Rachel, Ido's mother, shows up at Ruthie's apartment the following day, upset about the love affair. In this fateful conversation Rachel tells Ruthie, and then Or too: 'I'm not comfortable with that . . . it's just not right.' Rachel implicitly blackmails and threatens them: 'everything could go on as usual . . .'.

'Mum!', Or pleads for support. 'Maybe Rachel is right,' Ruthie, who had been delighted to watch Ido's and Or's love, meekly says. She is helpless, defeated and broken, and conveys to Or that she will have to acquiesce to Rachel's demand. We realize that Rachel actually forbids Or to be the girlfriend of her son because Or is identified by the society surrounding her as the promiscuous daughter of a prostitute. She cannot be loved for the person she is. Her and Ido's love is doomed.

Or withdraws from Ido, without explaining why (he is not aware of his mother's brutal intervention). Soon afterwards, Or reluctantly agrees to have oral sex with Doudi, one of the local guys, who comes over when on leave from his army service, and clearly exploits her cynically. She appears to be saying, 'nothing makes a difference any more'. At this point she gives up something valuable and crucial, accepting the separation between body and emotions, already accepted by her mother. Despairing at having love, she turns to self-destruction and self-hate. Having betrayed Ido, she pretends not to hear him when he calls her from downstairs.

The next scene is also crucial. Ruthie comes home from the street wounded and traumatized, and Or washes her tenderly. Or seems to realize now that she has not succeeded in curing the addictive repetition-compulsion of Ruthie, who goes on with her work in prostitution in spite of all its dangers (we are reminded here that she may be endangering her life too). She tells her mother: 'You are never going out again.' At first, this seems similar to numerous such moments in the past, but it is different, as Or adds: 'Tomorrow you will stay home and rest.' In other words, she no longer believes that working as a cleaning woman will save her mother. Another solution is needed, and it seems to crystallize during Or's following, sleepless night.

Or washing her traumatized mother Ruthie (Ronit Alkabetz)

In the morning Or goes single-mindedly to the apartment of their sleazy landlord, Shmuel. While Shmuel earlier rejected Ruthie's offer to pay the overdue rent with sex, something she used to do in the past, he gladly accepts such an offer from Or. This is her first experience of selling herself – body and soul – in order to gain economic advantage. Or belittles the meaning of this experience for her, by cheerfully boasting about it to her girlfriends in school, even inventing various details to make the story hilarious. But this time – unlike on other occasions – we cannot enjoy the girls' laughter. We realize something very destructive has happened. Or, apparently, was torn between two painful possibilities: either continuing to be her mother's mother (counter-identification), or becoming her mother's daughter (back to primary identification). Parental children, if they 'fail' in their parental task, may re-identify with the parent, and become in some way like that parent. Having understood, after Rachel's visit, that she is not seen as a person in her own right, and will always be stigmatized by society, Or now gives up the hope of being different, and adopts her mother's fate. If she is treated as a whore anyhow, she might as well enjoy the 'benefits' of this identity. This also becomes her new strategy for rescuing her mother, the most heroic strategy: fighting fire by fire.

As we said before, at first this appears to be a shocking transformation. Only with hindsight can we figure out how this fate was foreshadowed earlier, in what could be described as the latent contamination plot, initially disguised by the plot of 'clean/cleaning Or'. The two intertwined plots express two sides of Or's emerging sexuality. While the friendly sexuality with maternal Ido (who often feeds Or) arouses our joy and identification, being part of a warm object relationship, there are other moments where Or's sexuality with the group of local guys arouses restlessness in the viewer, even without realizing where it may lead.

In a key early scene, Or is kissing and necking with Doudi, who asks her – once his girlfriend Noa is approaching – to leave unnoticed through a back alley. Or acquiesces. Her need to be desired appears to blind her to the fact that she is being taken advantage of.

Rachel, who in some ways has been both Ruthie's and Or's caretaker, sarcastically exposes this side ('Ido loves her? But everyone loves her, and she loves everyone'). Or is devastated by the rejection, and abandons her 'clean' identity. Or may have also realized that her mother was right in claiming that money made in cleaning work, by either of them, is 'peanuts' in comparison to their financial needs (if the rent is not paid, they may be evicted), and to the money available in prostitution. And, in view of Ruthie's ageing, at least in terms of the cruel world of prostitution, her deteriorating health and the fear that she might get killed in the streets one night, Or's rescue project – never abandoned – is now radically transformed. She can rescue mum only by becoming mum; by turning into a younger, more glamorous prostitute.

Unlike Ruthie, the plebeian streetwalker, Or (who pretends to be over 17) becomes a classy call-girl, joining the 'Sexclusive Escort Service', under the assumed name 'Sivan'.[7]

Or, like every teenage girl, is confused by the power, danger, excitement and embarassment related to her budding sexuality. She can use her sexuality, but more likely in Or's case, she can be used and abused because of it. One of the touching and sad images of this film is Or sitting by herself in a Tel Aviv café, dressed in a way which is supposed to make her look older ('the veneer of adult, feminine activity'; Hollander 1961: 412). Or is more of a child than a woman, which makes this film even more sad and heartbreaking.

Or's first steps in the direction of prostitution are taken in order to rescue her mum from the vicious cycle of enslavement, subjugation, exploitation and addiction. But her need to be seen is still enormous – and it is once more frustrated. When Or comes back from her first prostitution job (this is the scene when we see her nude again, now with a lustful client who admires her young body), she is dressed like a prostitute and she weeps helplessly. Ruthie, on her way to work, does not hear her daughter's cry for help. Instead, she admires and compliments Or's appearance ('You look pretty like that with a dress on'), turning a deaf ear to her anguish. When Ruthie notices Or is crying, she attributes it only to Or's concern for her ('Don't cry, my love, I'll be OK'), and does not ask her what is the matter. Ruthie still does not see Or, in the same way that children may not see their parents, even though there is a strong bond between them. Or gets out of her stupor and runs after her mother in the street, begging her desperately to come home. This plea – made when she is herself dressed as a prostitute – brings to a climax her paradoxical fate as a parental child. But Ruthie pushes her aside, again ignoring her pain.

Is Ruthie oblivious to the fact that her daughter now walks in her footsteps? We could also think of her admiration of Or's new dress – never asking where the money to buy it comes from – as part of Ruthie's long-term enigmatic messages to Or. Maybe Or interprets the unconscious message that she, young Or, now has to replace her mother, or that, by joining her, she will no longer condescend her (clean Or as superior to dirty Ruthie) and thus their love can be less conflictual? Maybe mother's message is: we are both outsiders, and will never be able to be accepted by society.

Ruthie's excitement about Or's new appearance – a total change from her former tomboy style – is an extension of her own narcissistic pleasure in her own appearance as a prostitute, which we noted before. The combination of excitement and denial is a factor moulding the enigmatic message to Or, which Or attempts to decipher. In this context, Or's 'choice' to become a prostitute may be a way to receive her mother's approval and love.

We may now wonder: did Or in fact go through a process of transformation, or was this an inevitable path, a fate she could not escape? These two options coexist throughout the film and remain unresolvable. While our

Or fails to stop Ruthie

psychoanalytic viewpoint seeks individual motives and psychological processes, a feminist point of view focusing on social criticism, clearly central for these young filmmakers, suggests that within a certain social and cultural context Or's fate is far from unique, that she was doomed from the day she was born. There may be many Ors in Tel Aviv, and in other big cities. This viewpoint leads to social activism: perhaps, if the world of adults would notice these teenage girls in distress, there is a chance that they might be saved . . .[8]

At the same time, Yedaya and Ezouz, through their attempts to help prostitutes find another life (Ezouz, personal communication) are fully aware that intra-psychic dynamics may play a role in women's clinging to prostitution even when other options are made available.

The film ends most powerfully, offering no relief, no catharsis and no salvation. After Or gives up on stopping her mother from going on the streets, thus possibly realizing that contrary to her fantasy she has not replaced her mother but only joined her, Or calls 'Sexclusive' for another job. Now, Or and another young call-girl are about to undress for a paid orgy, a 'bachelors' party' celebrating a wealthy youngster's wedding. The party music becomes louder.[9] Or sits on a sofa, looking aside sadly, seeming disconnected from what goes on around her. Then, for the first time in the film, she turns her piercing eyes towards the viewer, seemingly asking now something of us. It is difficult not to contemplate Or's future. Will she have the strength to get out of the vicious circle she has now entered? At the same time we may ask ourselves: could we participate in that carefree, 'jolly' party? Are we part of a culture which – actively or passively – goes along with the harsh exploitation of teenage prostitutes? Are we responsible too?

Notes

1. Yedaya and her editor Sari Ezouz made an earlier, shorter film, *Lulu*, describing the life of a call-girl. Lulu is repeatedly shown washing her hands and brushing her teeth.
2. This could serve as a good example of the limitations of psychoanalytic discussions of film which deal with content while disregarding aspects of cinematic technique, although the latter strongly influence the viewer's experience (Berman 1998b). Due to the importance of voyeurism and its sublimation in the dynamics of filmmaking and film-viewing (see Mulvey 1975; Sabbadini 2000), the way the camera (representing the spectator's eye) is handled, and parallel technical choices in editing, are of crucial importance.
3. This could also be understood as indicating that Ruthie and Or are both seen and unseen, as part of their marginality.
4. Yedaya and Ezouz are feminist activists, and they are personally involved in helping prostitutes who wish to get out of prostitution. They plan to use part of the film's income to set up a place where such women can live and get help (Ezouz, personal communication). Still, their film has no didactic or propagandist quality whatsoever, its ideological level being fully integrated.
5. In Hebrew, the term addiction is derived from the verb 'to sell'. In that sense, prostitution as the 'selling of oneself' can also be understood as a form of addiction. In preparing this chapter we searched for psychoanalytic interpretations of prostitution, and were amazed to discover how little this topic was explored in psychoanalytic literature (for rare exceptions, see Agoston 1945; Hollander 1961; Gilman 1981). Psychoanalysts too apparently turn a deaf ear to the despair of the poor and the outcast, in spite of Freud's (1919) hope.
6. The continuity of these two scenes, separated by many others, makes them an example of Eisenstein's extended notion of montage (Berman 1998b).
7. We may be reminded of Agoston's (1945) interpretation of prostitution, relating it to a 'pseudo-personality', to an experience of 'I am not I'.
8. In this context it is interesting to mention two women who in fact were one – Anna O and Bertha Pappenheim (Rosenbaum and Muroff 1984). Her personal history combines psychoanalysis, feminism, and social awareness. Freud saw the starting point of psychoanalysis in Breuer's experience with Anna O, who invented the term 'the talking cure'. Anna O, whose real name was Bertha Pappenheim, subsequently became one of the founders of social work and a feminist activist. She was one of the first feminists to draw the connection between the exploitation of women in general and female prostitution. She founded centres in Germany and elsewhere for prostitutes wishing to change their lives. She travelled to different countries in her crusade against trading in women. On a visit to Palestine in 1911 she gave a fiery speech against 'white slavery' and prostitution. As a result, the Union of Jewish Women Workers in Palestine published their first pamphlet against trading in women. Unfortunately, this phenomenon is still widespread in contemporary Israel, where many women – including teenagers – are brought illegally from poor Eastern European countries and exploited as prostitutes under slavery conditions.

9   Here the film benefits from another deliberate radical technical choice: not using any music, except for the natural sounds of the situations filmed (Ezouz 2005).

References

Agoston, T. (1945) Some psychological aspects of prostitution: the pseudo-personality, *International Journal of Psychoanalysis*, 26: 62–7.

Berman, E. (1997). Hitchcock's *Vertigo*: the collapse of a rescue fantasy, *International Journal of Psychoanalysis*, 78: 975–96.

Berman, E. (1998a) Arthur Penn's *Night Moves*: a film that interprets us, *International Journal of Psychoanalysis*, 79: 175–8.

Berman, E. (1998b). The film viewer: from dreamer to dream interpreter, *Psychonalytic Inquiry*, 18: 193–206.

Ezouz, S. (2005) Contribution to panel on *Or*, 3rd European Psychoanalytic Film Festival, London.

Fairbairn, W.R.D. (1954) *An Object-Relations Theory of the Personality*. New York: Basic Books.

Freud, S. (1919) Lines of advance in psycho-analytic therapy, *Standard Edition*, Vol. XVII. London: Hogarth Press.

Gilman, S. (1981) Freud and the prostitute, *Journal of the American Academy of Psychoanalysis*, 9: 337–60.

Greenberg, J. and S. Mitchell (1983) *Object Relations in Psychoanalytic Theory*. Cambridge, MA: Harvard University Press.

Hollander, M.H. (1961) Prostitution, the body, and human relatedness, *International Journal of Psychoanalysis*, 42: 404–13.

Mulvey, L. (1975) Visual pleasure and narrative cinema, *Screen*, 16: 6–18.

Rosenbaum, M. and Muroff, M. (eds) (1984) *Anna O: 14 Contemporary Reinterpretations*. New York: Free Press.

Sabbadini, A. (2000) Watching voyeurs: Michael Powell's *Peeping Tom*, *International Journal of Psychoanalysis*, 81: 809–13.

Searles, H. (1979) The patient as a therapist to his analyst, in *Countertransference and Related Subjects*. New York: International Universities Press.

Winnicott, D.W. (1969) The use of an object, *International Journal of Psychoanalysis*, 50: 711–16.

4

THE ANOREXIC PARADOX
Matteo Garrone's *First Love*

Maria Vittoria Costantini and Paola Golinelli

Primo amore (*First Love*) (Italy, 2004)
Director: Matteo Garrone
Distributor: Medusa Video

In our clinical work, psychoanalysis provides us with the wherewithal to raise unexplored or repressed areas of the psyche and emotions to the level of consciousness.

What can it give us when we watch a film? Immersed in the dark, in the dreamlike atmosphere of the cinema, intent on watching the flickering images together with the rest of the audience, the analyst finds himself in the ideal situation to use the tools of his work to facilitate the workings of the preconscious. Certain visual images provide a fresh representative stimulus which enables the analyst to make contact with parts of the self. A partially or totally inhibited representative process – or one which had remained unknown or 'deactivated' – can then be set in motion again thanks to the evocative force of the moving pictures and the complexities of the cinema as an artistic form, with its ever more sophisticated techniques, encompassing words, music, noise, sounds and silence. It becomes the means to carry on the mind's journey from sensations and perceptions to representation, providing a continual flow of 'representations of things'. From this viewpoint, cinema can reactivate the representation function, enriching it and presenting (or re-presenting) aspects which would otherwise remain obscure.[1]

Compared to the average filmgoer, the analyst is more aware and more accustomed to reflecting on his emotions. Thus, he can shift from seeing the object/film from the outside to an inner view of himself. This does not mean that the filmgoing analyst must deliberately take up a special type of mental

The anorexic paradox

mindset aimed at analysing the film, which would be largely incompatible or intolerable vis-à-vis the preconscious (Bolognini 2002). Rather, the analyst may make use of a mental disposition which is familiar to him through his work. He may respond to the disturbing elements of the film, instead of rejecting them or letting them slide into a general impression of well-being or discomfort, later to be stored away, formless and undifferentiated, along with many other such stimuli.

Through identification, the analyst is drawn to the psychic world of the artist (the filmmaker). This is not in order to discover possible pathological elements. Rather, it is to answer a call that both psychoanalysis and art have in common; a call to seek out 'truths' yet to be revealed, elements still undifferentiated, at the very limit of the sensorial, of the corporeal. The analyst is fascinated by a psychic movement that leads him from 'looking [at the artistic object] to taking a disturbing look at oneself' (Di Benedetto 2000: 38).

With reference to Matteo Garrone's intensely dramatic film *First Love* (*Primo amore*), we will be focusing on the representation of the exhausting struggle between the need for control over emotions and the libidinal expression of the body.

It is the skin, the flesh, the body as a whole as the seat of both senses and affects, that first accomplishes the world and remains marked by it. The history of every individual develops from the relationship with the mother's body, a unique bond of which both parties retain a memory in the flesh. Mother and baby co-penetrate, united in an embrace which gives a special significance to both. The signs of that primary relation are, for the most part, unconscious, not repressed but forming part of the memory which is called 'implicit' or 'procedural' and which we might call 'somatic', as it is inscribed in that individual's body and constitutes his or her individuality and otherness. The sense of this primary relation imbues all subsequent relations, which are thus affected by the corporeal imprint, since in the initial stages of development object relations and corporeal experience coincide.

In *Inhibitions, Symptoms and Anxiety* Freud (1925) wrote that the word is born from the flesh. What we carry in our bodies is 'our flesh', i.e. the primordial affective experience. 'Metaphorically speaking,' writes Racalbuto (1994), 'I would venture to call this type of knowledge "carnal knowledge" (also the title of a Mike Nichols' 1971 film); it is the basis for what first constitutes psychic reality, reality accomplished through affective sensations, i.e. sensorial experiences with a marked emotional connotation'. The body is the front and back door of the emotions, the source of sensations: man's body is history incarnate.

Through his films, especially *L'imbalsamatore* (*The Embalmer*) (2002) and *Primo amore* (2004), Matteo Garrone deals masterfully with the theme of the body: it becomes the battleground which, by eliminating all that represents

47

the libidinal-emotional *sexual* aspects of the body, aims at nullifying the affective dimension which the subject paradoxically perceives as the greatest threat to his or her self-integrity.

The idea of *First Love* is taken from a news item, narrated in the novel *Il cacciatore di anoressiche* (*The Hunter of Anorexic Women*), written by a convict (Mariolini 2001). One of the themes the film takes up is that of the conflict between, on the one hand, the fantasy of body-mind perfection which can only be achieved by eliminating the living matter, and on the other, the impossibility of accomplishing such a goal. It would mean eliminating Eros, i.e. eliminating the life instinct and therefore life itself.

First Love tells the story of a relationship between a man and a woman which starts with a blind date, devoid that is of affects. What lies behind this, on the man's part, are fantasies stemming from a perverse, delusional project, whereas the girl seems to be driven more by a need to break out of her loneliness and emotional void, within a borderline pathology. She manifests aspects of dependence, insecurity and inner narcissistic emptiness which constitute the gap through which he is able to insinuate himself and attempt to empty her. The film starts with the two protagonists declaring their standpoints: 'I thought you were thinner,' says the hunter of anorexics; 'In that case, I'll go,' replies Sonia. However, evidently she cannot bear the separation from and loss of the object; the fact that she stays seals the perverse contract and sets in motion the *folie-à-deux*.

The director has a special skill in reconstructing the environment and making the actors play their parts in a crudely authentic manner. Michela Cescon, who plays Sonia, actually lost 15 kilograms (over 30 pounds) in

Vittorio (Vitaliano Trevisan) and Sonia (Michela Cescon)

weight during the making of the film, as the director wanted. Vitaliano Trevisan, who plays the part of the male protagonist Vittorio, is from Vicenza, where the film is set, and helped in the writing of the screenplay to make it more realistic. The use of a shoulder-held camera also shows the director's desire to really get inside the story. As analysts, we can recognize ourselves in this identificatory modality which lies at the foundations of our work. Both in the analytic relation and in the film, we are immediately captivated by the characters and enter into their minds, experiencing ourselves their dramas and anxieties.

Vittorio, who has inherited a small goldsmith's workshop in the city of Vicenza, world famous for its gold jewellery, is immediately presented as suffering from a serious illness which entails the need to control the object, even as regards its material aspects: gold as well as women's bodies. We are immediately struck by his anaffectivity and by the fact that he seems to replace his affects with a desire for perfection, which leads him to empty the female body and strip ever more flesh from the stylized gold figures produced in his workshop. He appears to be incapable of a real process of mentalization, and so his attempt to control the incandescent matter (gold) – which represents carnality – is performed by concretely reducing bit by bit both the woman and the statuettes. They grow thinner and thinner, finally becoming fetishes stripped of any flesh. The story is masterfully narrated on two levels: the working of gold represents the metaphoric, while the real is the 'working' of a woman's body.

Vittorio's plan is revealed in the course of two interviews with a psychiatrist. In the first he states that he would be fine if he could only find a woman who would allow him to join mind and body together, meaning an anorexic body. He is looking for a mind without desires, emotions or needs. In the course of the second interview, Vittorio tells the psychiatrist he has found 'a mind', but that he has to remodel the body. The psychiatrist makes a clumsy attempt to get him to see reason and make him understand that the body of a human being cannot be omnipotently modelled as if it were gold. The psychiatrist's attempt fails and only seems to consolidate the dissociative aspect, as shown in the dialogue with his patient which ends with the psychiatrist saying: 'Does Sonia know what you are turning her into?', to which Vittorio replies: 'I know what I don't want her to turn me into.' Our clinical experience tells us that it is highly unlikely that this type of patient would refer himself to the psychiatric services, given that he shows no signs of suffering, nor concern for others. We think that it is also rather improbable that a psychiatrist would respond to such a patient by laying down the law, appearing to sit in judgement and relating so little to him, as if he had no understanding at all of basic psychiatric and psychoanalytic principles.

Rather, these scenes appear to be the externalization of an internal dialogue between one part of the protagonist which silences the healthy aspect of the ego trying to bring him back to reality, and his other split off part. Indeed, the splitting in Vittorio's self is made clear when, denying an aspect of reality, he attempts to push forward the 'frontiers of the possible', to cross the narrow borders of the human condition. According to Chasseguet-Smirgel, 'there is a "perverse core" latent within each one of us that is capable of being activated under certain circumstances' (1983: 293). Indeed, when Vittorio meets Sonia, he seems to lose sight of the boundaries between self and other and to try to build his own personal 'neo-reality'.

The creative potential of the drive towards modelling reveals the failure of the fetishistic production, which serves to guarantee the image of a body refuting gender differences, male and female, and separation. Vittorio wishes to reduce Sonia's body to a mere skeleton. Like his slender and elongated gold sculptures, this for him is absolute purity, achieved by the elimination of all dross and of all shapes; it is a fetishistic part object. Fetishistic construction is Vittorio's extreme and desperate defence against the anxiety of fragmentation of the self, in an inner world where defences against persecution become increasingly rudimentary. In order to satisfy his deadly fantasy, Sonia must be reduced to an ego-skeleton, with no dross/flesh, nor desires or forms, and therefore as perfect as an abstract idea. Affectivity seems to coincide with the flesh, and therefore the mind must belong to a body stripped of its flesh to avoid being made impure by emotional contamination. As a result, the body can be omnipotently freed from its limitations. When Sonia gives in and eats some food, Vittorio tells her: 'It was your body that wanted to eat, not your mind.'

The fantasies present in perversion cancel out the anxiety of passivity and powerlessness, denying the existence of human, maternal control over the subject. These fantasies deny that the mother may have harmed the baby. We could say that an individual can create a perversion instead of forming a relationship (Bach 1991). The perverse individual confuses past and present and denies the boundaries of separation. He needs the pretence, deception and illusion created by the fetish; he needs to dominate and manipulate.

In *Alienation in Perversions*, Masud Khan (1987) describes the technique of intimacy to indicate the character and emotional atmosphere of object relations concerned with perversion. By means of this technique, the subject would seek to 'push inside' another person something which belongs to his deeper nature. The author maintains that one of the few talents a pervert has is the ability to create an atmosphere which can induce another person to voluntarily surrender to his perverse logic. This brings about a suspension of judgement and a resistance as regards guilt, shame and separation. According to Khan, a fictitious situation is offered in which two individuals temporarily give up their identities and their boundaries and try to create corporeal (physical) intimacy, with the aim of achieving the highest degree of orgasm.

This 'technique of intimacy' is accurately portrayed by Garrone in *First*

Love, both in the indoor claustrophobic and suffocating scenes, and in his making the woman act out the man's perverse nucleus. Vittorio's house and workshop is like a fortress with barred windows to protect the gold, not unlike a bank vault. It also serves to represent the inner prison in which his ego paces restlessly until he meets Sonia. This enables the perverse/deluded nucleus to take shape. Even the purchase of a new house only shifts the location; the setting is the same. It is not a place for freedom or to build a loving relationship, as Sonia, after some initial hesitation, believes. Rather, it is an isolated fortress (on the beautiful hills near Vicenza) within which to lock her up. One could say it is a new workshop in which to terminate the final work on her body, by 'pushing inside', as Khan says, his perverse part. As the film progresses, the folly of Vittorio's project is revealed.

McDougall (1989) states that psychic life begins with a fusion experience from which there derives the fantasy that a single body and a single psyche exist for two (the mother/child dyad). Deeply buried within us is the fantasy of the single body, together with nostalgia for a return to this illusory 'fusion', and the wish to become part again of the mother or of the world of early childhood: without any frustrations, responsibilities or desires. In order to achieve this, Vittorio must strip the primary object, the frightening, omnipotent maternal body, to the bone. From this point of view we could consider that he, not she, is the real anorexic, because he cannot live with the desire for fusion with a primary object, experienced as a pernicious maternal body to be expelled. It is thus split off and 'pushed inside' an object-ego-skeleton, deprived of flesh.

Of course, one may ask why Sonia is prepared to offer herself as the object of his madness and why she cannot free herself from him, even as she gradually realizes that she is being imprisoned and used as a goldsmith's object, according to the symbolic equation which persecutes him. From the start of the film, Sonia is shown as fragile, insecure and dependent; she creates dependence and is unable to stand separation and object loss; she is masochistic and captivated by his disapproval. Within Sonia, there also seems to be a strong nostalgia for a return to illusory 'fusion', which would protect her from separation anxiety. The masochist is a depressed subject who still hopes not to lose the object (McWilliams 1994). That is why masochists take on the guilt of the other's disappointment, carry out every task that is imposed upon them, in the hope that the more they adhere to the other's requests by sacrificing themselves, the more they will be loved.

Sonia immediately accepts Vittorio's sadistic fantasies and allows him to carry them through in the masochistic attempt to maintain the illusion of fusion. Her reaction in so doing triggers off a psychotic breakdown in Vittorio. The idea of accomplishing what would bridge the gap between the symbolic and the real – or in his own words, having a mind and a (non) body joined together – seems to make the fantasy come true of the union of a body deprived of its dangerous flesh (affects). Vittorio loses his workers, his connections at work, his customers and his friend, a sales representative, while Sonia, as she becomes thinner and thinner, loses along with her flesh also her affectivity, mobility and vitality. As with real anorexic patients, her mood changes and she becomes irritable, aggressive and withdrawn. As her ribs begin to protrude, the actress who plays Sonia seems possessed by the anorexic obsession, as if she had totally identified with her character.

We, the spectators, become prey to anxiety, just as we are whenever faced with real-life anorexics. Sonia becomes ever more passive and gives up what little remains of her autonomy to Vittorio, just like anorexics do with the tyrants inside them, obsessed as they are with food, scales and calories, but most of all by the fictitious illusion of feeling fulfilled by holding on to an object which is already lost. Once Sonia has begun her life as an anorexic, she absorbs from Vittorio the anorexic way of thinking and appears to take on that role with all its modalities, rituals and cavings-in, which culminate in the dramatic scene at the restaurant. Here Sonia, having ordered just a green salad without any seasoning, gets tempted by Vittorio's dish of *tagliatelle coi funghi* and, while he is for a few minutes at another table with some friends, she furtively takes a forkful of it, then another, then another . . . Soon she is overwhelmed by the desire to stuff herself and she greedily devours the whole plate. As Vittorio realizes what she is doing, she gets up from the table and runs to the kitchen, followed by him. Here her orgastic need for food comes to its climax: in the general pandemonium ensuing, Vittorio tries to physically constrain her, the cooks get upset, crockery gets smashed to the floor, Sonia frantically grabs and gobbles down directly from the saucepans anything she can lay her hands on, shouts, runs around . . . In the next, squalid scene, we see Sonia naked, kneeling down in front of a toilet, throwing up under Vittorio's accusatory eye.

The substantial difference between Sonia's psychic set-up and the central nucleus of the anorexic condition is the moral law to which the real anorexic submits and which recalls Kant's 'imperatives'. It is an absolute and necessary transcendent demand to which she owes blind obedience, a primitive superego. It is, in fact, more of an ego ideal, so imbued with a corporeal ideal ego as to prevent any form of growth that would bring it up against the primitive mother and therefore death.

We know that anorexic patients in analysis, when they begin to establish an affective relationship with the analyst and to feel dependent, are seized by anxiety and often interrupt the treatment. By contrast, faced with Vittorio's excessive sadism, Sonia realizes that she is in mortal danger and begins to react like a trapped animal (witness the scene in the restaurant). Even her vomiting, following her binge, is provoked not by guilt but by the sadistic control which he imposes upon her. It is a paradox that anorexics die in order to live, because by dying they kill the persecutory primary object. They reduce themselves to

The anorexic paradox

the bone in order to have a body, experiencing such a great anxiety that the affects of the fleshed body will kill them. Sonia, on the other hand, rebels as soon as she becomes aware that she is being used by Vittorio in order to realize his fantasies of annihilation and death. When she realizes that she is really losing herself, mentally and physically, and that there is no escape for her, she attempts to kill Vittorio to save her own life. If the borderline solution cannot consist of separation from the object, all that remains for Sonia to do is to physically eliminate the other. In order to live, she has to eliminate her partner, i.e. the aspect that he puts inside her, necessarily a part colluding with her most primitive, fusional and persecutory one.

In fact, the film's ending is left ambiguous; we do not know what really happens. Vittorio is struck on the head and falls to the ground, but we hear his voice ranting and raving about his project. Garrone exploits the confusion that exists between the two protagonists: the spectator can no longer tell whether the voice is that of the man who is still alive but delirious, or of the woman who has absorbed the delusion of her dead partner. Not even now is Sonia able to leave, perhaps because the persecutory object has really become part of her. We could even state that this explicitly ambiguous ending reveals another possible interpretation of the film: it could be seen as a metaphor in

Sonia (Michela Cescon) and Vittorio (Vitaliano Trevisan)

which Vittorio, since the beginning of the story, is nothing more than the externalization of the internal, perverse, persecutory object of Sonia, the real anorexic.

When the splitting fades, Sonia – following the anorexic paradox – can only kill him, that is, kill herself, in order to save herself.

Conclusion

Cinema, and more generally art, can provide psychoanalysts with extra tools for dealing with uncertainty and stress when, in the course of their daily practice, they may feel overwhelmed by confusion. What is thus made available to them is 'a material that allows them to think and represent what had not, and could not have, been thought and represented before' (Golinelli 2004).

Anorexic folly remains as much unknown as it is painful. We may have learned to master delusional ideas or psychotic disintegration, but we still find it unacceptable that fully clear-minded and well-structured individuals could coldly plan their death by starvation out of the despairing conviction that this is their only way to survive.

Through its narrative and its images – cruel and often upsetting, but so realistic as to truly 'capture' its audience – *First Love* forces us to reflect about and to enter into the anorexic folly, in itself repulsive and unthinkable because of its almost inhuman quality, and to attempt to give it meaning. Through our identification with the two protagonists, Sonia and Vittorio, and with their split off parts, it is possible to make sense of the anorexic paradox of depriving the internal persecutor of food to the point of starving it to death, in order to save one's life.

Note

1 An analyst with a passion for cinema, Alain De Mijolla (1999) refers to his autobiographical experience of reinterpreting in *après coup* a childhood memory linked to a film he had seen as a child. Watching the film again as an adult, one scene that had particularly struck him became the keystone for his professional choice to become an analyst.

References

Anzieu, D. (1985) *The Skin Ego*. London: Hogarth Press, 1989.
Bach, S. (1991) On sadomasochistic object relations, in G. Fogel and W. Myers (eds) *Perversions and Near-Perversions in Clinical Practice*. New Haven, CT: Yale University Press.

Bolognini, S. (2002) *Psychoanalytic Empathy*. London: Free Association Books, 2004.
Chasseguet-Smirgel, J. (1983) Perversion and the universal law, *International Review of Psycho-Analysis*, 10: 293–301.
De Mijolla, A. (1999) Freud and the psychoanalytic situation on the screen, in J. Bergstrom (ed.) *Endless Night: Cinema and Psychoanalysis, Parallel Histories*. Berkeley, CA: University of California Press.
Di Benedetto, A. (2000) *Prima della parola*. Milan: Franco Angeli.
Freud, S. (1925) Inhibitions, symptoms and anxiety, in *Standard Edition*, Vol. xx. London: Hogarth Press, 1960.
Golinelli, P. (2004) Per una lettura psicoanalitica dei film, *Rivista di Psicoanalisi*, L, 2: 449–60.
Khan, M. (1987) *Alienation in Perversions*. London: Karnac.
Mariolini, M. (2001) *Il cacciatore di anoressiche*. Legnano: Gruppo Edicom.
McDougall, J. (1989) *Theatres of the Body*. London: Free Association Books, 1996.
McWilliams, N. (1994) *Psychoanalytic Diagnosis: Understanding Personality Structure in the Clinical Process*. New York: Guilford Press.
Racalbuto, A. (1994). *Tra il fare e il dire*. Milan: Cortina.

5

REPARATION AND THE EMPATHIC OTHER
Christian Petzold's *Wolfsburg*
Ralf Zwiebel

Wolfsburg (Germany, 2003)
Director: Christian Petzold
Distributor: Peripher Film

As a specific psychoanalytic way of approaching the understanding of a film, Gerhard Schneider proposed to consider it as a 'quasi-person'. In this way one develops a 'quasi-personal' relationship to the film that induces different emotional-cognitive reactions, related especially to the strangeness, the unknown and the mystery of the Other.

Much as in the encounter with the analysand in the analytic situation, the psychoanalyst approaching a film wants to understand his emotional experience by asking two fundamental questions: Who is he (the film)? And what is its meaning for him? (Schneider 2006). Or, in other words, the psychoanalyst dealing with films wants to decode the film's unconscious message (Zwiebel and Mahler-Bungers 2006). Developing such an emotional-cognitive relationship with the film involves watching the film again and again, reading about the problems that are raised by it, comparing it to other productions by the same director, and engaging in self-reflection or self-analysis: this is of course a never-ending process with no definite outcome. This methodological procedure can be compared to the inner working process of the analyst in the clinical situation: by assuming a kind of bifocal attitude, the film analyst oscillates between an *object-perspective* (the observation of the formal structure, the images and the narrative of the film) and a *subject-perspective* (the awareness of his own emotional and associative reactions).

Through a form of 'intercontextuality', this can provide different, and partly new and unique, meanings to the film.

Before considering my own observations, responses and reactions to Christian Petzold's *Wolfsburg*, it might be useful to look at the background to the film and its director. Born in 1960, Christian Petzold is a young and successful German filmmaker, having so far made films for television and more than ten features, including *Die Innere Sicherheit* (*Inner Security*) (2000), *Toter Mann* (*Dead Man*) (2001) and his latest, *Gespenster* (*Ghosts*) (2005).

Wolfsburg, which was released in 2003, tells the story of a man, Phillip, who hits a young boy with his car and drives away from the accident without helping him. The boy's death increases the protagonist's struggle with his conflictual wishes to confess his guilt and to deny it, as he seeks relief in a relationship with Laura, the single mother of the child, who is searching for the perpetrator and is after revenge. Eventually they fall in love, but at the end of the film Laura discovers the true identity of the protagonist and stabs him while driving together in his car. Petzold describes his film as a movie about love and cars, and the development of a man who leaves his car to become a human being.

What strikes me about the film is how, even after repeated viewings, it remains difficult to establish a confident and close relationship to it; there remains a feeling of distance, strangeness, coldness and ambivalence. The film as a 'quasi-person' does not develop into a trustworthy and well-known human being whom one wants to get close to, and attempting to do so is a painful, even torturing, experience. The film conveys an emotional atmosphere of desolation and inner emptiness, which makes it difficult to develop an empathic identification with its protagonists. The only way we can interpret their inner worlds is through their actions.

This 'social coldness', or sterile reserve, is also evoked by the film's formal structure. All drastic and direct descriptions are avoided except at the very end, and in many scenes it is difficult for the spectator to get close to the action. When the boy is hit by a car we hear the collision, but we do not actually see it. As spectators we are kept at a distance from the injured child, a position perhaps resembling Phillip's own. When Laura hears that her child has died, the scene is immediately interrupted; her subsequent attempted suicide is only revealed to us in the doctor's medical report; and the sexual encounter between Phillip and Laura is left to be imagined by the spectator. Most of the sequences are short and many of them are interrupted. As a result the situations and interactions among the characters are suggested, but cut short before the spectator can develop a strong affective involvement with them (Moser and v. Zeppelin 1996). A similar effect is achieved by the near-absence of music in the film – only in the last sequences can music be heard, and that is only a very discreet melody in the background. A sense of sterility is also created by the film's settings, in particular the couple's living room, which seems empty and impersonal. In this respect the short and laconic dialogues suggest a kind of speechlessness and do not reveal much about the characters' personal histories. We find out, however, that Phillip is a 'womanizer' and that Laura wanted to give her baby away for adoption. There are no real or inner parents to which the protagonist can turn for help or assistance. And, finally, there is the constant presence of the motor-car, which probably gives the film its title, *Wolfsburg*, the city of the German Volkswagen. We could interpret the motor-car as a metaphor for the isolation and reserve of human beings, for the conflict between sheet metal and flesh, between cold and technical abstraction on the one hand, and the loss of emotional and human contact and empathy on the other. Or, in other words, the motor-car seems to represent the claustrophobic inner world of the modern subject. We are also reminded of Cronenberg's *Crash* (1996) in which the fetishistic bond between cars and sexuality is manifestly clear.

All these formal and structural elements of the film contribute to the emotional impression of 'social coldness', and the reserve of the images can be interpreted psychoanalytically as hinting at the lack of human empathy. These reflections could be deepened by considering political, historical or socio-psychological contexts, and especially German history; but keeping my focus on the psychoanalytic perspective, I would like to consider my emotional response to the film narrative, and discuss in greater detail the relationship between real and unconscious guilt, empathy and reparation. The issue of reparation for me is one of the central aspects of the film, and is also a key feature of Kleinian psychoanalysis. Although I do not consider myself a Kleinian analyst, I find this issue to be of great importance in clinical psychoanalysis. Plenker (2002) discusses this problem in his paper 'On reparation' as the inner work on damaged inner objects, which is often transferred to real persons. The main point he makes is about the ability to cope with the sense of guilt about one's own destructiveness and that the wish for reparation is connected with the depressive position described by Melanie Klein.

There are two main questions that move me as a spectator of *Wolfsburg*: Why does the protagonist not get out of his motor-car after hitting the boy and help the injured child? And why does he want to have a relationship with the child's mother? In my view some of the answers can be provided, as we have seen, by the formal and structural aspects of the film. The film's accident sets in motion the following events: Phillip argues with his girlfriend who reproaches him for being cold and not paying attention to her, and threatens to leave him. He swerves his car, dropping his mobile phone on the floor; and as he bends down to pick it up, he knocks the boy off his bike. Following the collision, we see Phillip looking back in shock at the hurt child: his first impulse is to get out of the car to help him, but then, realizing there are no witnesses, he decides to drive away. Psychologically we can speak of a double guilt – that is, the hitting of the child and his decision not to help him.

The protagonist's shock is also felt by the viewer, who – from a safe distance – asks himself why Phillip does not get out of his car to help the child. Many of the spectators will probably identify in some way with his conflict of conscience, especially with the moral duty to help the child. They may feel indignant about Phillip's flight, but to do so is to forget that all human beings have been and always will be in similar situations, even if not quite as dramatic and traumatic as this one. In other words, we are all guilty: we all hurt and harm other people, whether we are conscious of it or not, whether we do it willingly or not; and we have to find a way to cope with the conflict between acknowledging our real guilt and our wish to deny, repress and project it. But, as spectators of the film, we are neither given much time to reflect on our emotional reactions in greater depth, nor to consider Phillip's inner state of mind or experiences of real guilt in our own lives. There is also not much time

Phillip (Benno Fürmann)

to reflect on the fact that a child has been hit by a car and injured. This leads to a form of vagueness or obscurity that can be linked to the protagonist's inability to understand his own reaction to the accident, why he ran away and was unable to help and empathize with the injured boy.

We only realize just how little Phillip understands this reaction in a later sequence, when he is on his way to the police in order to confess his crime. He seems to be aware of his double guilt and cannot understand why he did not help the child, yet despite this insight his own actions are alien or unconscious to him – I referred to the emptiness of his inner world – although his motives seem to be less difficult to understand: he wants to save his bacon! We could also suggest that through the unforeseen accident Phillip is suddenly confronted with his own self-centredness and hostility towards the Other, or in other words with the loss of his social 'mask'. The accident and his escape lead to the injury of the real child, but also to a shattering of Phillip's self-image, which forces him to come face to face with the destructive and narcissistic parts of his personality. The outer reality of the accident and his flight from it, therefore, resonate with Phillip's inner reality, something that can be described as a confrontation with the 'bad parts' of his self.

This effectively constitutes the central proposition of psychoanalysis, namely the intertwining of inner and outer reality. As the story unfolds, it seems to describe the destiny of these inner and outer conflicts: the outer conflict consists of the protagonist's wish to acknowledge his real guilt and to avoid real punishment; the inner conflict can be seen in his wish to gain an insight into his self: to acknowledge and accept his 'badness' on the one hand, and to hold on to his idealized image and repress the rejected parts of his self on the other. As spectators we experience Phillip's agonizing difficulty of coping with his real conflicts, to confront his real guilt, which he is always attempting to do.

There are, I think, a number of reasons why he cannot cope with this, which can be seen again in the intertwining of inner and outer reality: the outer conflict of real guilt seems to have a complicated connection with the inner conflict of unconscious, imagined guilt (originating from his relationship with his girlfriend and perhaps, we could speculate, from his childhood). Furthermore, he seems unable to cope with his real guilt in the absence of an empathic Other. And, lastly, the awakened drive for reparation precipitates a sort of 'perversion of reparation' when he meets Laura and falls in love with her.

Let us now take a more detailed look at some specific scenes in order to illustrate what I have been discussing so far. In the sequence where Phillip returns home after the accident and goes to make a telephone call to confess his crime, he is interrupted by his girlfriend, who tells him she wants to leave him because of his self-centredness and hostility towards her. Following this accusation, and because under the surface he does feel a real sense of guilt, he rushes to embrace her, but is unable to confess his guilt, probably because at that moment the loss of his self-image, and of the respect of his girlfriend which would accompany it, seems unbearable to him. In one of the scenes that follow we see Phillip on his way to the police, rehearsing his confession, but in the next sequence he is in the hospital where the injured boy is being treated. We can imagine Phillip praying that the boy recovers, that his injuries are not serious, so that he doesn't need to confess his failure and can repair his damaged self-image.

But in this scene we are also alerted to his activated impulse of reparation, seen in his repressed concern for the boy and his desire to make up for the harm he has caused him. In the hospital he meets the child's mother, Laura. Just as he is about to introduce himself to her and reveal what he has done, she is called away by a nurse and informed that her son has woken up. Again, chance prevents him from confessing his actions, but probably at the same time it calms down his inner anxieties and assures him that after all his crimes are not that serious. His journey to Cuba soon after and his unexpected marriage seem to be a kind of escape from his outer and inner conflicts, like 'a flight from conscience', to use Leon Wurmser's (1992) phrase.

Again we see the intertwining of inner and outer reality: Phillip tries to flee from his real guilt by repairing his damaged relationship with his girlfriend, which is what had caused his unconscious feeling of guilt in the first place, and also to repair his self-image. After his return, Phillip is confronted with the death of the child and must accept the failure of his flight from his outer and inner conflicts. Yet again, his attempts to confess to his wife fail, this time because she misinterprets what he tries to say as being about his infidelity, and so refuses to accept the role of the empathic Other: 'I do not want to be your garbage container,' she tells him. As spectators we feel for a moment the despair caused by this misunderstanding. Even in one of the last scenes, when Phillip and Laura, by now lovers, are at the seaside, Phillip makes a final, if hesitating, attempt to tell Laura the truth, but she embraces and kisses him and, yet again, his confession is interrupted. So we witness an oscillation between his wish to acknowledge his guilt, and to deny and repress it, both chance and the lack of an empathic Other reinforcing his tendency for repression.

After the boy's death Phillip's inner and real conflicts intensify, and his desperate wish for reparation becomes compelling, especially after he meets Laura by chance in a restaurant. Since he can offer no real reparation for the death of her child, he focuses his wishes for reparation on to her. In a scene that is reminiscent of Hitchcock's *Vertigo* (1958), he saves her from suicide, takes her home and invites her for dinner. At this point it is likely that she suspects him, and he probably realizes it. Again we can see the close intertwining of inner and external reality, and we ask ourselves why he should want a relationship with Laura.

Phillip's attraction to Laura has a psychodynamic complexity which cannot be simply attributed to his being a 'womanizer'. With regard to the real conflict, it may be that he wants to stay in close contact with his 'enemy' and his persecutor, so as to be able to control her; at the same time his repressed wish for confessing to an empathic Other becomes progressively stronger. Laura, on the other hand, is attracted to him because she also suffers from guilt and unconsciously considers herself her own son's killer. No forgiveness can be as effective as the forgiveness of the victim! But Phillip's wish to confess is at this point corrupted by his need for unconscious punishment which was already evident in the lack of resistance Phillip had put up after his wife had left him and when he lost his job.

Since Laura is looking for the culprit and is after revenge, Phillip unconsciously offers himself for punishment. His attempts to rescue the depressive and suicidal Laura may also have a self-centred component, for her successful suicide would turn him into a 'double murderer'. Finally, I would like to suggest that his need for reparation is erotized and perhaps expresses his unconscious phantasy to give Laura a child by making her pregnant, thereby undoing and repairing his destructive deed. His yearning for a good, inner object in the real person of Laura is significant, since the lack of an empathic Other reflects also the lack of a good inner object. Reparation would be impossible in the absence of such an object.

Considering this complex pattern of motivations, one can truly speak of an 'impossible love' or a 'perversion of reparation', because the relationship consists of lies and a denial of reality, erotization of destructiveness, and self-centredness. A reconciliation under these circumstances seems impossible, and the return of the repressed unavoidable. Again, chance has a role to play when Laura discovers the car licence number and deduces that Phillip must be the culprit. Eventually Phillip is, fittingly, punished for his crime by undergoing the same fate as his victim. Since he could not meet an empathic Other, the total identification with the victim is all he is left with: stabbed by Laura with a knife, he lies badly injured on the road like the child he had run over. Laura can at last prove his guilt as she calls the police, but at the same time fulfils her revenge by abandoning the badly injured Phillip on the road.

It would be fascinating at this point to compare this movie with the already mentioned *Vertigo*, a film also much admired by Christian Petzold. In my own comments on this film I discussed the issues of trauma and melancholia which are, in my opinion, central to *Vertigo* and to Hitchcock's work in general (Zwiebel 2003, 2006). The tragic problem of 'perversion of reparation' and the compulsion to repeat are also found in the relationship between the protagonists, 'Scottie' Ferguson and Madeleine Elster: Scottie's trauma leads to guilt feelings which manifest themselves in his acrophobia and in his unconscious wish to fall and let fall. In the meeting with the beautiful Madeleine, who seems so attracted to death, Scottie first wants to rescue his own self from this destructive self-punishment, but what then develops is an 'impossible' love relationship that contains all the elements of a 'perversion of reparation': denial of reality, erotization, hidden destructivness, narcissistic and fetishistic aspects of the relationship and the final breakdown of the rescue phantasy. It would also be interesting to discuss the apparently different endings of both films – Scottie has overcome his acrophobia but lost his beloved Madeleine, while Phillip lies heavily injured and helpless next to his car as Laura leaves him. This, however, would require a much closer examination of both films.

The issues raised in this chapter – the conflict between real and neurotic guilt feelings, the intertwining of inner and real conflicts, the urge for reparation and the role of the empathic Other – are also of central concern to psychoanalytic, especially Kleinian, theory. With regards to the understanding of the psychoanalytic process, in particular the importance of working through the patient's depressive anxieties, Plenker discusses the differentiation between guilt feelings from the perspective of superego and guilt stemming from archaic object relations, as well as the tendency of the analyst to avoid this latter problem, and the analyst's need to tolerate his own guilt. This could open up an 'intercontextual' discussion about the film's contribution to these themes, but while in a clinical context the inner processes are emphasized – Plenker writes 'reparation is mainly an inner process, which is connected with painful inner work' (2002: 351) – in *Wolfsburg* these inner processes are less central, even though Christian Petzold emphasizes the protagonist's inner development.

Nonetheless, *Wolfsburg* offers an impressive description of a social climate of human relations that is characterized by speechlessness, isolation and repression of emotions, inner emptiness and absence of social warmth. The omnipresent motor-car can be seen as a metaphor for this condition of modern, and especially modern German, human beings. This could be connected with German history and the fundamental themes of collective guilt, denial and the repressed wish for reparation. My focus here, however, is primarily on the existential dilemma of human beings. The sense of desolation I felt when watching *Wolfsburg* is, I think, connected with this 'social coldness' and with the failure of reparation in the absence of an empathic Other, which inevitably leads to hopelessness and despair.

In this involvement with the film, another creative aspect comes to light: the appreciation of the overdetermined complexity of human experiences and actions, which is much emphasized by psychoanalysis; or to be more specific, the repudiation of quick patterns of interpretation and one-sided perpetrator–victim definitions, as well as the insight that the inner healing process in the struggle with the narcissistic and destructive parts of the self is a painful and often avoided process. In order to tolerate one's own 'badness' one needs the empathic Other, and when this is missing, the desperately needed reconciliation will fail, especially when there is a social climate of coldness that generates isolation and claustrophobic emptiness.

Reconciliation and reparation are closely connected with empathy. The tolerance of the self-centred and destructive aspects of one's own personality, and of one's subsequent guilt and shame – metaphorically represented in Petzold's film by the death of the boy – needs empathy for one's own 'inner child' and for the 'inner child' of one's objects.

References

Moser, U. and v. Zeppelin, I. (1996) *Der geträumte Traum*. München: Kohlhammer-Verlag.
Plenker, F.P. (2002) Über Wiedergutmachung, *Forum der Psychoanalyse*, 18: 350–66.
Schneider, G. (2006) Film und psychoanalytische Theorie, in U. Pfarr *et al*. (eds) *Lexikon Psychoanalytischer Begriffe für die Kuntwissenschaft*, in preparation.
Wurmser, L. (1992) *Die Flucht vor dem Gewissen*. Berlin: Springer.
Zwiebel, R. (2003) Höhenschwindel – psychoanalytische Anmerkungen zu Trauma und Melancholie in Hitchcocks *Vertigo, Psychoanalyse im Widerspruch*. 30(S): 45–62.
Zwiebel, R. (2006) Freud und Hitchcock – filmpsychoanalytische Reflexionen zu Trauma und Melancholie, in *Tagungsband der DPV*. Tagung in Bad Homburg: Geber und Reush.
Zwiebel, R. and Mahler-Bungers, A. (2006) *Projektion und Wirklichkeit. Die unbewusste Botschaft des Films*. Göttingen: Vandenhoeck und Ruprecht.

6

THE TALKING CURE, FROM FREUD TO ALMODÓVAR
Hable con Ella
Andrea Sabbadini

Hable con Ella (*Talk to Her*) (Spain, 2002)
Director: Pedro Almodóvar
Distributor: Pathé

Psychoanalysis was born, circa 1895, with the publication of the *Studies on Hysteria*. The central case history in that book is that of Joseph Breuer's famous patient Fräulein Anna O. At that time, the common form of treatment for hysterical patients like her was hypnotherapy; but, in Anna O's case, and on her own request, Breuer replaced hypnosis with what later became known as the method of free associations. As Anna O's traumatic memories started to emerge, such recollections had the effect of making her hysterical symptoms disappear. She wittily described this cathartic process as 'chimney-sweeping' and as a 'talking cure' – a quite accurate definition that has remained attached to our profession ever since.

Talking about oneself – about one's thoughts, feelings, memories, dreams, fantasies, fears and desires – may well be therapeutic then, but only on the condition that it occurs in the presence of a listening other. Indeed, rather than as the 'talking cure', it would be more accurate to refer to psychoanalysis as the 'talking and listening cure'.

I remember some years ago one of my patients noticing a 'For Sale' sign outside the house where I had my consulting room. At first she had panicked at the idea that I might sell up, move abroad and abandon her; but then, as she realized that the sign did not refer to my house but to the one next door (which, being in a terrace, was identical to mine), she expressed the fantasy of buying it herself, furnishing its top floor where I had my consulting room exactly like my own and then lying there every day by herself for 50 minutes on the couch, at the precise time of her sessions, to say all the same things she would have told me. At that point she realized that such a solitary form of self-analysis would be impossible. Talking would have been meaningless to her unless I was there to listen to her words.

The *quality* of the analyst's listening is, of course, of crucial importance. Freud recommends it should take place in a state of 'evenly suspended attention' that would be the counterpart to the patient's free associations, and Theodor Reik suggests it should be done with what he calls 'the third ear', the one tuned into the same wavelength as the analysand's unconscious communication.

Let me add here a few more general considerations. Firstly, in the psycho-analytic couple it is not the patient who does all the talking and the analyst all the listening. Their roles can be reversed. Insight and therapeutic progress may occur when the patient listens, and then responds verbally or emotionally, to the analyst's interpretations and constructions. Secondly, the analysand who talks with the analyst, and is listened to by him, is not the only one to benefit from such an interaction: the analyst benefits also. In other words, being in the position of the listener can itself be therapeutic. Thirdly, as we know from personal experience, it is in *all* relationships, and not just in the context of psychoanalytic encounters, that talking and listening can be helpful: between partners, in families, among friends, in the classroom or at the workplace.

And, perhaps, also at the bedside of a patient in a coma.

Pedro Almodóvar, the Spanish screenwriter and director of *Talk to Her* is a sophisticated observer of hysterical and other psychologically disturbed women, many of the characters in his previous films (such as *Women on the Verge of a Nervous Breakdown*, 1988) comically displaying such neurotic features. With *Talk to Her* he confirms his progression to a less idiosyncratic, yet still highly original and more mature style of filmmaking, already noticeable in his previous two works, *Live Flesh* (1997) and *All About My Mother* (1999). Departing from many of his earlier films, characterized by flamboyantly kitsch and outrageously punk and camp comedy, he uses here a mostly restrained melodramatic language to represent a series of multiple parallel stories, characters and themes, in a fascinating play of mirrors.

Two men, young nurse Benigno (Javier Cámara) and 40-something journalist Marco (Dario Grandinetti), love two women who lie in a state of coma in the same clinic. It was in similar fashions that both these women were nearly killed: Lydia (Rosario Flores), described in the screenplay as 'brave, almost suicidal', was hit by a charging bull in a *corrida*; Alicia (Leonor Watling) was hit by a charging vehicle in a road accident. Indeed their respective activities, bullfighting and dancing, have plenty in common. Their lives are reconstructed for us through a series of flashbacks, and are constantly interpreted in the light of the 'material' that emerges as the film's narrative develops,

The talking cure

challenging our assumptions and forcing us to reconsider our initial constructions.

The film title, *Talk to Her*, sounds like a piece of advice, almost an injunction. It is interesting to notice that the Spanish original *Hable **con** ella* means 'talk **with** her'. The inaccurate English translation, therefore, misses the dimension of mutuality. In either case, however, the title refers to the different attitudes that the two male protagonists, for reasons of character and personal history, have towards the two women. Benigno talks incessantly *to* his comatose patient Alicia, though in fact he is convinced he is talking *with* her, and that she can hear him, enjoy his stories and even see what he shows her.

The less talkative, but more prone to tears, Marco, on the other hand, finds it almost impossible to address his words to Lydia, feeling certain, especially after his conversation with Dr Vega, that patients in a coma are unreachable with words: 'We don't know if vegetative life is really life . . . Alicia is practically dead! She can't feel anything for anybody, not for you, not for me, not even for herself!', Marco tells Benigno, as the latter tries in vain to convince him to be less 'secretive' with her (*hermetico* in the original Spanish).

It is interesting to note that before her accident Marco *was* talking, but not listening, to Lydia: in the car on the way to her fatal bullfight she insists they should talk. Marco says they have already been in conversation for an hour, and Lydia points out that it was him doing all the talking while she had no chance to get a word in edgeways.

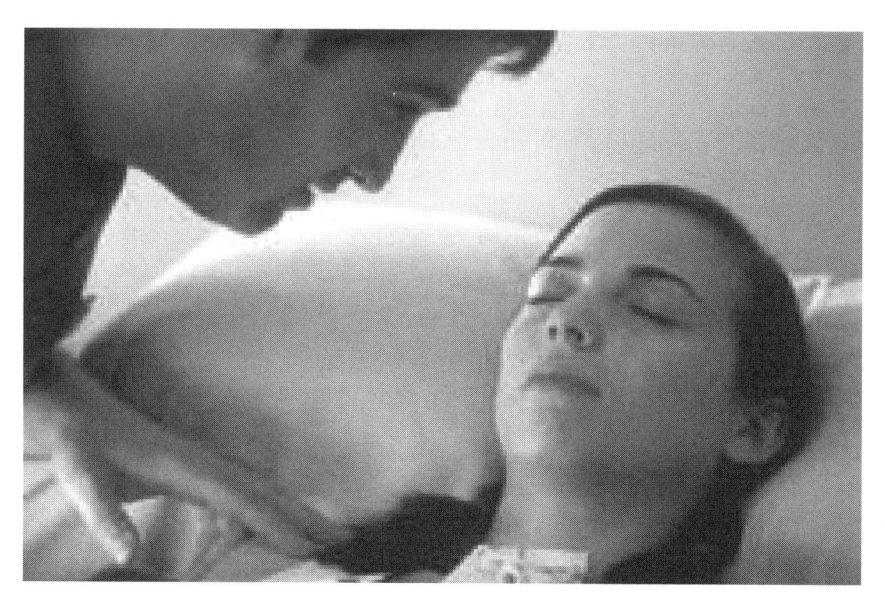

Benigno (Javier Cámara) and Alicia (Leonor Watling)

Benigno and Marco (Mario Grandinetti), with Alicia and Lydia (Rosario Flores)

Monologue or dialogue? This question, relevant to the psychoanalytic situation, is also central to Almodóvar's film. Not just because the subject of *Talk to Her* concerns the depth of communication that is (or that we believe is) possible with another individual in a state of coma, but also because the film – as indeed any other artistic creation – draws us into an intellectual and emotional engagement, a sort of 'conversation' with itself. In other words, *Talk to Her* talks to *us*. Such one-way dialogues, or perhaps two-way monologues, with art products can be enormously rewarding. This is why, after all, we go to concerts, read books, visit art galleries and watch movies. It is remarkable how Almodóvar invites his audience *of Talk to Her* (us, that is) to join in and share the enjoyment of his audiences *within Talk to Her*, as the film not only is a show in itself, but also offers us a number of other spectacular performances within it: Pina Bausch's moving ballet choreographies, containing the film like two bookends, on the Lope de Vega stage; a dramatic *corrida* in the bullring of Brihuega; the screening of a delightfully funny silent movie at the Cinematheque; Caetano Veloso's seductive interpretation of a traditional Spanish melody; and what is, among such performances, perhaps the most theatrical of them all, a wedding in the church of Our Lady of Aracoeli.

Benigno, desperately and pathologically enamoured of Alicia, often left on his own all night to look after her beautiful comatose body, will end up making love *to* (rather than *with*) her, as a result of which she will become pregnant, with inevitably tragic consequences. Here and elsewhere (e.g. in his masterpiece, *All About My Mother*) Almodóvar is a master at challenging some of our conventional moral preconceptions, offering us his own original off-beat view of life and relationships, of sexuality and friendship. In particular he draws the spectators of his films into reconsidering their assumptions about what is normal and what perverse – or, in other words, into thinking about what we can, or cannot, justify in the name of 'love'.

After watching *Talk to Her* many of us may no longer so easily dismiss Benigno as a psychopath and his behaviour towards Alicia as a case of necrophilic rape deserving our contempt and the harshest of punishments. We are invited, instead, to understand such an act, disturbing and abusive as it is, in all its complexity, drawing us personally into it in the process. 'What are we to do, men and women alike,' asks Lichtenstein in a recent psychoanalytically-informed review of the film, 'with the erotic fascination generated by extreme helplessness, and especially by a helpless woman?' (2005: 905). Almodóvar revealed that one of the sources that inspired him to write this screenplay was the intriguing story of a ward in a Romanian morgue who brought back to life the only apparently dead body of an attractive young woman by making love to her. While the girl's own family were extremely grateful to him, public justice had him put into prison.

The moment one dies, in that instant of profoundly silent transition, one stops being a person and becomes a body. This sudden transformation leaves those who find themselves near the dead (and who are still persons) in a state of awesome confusion, faced as they are with something intangible, emotionally charged with a sense of mysterious finality.

There are other situations, though, where death is not so absolute, or certain, and which therefore evoke different responses. I am thinking, for instance, about the tragic condition of the relatives and friends of those 30,000 *desaparecidos* kidnapped during the Argentinean military dictatorship between 1976 and 1983. They had reasons to believe that their dear ones had been tortured and murdered but, deprived as they were of reliable information, went on for months or years hoping they may still be alive. Left in a state of a most painful uncertainty, they could not even have the comfort of mourning their losses.

The situation that concerns us here in relation to *Talk to Her* is that of people who, following an accident or an illness, fall into that state of deep and prolonged unconsciousness which we call coma. 'Her brain is dead,' says Dr Vega of Lydia, 'she's got no ideas or feelings.' Yet these patients are somehow still alive in so far as their vital physiological functions are operating – no longer 'persons', maybe, but also not yet 'just bodies'. Of course, just as a few *desaparecidos* did return home, doctors' prognoses can sometimes be wrong and some comatose patients, such as Alicia in the film, do miraculously come back to life: 'I believe in miracles!', says Benigno to his incredulous colleague Rosa.

A recent article in the *Guardian* reported the following story:

> A man who began speaking again after two years in a coma says that he had heard and understood everything going on around him. Salvatore Crisafulli, 38, has had great difficulty in speaking since recovering, but, asked if he could remember the past two years, he replied '*yes*' and wept. In true Italian style, his mother told reporters that his first word had been '*Mamma*'.
>
> (Hooper 2005: 15)

A condition similar to coma is *encephalitis lethargica*. These patients woke up after many years of deep sleep thanks to a newly discovered drug (L-DOPA), as described by psychoneurologist Oliver Sacks in his book *Awakenings*: 'The terror of suffering, sickness and death,' he writes there, 'of losing ourselves and losing the world are the most elemental and intense we know; and so too are our dreams of recovery and rebirth, of being wonderfully restored to ourselves and the world' (1973: 202).

At one level Almodóvar's powerful film could be read as a conventional narrative of unrequited love, set however in the most unconventional of circumstances. At another level, it could be seen as an in-depth exploration of the conflict, represented by the contrasting attitudes of the two male protagonists, between hope and hopelessness. The ancient Romans used to say *Spes ultima dea* ('Hope is the ultimate goddess'), meaning that human beings have a tendency to hold on to hope even when reason – or, in the case concerning us here, medical science – suggests that a specific situation is, to all intents and purposes, hopeless. At yet another level, the film is a compassionate description of the beautiful, if desperate, friendship which grows between the two men from such tension, even more than as a result of homoerotic attraction or the coincidence of finding themselves in a similar situation.

I would like to suggest that Benigno's life is conditioned by his regressive hope to reunite with his primary object, via his fantasy of returning into his mother's womb. Before looking after his beloved patient Alicia, Benigno had cared for his ill mother for 15 years, until her death. Anna O herself, it may be remembered, had developed her hysterical symptoms at the time of nursing her terminally-ill father. Both are instances, it could be argued, of failed resolutions of Oedipal attachments.

This regressive need is related to another central theme in the film, that of multiple losses and replacements. Benigno has lost his mother and replaced her with Alicia; Lydia has lost her lover El Niño and replaced him with Marco, before replacing him again with El Niño; and Marco, having recovered from the loss of his girlfriend Angela and having replaced her with Lydia, after she dies will perhaps replace her with the resuscitated Alicia.

As a touch of his playful genius for paradox, Almodóvar has Benigno – the man who believes in talking – become an enthusiastic spectator (as Alicia had been herself) of *silent* movies. As he watches the seven-minute *Amante menguante*, Benigno identifies with the shrunk Alfredo, its protagonist, who climbs, or rather dives, inside the body of his sleepy girlfriend Amparo. 'That door,' writes Almodóvar in the screenplay, 'source of life and pleasure, the first door, will also be the last.' This scene in the movie-within-the-movie, and its accompanying regressive fantasy, are then enacted in Benigno's sexual penetration of, and merging with, his comatose patient Alicia – the centrepiece event of *Talk to Her* which Almodóvar, however, sensitively withholds from his spectators' voyeuristic curiosity. We only find out about it as a *fait accompli* when Marco himself is informed of Alicia's pregnancy over the telephone. Benigno is arrested and then, having been told that the son he conceived in such an exceptional way and with whom he identifies has died, and having been deceived into believing that Alicia herself will never awake back to life again, makes the final regressive and identificatory step of killing himself.

Throughout the film we can also detect a clear, if only implicit, reference to the Christian narrative of death, resurrection and salvation – a variation on the vast theme of 'rescue fantasies' which I have elsewhere illustrated with the Greek myth of Orpheus and Eurydice (Sabbadini 2003). Benigno – who

Benigno

talked to Alicia with the same fervour of the faithful praying to mostly silent gods – is ready to sacrifice himself on the cross of his own suffering for his mother and then for Alicia; and indeed his final sacrifice, taking him first to jail and then to a lethal overdose, is what makes her resurrect from (near) death. As Marco says at Benigno's grave (talking to his dead male friend as he had never been able to do to his half-dead girlfriend): 'Alicia is alive. You woke her up': a variation on the theme of the fairy-tale of *Sleeping Beauty*.

By then, Marco has already moved into Benigno's flat, where, like him four years earlier, he spends time at the window observing Alicia in the dance academy. The relationship Marco may develop with her would be but the organic continuation of his already advanced identification with Benigno. Their actual meeting, in the same theatre of the film's first sequences, and the caption 'Marco y Alicia' that goes with it, suggest that this will be the beginning of Almodóvar's next movie.

Almodóvar's next movie, however, as we now know, was *Bad Education* (2004), which has nothing to do with Marco and Alicia's vicissitudes. Anyone familiar with the Spanish director's sense of humour could have predicted that a sequel to *Talk to Her* was unlikely. Instead – just as Almodóvar remembers doing himself as a child when he was retelling and changing for his sisters, much to their enjoyment, the films they had watched together – it will be up to us to use his postmodern generous gift of an open finale and our own creative imagination to invent a new narrative.

References

Hooper, J. (2005) I could hear everything, says man after two years in coma, *The Guardian*, 6 October.
Lichtenstein, D. (2005) Talk to her, *International Journal of Psychoanalysis*, 86(3): 905–14.
Sabbadini, A. (2003) Not something destroyed but something that is still alive: *Amores Perros* at the intersection of rescue fantasies, *International Journal of Psychoanalysis*, 84(3): 755–64.
Sacks, O. (1973) *Awakenings*. London: Picador, 1982.

7

INTERGENERATIONAL TRANSMISSION
The holocaust in Central European cinema

Catherine Portuges

The topic of this chapter is prompted in part by my experience as the Hollywood-born and raised daughter of a Hungarian father and an Austrian mother who had fled Hitler's Europe for the heart of the movie colony founded by Jews from the former *shtetls* and cities of East-Central Europe. These intersections of European memory, history and complicated, often repressed, identity are worth revisiting today, in the shadow of the 60-year commemorations of the end of the Second World War. But, as I later came to discover in Vienna and Budapest, my own Jewish heritage had been kept silent within the family, and so it was not until my first trip to Hungary in the mid-1980s that I discovered that I, too, had relatives who had disappeared during the Holocaust. Since then, my research has taken me throughout Eastern and Central Europe, screening and writing about films that seek in different ways to come to terms with the complex and ongoing issues of post-Holocaust Jewish identity, and its transmission from one generation to another in first-person narratives, whether documentary, experimental or fiction. Contrary to earlier ideas of documentary that tended to be fixated on the notion of objectivity, I want to propose that a hallmark of contemporary non-fiction and fiction filmmaking is the undisguised, deeply personal and passionate interests of filmmakers: indeed, over the past 20 years, the best of these productions often take a strong stand, expressing the filmmaker's own voice, positionality and point of view – staking a claim, unapologetically claiming a self, yet engaging openly with the world beyond that framed on screen. When the Holocaust is the subject, how, then, does this subjectivity make itself felt?

European commemorations of the anniversary of the Holocaust

acknowledged, often for the first time, the suffering of the Romany people, of homosexuals, the disabled and political dissidents. The deportation of nearly half a million Hungarian Jews in the most intensive process of extermination was commemorated by the inauguration of a new Holocaust Memorial Centre in Budapest and a conference in which I participated on 'The Holocaust in Hungary Sixty Years Later' at the US Holocaust Memorial Museum Center for Advanced Studies in Washington DC. The liberation of Auschwitz and related events were accorded weeks of programming on European television. Sixty years after Germany's unconditional surrender to the Allies, and 40 years after the establishment of diplomatic relations between Israel and Germany, a controversial Memorial to the Murdered Jews of Europe, first proposed in 1988, just a year before the Berlin Wall fell, was dedicated in Berlin. Undeniably, such commemorations share with the psychoanalytic project a profound concern with the experience of trauma, with dreams, symptoms and parapraxes, interrogating representational modes of narration, the structure of memory and questions of identity. These memorial occasions have been marked by a period of solemn reflection, remembrance and often intense and sustained public debate surrounding the images, objects, documents and sites of Jewish memory in Central and Eastern Europe, and accompanied by an outpouring of historical studies, memoirs, films and conferences that can offer a productive space for intervention in reconsideration of the legacies of those events and their resonance, both in post-war and post-communist cinema.

For 20 years after the end of the Second World War, the West responded to the Holocaust with relative silence; more recently, Western cultural media have sought to make the Holocaust part of history, a narrative within a larger narrative, an event described and interpreted through the eyes and sensibilities of individual and collective witnesses. And as the historical episode has become more distant, responses to it have become ritualized. It is in fact this very ritualization that has motivated historians such as Saul Friedlander (1992) to argue that the trauma of the Holocaust has not yet been worked through on either the individual or the collective level. Lawrence L. Langer writes that 'before 1939 imagination was always in advance of reality, but ... after 1945 reality had outdistanced the imagination so that nothing the artist conjured up could equal in intensity or scope the improbabilities of *l'univers concentrationnaire*' (1994: 97–8).

What Auschwitz may signify for the theory and practice of psychoanalysis as well as that of cinema, both of which were elaborated prior to and beyond the experience of deportation – indeed, what Geoffrey Hartmann (1996) has called 'the longest shadow' – remains a focus of ongoing meditation, some three generations after the fact. The Polish-Yiddish film, *Unzere Kinder* (*Our Children*, 1948) demonstrates most painfully the struggle and inability to comprehend and mourn that were to mark responses to the Holocaust for decades. It is a remarkable document in part because of what it reveals about the limitations of art. *Lang ist der Weg* (*Long Is the Road*, 1948), the first of these films to receive theatrical distribution, concerns displaced Jews waiting to find a home in Israel in the years after the war. Produced by the US Army Information Control Division, the film was shot during 1947 and 1948 at film studios in Munich and at Camp Landsberg, a temporary settlement in Bavaria for Jewish displaced persons. The screenplay, written by Karl-George Kulb and Israel Becker, with dialogue in Yiddish, German and Polish, features Becker himself, upon whose life the story is loosely based and who had been active in Poland's Yiddish theatre before the German invasion, along with performers from the Yiddish theatres in both Germany and Poland, directed by Herbert Fredersdorf and Marek Goldstein. The first half of the film focuses on the Holocaust directly by tracing the history of the Yellins, an affluent, religious, middle-class Jewish family in Warsaw. Their peaceful existence is destroyed by the bombing and invasion of Poland (shown in documentary footage). David Yellin, played by Becker, comes home to tell his parents that they must move into the ghetto. Resigned, the family welcomes the Sabbath with the father's soulful prayer. After a period of time in the ghetto, the family is placed on a train to be taken to Auschwitz. David jumps to freedom from the moving train; his parents arrive at Auschwitz, where his mother is allowed to live but his father is sent to his death. David makes his way to the partisans, who persuade him to kill a German soldier for his rifle. After a few dramatized scenes at Auschwitz, we see documentary footage of the Allied soldiers liberating the concentration camp and caring for the prisoners. The National Center for Jewish Film at Brandeis University has claimed this work to be 'the first feature film to represent the Holocaust from a Jewish point of view'.

However, many Jews were still trying to convince themselves that they had a home in Europe. Some 60,000 to 70,000 Jews in Poland at the end of the war were joined by another 175,000 who returned, mostly from the Soviet Union – some 245,000 survivors of an original 3 million people. And in spite of Poland's continuing anti-Semitism and the large number of those fleeing the country, a significant group still remained, trying to forge a new life under the banner of communism. Since a popular and successful film industry had existed as part of the Yiddish culture in Poland before the war, it was perhaps to be expected that Jews would turn to the cinema as a means of expressing their hopes about the future while also attempting to cope with the horrors of the past. The location for much of this section is the Helenowek Colony, near Lodz (also the central location for *Unzere Kinder*). These scenes foreground the extent to which acts of denial were a necessary component of the post-traumatic process. The fact that these children are without families, with a past of inescapable nightmares, is mitigated by shots of them learning, working, singing and performing together: as if the past were effectively finished, its negative impact minimal, their suffering at an end. The film seems to argue that a better Poland is the result of past horrors, suggesting that children might live in a less divided world than they might otherwise have experienced.

With this framework in mind, I consider selected films in which Jewish identity is inscribed primarily in first-person narratives. What I intend by evoking a dynamics of intergenerational memory is a kind of memorial mapping characteristic of selected documentary films, home movie footage, archival materials and fictional narratives that address this traumatic history. Some of these films resonate with other, earlier films, creating a kind of intertextual dialogue intended at once for the filmmakers' own generation, that of their parents and that of their successors: Péter Forgács' *Private Hungary* (1989–2005) deploys an experimental approach using diary and home movie footage shot by amateur photographers, attracting the attention of younger audiences without direct experience of such trauma. A still younger director, Diana Gróo, explains that today's filmmakers are searching for new topics and new stories, in some sense having been denied the freedom to retell the stories of the past:

> We are the third generation after World War II. Our parents' generation could talk about communism and they were closer to their parents' war experience. For us to talk about the past is very unusual. As a result, our generation is not just searching for funding, but also for an identity and topics that will appeal to a broad audience. We no longer have a common landscape. Everybody is searching to express him- or herself. The style of a contemporary director has to be completely different from that of Szabó, Károly Makk, Miklós Jancsó, Judit Elek or János Rózsa.
> (Personal communication, Budapest, February 2005)

These works at once interrogate and articulate unresolved questions of intergenerational transmission of Central European and Jewish identity in the region, focalizing narrative structures through the point of view of historically located, specific individual voices, rather than an omniscient camera-narrator. After all, autobiographical cinema is capable of offering uniquely intimate access to a historical moment and of posing a challenge to the transmission of knowledge: drawing attention unapologetically to the subjectivity that is always already there, with its ambivalence, anguish and contradiction.[1]

Poland, Hungary and Czechoslovakia were among the first East European cultures to devote attention to films about the deportation, ghettoization and extermination of the Jewish populations during the Nazi occupation; the preoccupation with themes of resistance and international solidarity, the cinematographic modalities and the variety of historical and individual perspectives deployed is particularly significant in those films produced immediately following the war, between 1947 and 1949, and between 1959 and 1968, and finally again when the regimes began to deteriorate. For some filmmakers, in addition to the personal motivation they may have had as Jews or former concentration camp prisoners or both, in the 1960s the subject of the Holocaust was at the same time appropriated as a vehicle for the expression of discontent about totalitarianism in Eastern Europe, as well as an opportunity to present, in a way that could be less immediately threatened by censorship, issues such as compliance with an authoritarian regime or conflict between individual and ideology, introducing the anti-hero as protagonist.

Somewhere in Europe (Géza Radványi, 1947)

The methodological parallels between psychoanalysis and cinema, both concerned with subjectivity and intelligibility, and undertaken in a context of historical consciousness, inevitably raise the larger question of witnessing and testimony, remembering and forgetting: memorials, like films and dreams, are fraught with symbolic meaning, often becoming contested terrain, as attested by the debates that inflame the discussion of psychologically acceptable ways of commemorating 11 September 2001 in lower Manhattan and elsewhere. Useful comparisons may, I suspect, be made between films written and directed by those who were witnesses and victims and those at one remove,

Somewhere in Europe

based on memoirs, archival materials, historical accounts, photographic documents or autobiographical novels, adapted or 'translated' to another medium by those who may not have witnessed the events first hand.

In *Valalhól Europában* (*Somewhere in Europe*), a group of homeless European children orphaned by the war or separated from their parents as the Soviet Union took power, band together for survival. This 1947 film was shot entirely on location in Hungary, then still freshly scarred by the war (the film is dedicated to the 'unknown children' who were victims of the war). Its proximity in time and space to the actual event gives the film an undeniable authenticity that transcends boundaries of fiction and documentary. The director's second feature, the screenplay was co-written in 1945 by the Hungarian film theorist Béla Balázs (born Herbert Bauer – his name change echoes that of many Central European film artists persecuted by antisemitism); two other major figures of Hungarian cinema, Felix Máriassy and Károly Makk, also contributed to one of the last post-war films to be released before the communist takeover of Hungary.

The film opens with a zoom that locates Central Europe on a period map of the world, followed by a rapidly edited sequence of wordless vignettes of children exposed to the horrors of modern warfare, symbolized by violent cuts and extreme camera angles. Tragedy is embedded in every sound and image, as the director emphasizes the insanity of war and its traumatic effects on his protagonists: a child flees a bombing raid by escaping into an abandoned carnival's House of Horrors, where baroquely expressionist cinematography foregrounds figures of surreal monsters and a melting wax Hitler that at once embody and exacerbate his terror.

Left to their own devices, the children wander aimlessly: one girl witnesses her own father being shot; others narrowly survive the bombing of a shelter for delinquents. Filmed in a style that Balázs has called 'fantastic realism' that evokes post-war Italian neo-realism, *Somewhere in Europe* is set in the war's wreckage, primarily in the ruins of a castle occupied by another displaced person – a shell-shocked musician and former orchestra conductor. When the gang of children set out at first to rob him, their leader intercedes: yet the humane impulse of the old musician is to protect them, and from this ground zero of their descent into anarchy they are offered hope in the form of a figure who serves as a paternal link back toward the humanity they have nearly been forced to surrender. Shifting from the more poetic realism and absent dialogue of the first half of the film, the narrative acquires an increasing verbal intensity and specificity, suggesting perhaps a trajectory away from the darkness and despair of a chaos to which silence is often the only possible response, in which protagonists are deprived of their ability to feel and to communicate, toward the potential of communication and verbal transformation of that experience, not unlike the arc of the psychoanalytic process. This dynamic was no doubt familiar to audiences of the time who themselves would have likely experienced the violence of war on Hungarian soil, powerfully fictionalized in this transformative cinematic meditation shot shortly after the mass deportation of Hungarian Jews. Indeed, Radványi had envisioned a trilogy of films about the homeless survivors of Europe following the war: although he did manage to make a second film, *Donne Senza Nome* (1949) on the subject of homeless women in an Italian displaced persons camp, the final instalment was never realized.

The Last Stop (Wanda Jakubowska, 1948)

A year later, in 1948, the same Béla Balázs who wrote the screenplay for *Somewhere in Europe*, claimed: 'We must first speak about the genre of this wonderful Polish film', thereby opening a discussion of *The Last Stop* (*Otatni Etap*), the first feature film to attempt to represent Auschwitz and the universe of mass extermination. Shot during the summer of 1947 on the very site of the camp itself and its still almost completely existing structures, directed and written by two former prisoners of the women's camp in Birkenau, Jakubowska herself and Gerda Schneider, an East German communist, the film is performed not only by actors but also by extras who either lived in the town of Auschwitz or had been deported to the camp themselves.

Arrested in Warsaw, Marta Weiss is deported to Auschwitz, where she is selected by the authorities to serve as an interpreter. She joins a resistance group composed of women of diverse nationalities struggling against the *kapos* (mostly Polish) and the SS. *The Last Stop* soon acquired the status of an iconic document through its portrayal of what became a cinematic iconography of the experience of Nazi persecution, thereby laying the groundwork for a new filmic genre that has since become ubiquitous: the docudrama.

Subsequently appropriated as an influential source for other Holocaust film narratives, the iconic images of Auschwitz-Birkenau and their effect on both individual subjectivity and collective experience include the arrival under cover of darkness of deportation trains, which became a standard reference for Alain Resnais' *Night and Fog* (1956), Gillo Pontecorvo's *Kapo* (1960), Steven Spielberg's *Schindler's List* (1993),[2] and Alan J. Pakula's *Sophie's Choice* (1982), among many others. The 'Appellplatz' sequence imparts the claustrophobic sensation of being anchored in a world of suffering and bondage, an image linked with neo-realist location shots framed in open spaces. In his treatment of *The Diary of Anne Frank* (1959), director George Stevens borrowed from the film a dream sequence of female prisoners standing together, transforming a moment of forced attention and solidarity among the prison community into a surreal, oneiric image.

The Last Stop combines the secondary dramas of female prisoners and their Nazi antagonists with dramatic visions of the camp in carefully composed long tracking shots, stark contrasts of light and symbolic choreography in cinematography by Boros Monastyrsjki, a student of Eisenstein. The central figure, that of a woman translator, incorporates the actual experience of Mala Zimetbaum, who was deported to Auschwitz from Belgium, worked for the resistance underground in the camp using her position as translator for the native languages represented, including Polish, Greek, Hungarian, French and Portuguese to gather and distribute resistance documents and succeeded, in June 1944, in escaping from the camp, only to be ultimately recaptured and executed as a martyr. Jakubowska's portrayal of the collective experience of the *univers concentrationnaire* was perceived as so authentic that it has been integrated by other filmmakers as actual footage of the camps.

Yet in the post-Holocaust moment we are aware that remembering and bearing witness are not necessarily self-evident processes, as theorists such as Shoshana Feldman (Feldman and Laub 1992) and Michael Rothberg (2003) have suggested. 'What if the tragedy of the messenger is that he could not deliver his message,' asks Elie Wiesel, 'worse, that he forgot the message. Worse, that he forgot he was a messenger. Or worse, that he delivered the message and nothing changed?' As Wiesel's parable reminds us, survivors of the Holocaust faced, and indeed may continue to face, troubling barriers, internal and external, when seeking to recall and narrate their past. In his study of *The Last Stop*, Stuart Liebman (1996: 43) asks: 'What type of narratives can replace classical film plots whose neat contrivances would seriously distort the astonishing primal and unpredictable truths of ghetto or camp existence? Indeed, is there a dramatic structure that can be conceived for a situation whose victims had so little chance to resist?'

Awarded numerous festival prizes, the film was an international success, screened in some 45 countries. For the first time, a mass audience was to confront the reality of the camps in the form of a fictionalized, internal mental representation that drew upon the imagination and the emotions rather than primarily on documents and footage shot by the American army during the liberation. The presence of the filmmakers as first-person witnesses to the very traumatic events they revisit remained a reference point thereafter in the intersecting theories of cinema, psychoanalysis and the Holocaust. In contemporary theoretical debates, the notion of trauma transcends disciplinary boundaries of psychoanalytic and psychiatric treatment to join the discourses of historical and artistic representation where it is symptomatically inscribed in texts such as these.

Father (István Szabó, 1966)

The phenomenon of post-traumatic autobiographical remembrance of the Holocaust has been explored, albeit intermittently and at times indirectly, by Central European directors such as István Szabó, one of Hungary's internationally renowned filmmakers born during the war. Some two decades after *The Last Stop*, *Apa* (*Father*) addresses a generation of Hungarians who came of age in the period that included the deportations, the war, the communist takeover and subsequent nationalization, as well as the uprising of 1956. Prefaced by these words: 'I confront your failure, you who look human', the film opens with a series of shots of the Chain Bridge in Budapest bombed by the retreating Germans in 1944–5; this documentary footage segues to a fictionalized sequence of a funeral, the burial of the father of young Takó, the film's narrator/protagonist. The fusion of documentary and fictional elements thus sets the stage for a narrative that integrates the public losses sustained by the war with a more private experience of mourning and loss, suturing the narrative structure that is to follow.

The first part of *Father* focuses on Takó's childhood neurosis as a consequence of his father's death. Fantasizing the absent figure alternately as cosmopolitan world traveller and heroic communist partisan, the boy acts out, through first-person point of view camera shots, what many of his contemporaries have experienced: in a classroom scene, the teacher asks how

Father

many of the pupils have lost their own father. More than half those present stand up, Takó hesitantly joining them.[3] Other filmmakers such as Pál Schiffer and Zsolt Kézdi-Kovacs have also addressed this phenomenon in both documentary and fictional form, exploring the painful consequences of the absent fathers in a society that discouraged, or for that matter suppressed, psychoanalytic investigation of the sequelae of these losses for a whole generation. Between the murderous character of Hitler, represented as a melting wax figure in *Somewhere in Europe*, and the patriarchal image of Stalin (figured as a 'good' father to children in 1950s Hungary, having defeated Hitler), the film powerfully evokes the post-war generation's profound psychological challenge and ultimate developmental task: to liberate itself from the repression that is both directly and indirectly a consequence of these oppressive and terrifying figures, and to take its rightful place in their own historical moment.

A closer reading of the film reveals another layer of hidden history: the fate of the Hungarian Jews, and the implication that Takó's father in some sense may have shared that fate. We know from *Sunshine* (1999) that Szabó reworked this theme in his epic of four generations of a Hungarian Jewish family, whose name, Sonnenschein, was changed to the more Christian-sounding Sors (meaning fate). The second part of *Father* depicts Takó as a university student active in the uprising of 1956; he accepts a role as an extra in a film in which he is to play first a Jew rounded up by the Hungarian fascist Arrow Cross, and then, in a gesture laden with irony, is made abruptly to switch roles, replacing the yellow star with the Arrow Cross armband. The sequence completed, he walks along the Danube with Anni, a friend and fellow student, on the very spot where Hungarian Jews were shot into the river by the Arrow Cross milita. We hear in her subjective monologue a profoundly conflicted and ambivalent stance toward her own Jewish identity and her attempts at assimilation, a conflict shared even today by many Central European writers, artists and intellectuals. This sequence was produced in 1966 when such questions were often repressed and far from commonly addressed in East-Central European cinema:

> It's awful, you know. For years I denied that my father died in a concentration camp. I'd make up a story rather than admit I was Jewish. I finally realized the futility of it and I faced reality. I even went to Auschwitz with an excursion group and I took pictures. All I got were pictures of well-dressed tourists milling around. Sometimes I still feel ashamed and pretend not to be Jewish. I am Hungarian, am I not? The forgotten past of my ancestors doesn't count. And I can't overcome it. I want to be proud of that Jewish past for which my parents gave their lives. I simply can't behave normally. I just don't know where I belong, where I want to belong, what I am, or where I should belong. The Pope at last forgave the Jews for their sins. That means that they were guilty of crucifying Christ 2000 years ago.

And those who 20 years ago let 6 million Jews be gassed and burned? How soon will they be absolved? You see how maddening this can be, and how idiotic this Auschwitz thing is! Part of me is there. My parents and relatives perished there. But I can't go on harping on it just to get sympathy. I feel ashamed for belonging to those who were slaughtered like sheep. I always feel as if I had to prove something . . .

Father – and its later incarnation as *Sunshine* – suggests that both documentary and narrative are potent vehicles of enacting and working through trauma and mourning, enabling filmmakers and viewers alike to engage in these processes whether directly (as survivors or witnesses) or indirectly, as vicarious participants after the fact. Both are forms of witnessing and testimony, capable of performing voyeurism, violence, comedy and propaganda. Both have become objects and agents of historical research. Since the beginning of the post-communist era in 1989, Central European cinema has undergone dramatic crises including that of filmmakers' sense of obligation and purpose with respect to their audiences. The years since the fall of the Berlin Wall have witnessed a renewal of interest in the traditions of Central European psychoanalytic practice, and the return of the history of discourse about Jewish experience to the centre of the cinematic stage. In successive decades, through ambitious historical frescoes as well as intimate, moving narratives, retrospective mappings onto the topography of cinematic representations sustain the intergenerational work of memory transmission. Despite the proliferation of publications, memorials, artistic works and memorialization, it is important to recall the silence that once surrounded discourse of the Shoah and that continues to inform the visual representation of Holocaust trauma.[4]

Free Fall (Péter Forgács, 1996)

A more recent instance of this multigenerational approach may be read in Péter Forgács's film *Free Fall*, a segment from his remarkable multipart series *Private Hungary*, composed entirely of home movie and amateur footage, some shot continuously by families from the late 1920s to the early 1940s. His innovative approach to experimental filmmaking on subjects from psychoanalysis to philosophy has earned him international acclaim. In this segment from his 1996 work, we witness an approach to memory created by the juxtaposition of text and image, sound and silence. Here, the imposition of the Jewish Laws (*numerus clausus*) on the lives of Hungarian Jewish citizens – seen in intimate daily life, celebrating birthdays and weddings, boating on the lake – is rendered through an operatic voice reciting the consequences of those laws which progressively deprived Jews of their livelihood and ultimately their lives.

Forgács edits footage taken of the upper middle-class Jewish family of György Petö, the cameraman of this footage, a successful Jewish businessman from a wealthy family in the Hungarian city of Szeged who made continuous home movies of his family, friends and lover beween 1938 and 1944. With a passion for music and speedboats, Petö acquired an 8mm camera at the age of 30 and quickly became an avid and prolific home movie buff. As in previous films in the series, Forgács reworks home movies to illuminate the hidden, repressed interstices of mid-twentieth century Hungarian history: with Hungary an ally of Nazi Germany, the Hungarian Jewish community was nevertheless virtually intact until the spring of 1944. In this tragic and disturbing piece, Petö's images of the banal and tender world of family gatherings, outings on the lake, his 33rd birthday party, erotic images of his lover in the bath and even of his early 'carefree moments' in the Jewish labour camps play disquietingly against radio reports, bits of newsreel footage, political speeches and the cool language of the ever more elaborate and cruel Hungarian anti-Jewish laws. One of this segment's most powerful 'narrative' strategies is its invocation of erosion of the false sense of security typical of Hungarian Jews (many of whom were non-observant) who, often ardent patriots, were nonetheless ultimately forced to comply with the instigation of the Jewish Laws of 1938–9, which effectively excluded them from professional and cultural life. Suggesting how deeply and pervasively most Hungarian Jews were integrated and assimilated into an idea of the nation, considering themselves proud Hungarian patriots, it becomes all the more inconceivable that they could be perceived as the other (the enemy) by their own compatriots. Combining newsreel footage and the viewers' own knowledge of historical circumstances, Forgács creates a documentary of ordinary life in extraordinary times, foregrounding the consequences of this tragic denial, perhaps more extreme than that of other Central European Jews.

What many commentators of his films call reverse, or parallel, history, however, is to Forgács primarily emotional, in large part because of his work with music, thanks to the creative collaboration with his composer, Tibor Szemzö. In what has become his signature style, Forgács evokes fragments of life stories, intercut with minimal explanatory material, by using home movie footage in much the same way as psychoanalysis creates a narrativized intertext of continuities and discontinuities, of transference and countertransference, of resistance and free association. To create these effects, the archival, amateur footage itself is manipulated by pausing on an image, creating an iris effect, coloring details within the frame, or toning entire sequences, lending the footage a sense of urgency and even doom which was clearly absent at the time of its original filming. The result is not merely a reassembled reconstruction of historical images, refashioned by technical manipulation and reprocessing from archival discoveries, but rather an original, independent work.

Free Fall requires the viewer to consider why, after so many Jews in Nazi occupied Europe had already vanished, the Hungarian Jewish community was still mostly intact in the early spring of 1944, foregrounding the radical disjuncture between Hungary's position as an ally of the Third Reich from the beginning of the war, and the fate of its Jews at the war's end. This 'paradox' in his view arises from the fact that Jews were not threatened until March 1944 with the Nazi occupation of Hungary:

> It took me time to understand this interesting and secretive part of Hungarian history ... property was confiscated earlier, but lives were not threatened. What was interesting for me was to see how one accommodates to these levels of degradation, how one accepts the degrees of discrimination and still remains a functioning human being, even happy ... Hungarian Jews assimilated, they had their illusions like others, such as the Dutch. But they were taken into deportation anyway, and the Szeged Jews were offered up. Anyone who tried to save one person was a hero in those dark days.

Of particular note is the director's reading of the deportation of Hungarian Jews, inviting the conclusion that non-Jews also suffered by portraying the links between these groups, both of whose experiences are handled with sensitivity in his avant-garde depiction of history which lacks any trace of ideological positioning. 'My works,' he says, 'are researches in the time archeology of private history.'

Can one imagine the indescribable sorrow of being prevented from practising one's chosen profession from the perspective of those who were active in all spheres of Hungarian life, only to realize finally that they belonged to the exiles – patriotic soldiers in uniform, successful businessmen in shops and companies, active family members, lively children? Forgács takes no political stance; rather, he chooses to trace this process of 'free fall' from an unexpected, intimate viewpoint, akin to that of a dream state, instead of documenting the bureaucratic mass homicide system from the outside, considering the process as experienced from within the future victims' quotidian subjectivity (Portuges 2001).

Fateless (Lajos Koltai, 2005) [5]

The last example of intergenerational transmission concerns a film based on Hungarian writer Imre Kertész' novel *Fateless* (*Sorstálanság*), first published in 1975 and translated into English 20 years later, the first Hungarian-language novel ever to win the Nobel Prize for Literature. According to the Nobel Committee, *Fateless* is a novel that upholds the fragile experience of the individual against the barbaric arbitrariness of history', and that admittedly has drawn upon the 'barbaric arbitrariness' of the author's own tragic experience as a 15-year-old Hungarian Jew in Auschwitz. During the 1970s, after a long period of repression and silence, Holocaust memory returned gradually to the public scene primarily in the form of literary texts produced by a generation of writers who had personally experienced deportation and incarceration as adolescents. Among them was Imre Kertész' 'In dark shadow', an essay from his collection *A Holocaust mint Kultúra* (1993). Kertész suggests that:

> nothing would [appear to] be simpler than to collect, name and evaluate those Hungarian literary works that were born under direct or indirect influence of the Holocaust . . . However, in my view that is not the problem. The problem, dear listeners, is the imagination. To be more precise: to what extent is the imagination capable of coping with the fact of the Holocaust? How can imagination take in, receive the Holocaust, and, because of this receptive imagination, to what extent has the Holocaust become part of our ethical life and ethical culture? . . . This is what we must talk about.
>
> (p. 171)

Kertész continues:

> I was not brought up as an observant Jew and I did not become a believer later on; at the same time, I find that Judaism is an absolutely decisive moment of my life, one I am attached to because, on account of it, I lived through a great moral test. But is it possible to rise above the experiences one lives through in such a way that we don't exclude them and at the same time manage to transpose them to a universal level? . . . My country has yet to face up to the skeleton in the closet, namely awareness of the issue of the Holocaust, which has not yet taken root in Hungarian culture, and those writing about it [still] stand on the sidelines . . . I think it is a success if my book has made even a slight contribution to this process.
>
> (p. 172)

Based on Kertész' semi-autobiographical first novel and his own screenplay, and with an eloquent score by Ennio Morricone, the film follows a 15-year-old Hungarian Jewish boy from Budapest, György Köves, as he is separated from his family and interned in a succession of Nazi concentration camps. This epic adaptation of the contemporary classic novel is set in 1944 as Hitler's final solution becomes policy throughout Europe. The narrative is focalized through the boy's first-person voice as he finds himself swept up by cataclysmic events beyond his comprehension. An ordinary metropolitan adolescent who has never felt particularly connected to his religion, he is suddenly part of the rushed and random deportation of his city's large Jewish population, as his father is deported to a forced labour camp. Köves finds himself in a cattle car on a train en route to Auschwitz and then Buchenwald. His existence suddenly becomes a surreal adventure in adversity and adaptation, and he is never quite sure if he is the victim of his captors, or of an absurd destiny that metes out salvation and suffering arbitrarily. Köves does not rebel against his fate: he evinces no surprise, nor does he attempt to escape.

Returning home after the liberation, he finds he misses the sense of community he experienced in the camps, feeling alienated from both his Christian neighbours who turned a blind eye to his fate, and the Jewish family friends who avoided deportation and who now want to put the war behind them. Throughout his experience of deportation and incarceration in the *univers concentrationnaire*, he makes passing friendships when he finds himself in the company of adults or children: some are terrified, others, compliant; still others, resilient or indifferent. The young narrator seems merely to observe the scenes unfolding before him. After a series of random experiences, fortunate and devastating twists of fate, he eventually returns home. While the writer and director convey the sense that human beings are capable of surviving even the unthinkable and unbearable, such scenes suggest the emotional impact of the trauma on multiple generations post-Auschwitz – indeed, the indifference of others when confronted by the returning deportee, so powerfully articulated in the literary works of Primo Levi (1986), Robert Anthelme (1990), or Charlotte Delbo (1995).

After his father loses his business and is deported to forced labour camp, György Köves soon finds himself alone in Auschwitz-Birkenau, struggling to find meaning in his tragic fate. György stoically endures the

Fateless

dehumanization of the concentration camp: in the midst of deprivation and brutality, he takes solace in the kindness of an array of characters, drawing on the memory of these small gestures of humanity when he returns to Budapest and realizes that the horrors he has experienced while interned have ultimately left him profoundly alienated from his post-war community. The young actor, Nagy, performs the role of the precocious György with an extraordinary depth of maturity, evolving over the course of the film from innocent young Budapest boy to adolescent Holocaust survivor. Kertész, who also wrote the screenplay, offers a nuanced, original and deeply philosophical exploration of occupation-era Europe that sets *Fateless* apart from other Holocaust dramas. Despite his obvious mastery of the epic sweep of his narrative, Kertész suggests that it is rather the intimate gestures, connections and observations that enable his protagonist to survive his devastating internment against all odds.

If the notion of 'second generation' is by now a familiar and fairly stable concept in Holocaust studies (the second generation, born in the immediate years after the war, are children of Jews who survived the Holocaust in Europe), a distinction is called for, one that Susan Suleiman (2002) has called the '1.5 generation', referring to child survivors of the Holocaust, too young to have had an adult understanding of what was happening to them, but old enough to have been present during the Nazi persecution of Jews.

> Unlike the second generation, whose most common shared experience is that of belatedness – perhaps best summed up in the French writer Henri Raczymow's rueful statement, 'We cannot even say that we were almost deported' (1979, p. 104) – the 1.5 generation's shared experience is that of premature bewilderment and helplessness. This characterization may appear inadequate, in view of the massive trauma experienced by both child and adult survivors during the Holocaust. The operative word, however, is 'premature' – for if all those who were there experienced trauma, the specific experience of children was that the trauma occurred (or at least, began) before the formation of stable identity that we associate with adulthood, and in some cases before any conscious sense of self. Paradoxically, their 'premature bewilderment' was often accompanied by premature aging, having to act as adults while still children (Brenner and Kestenberg 1996, Ch. 7); this was yet another form of trauma specific to the 1.5 generation.
>
> (Suleiman 2002: 277)

Conclusion

The subjective camera interrogates strands in current theories of documentary, autobiography and fictional narrative: here, the subjective artistic self – the self positioned behind the camera – is located as the source of questioning: for if, indeed, every film requires a lens in order to exist, the filmmaker may also be read as a source of light and motion (as in the French word for lens, *objectif*, or in Dziga Vertov's *Man With a Movie Camera*, 1929), determining what is to be shot, cut, edited, heard and seen by viewers implicated in this cycle of intergenerational transmission. If, then, all films have a source – whether documentary or fictional, literary or visual, experimental, ethnographic or avant-garde – and if autobiographical narratives draw attention unapologetically to that enunciative source or voice, we might argue that the subjectivity of witnesses, victims, survivors and those temporally distanced from the primary events must be taken into account as an element of interpretation. With the same etymology as 'transference', the concept of metaphor (*meta* = change, *pherein* = to bear) suggests associations among visual, aural and experiential layers of first-person cinematic representation. The film authors' layered and gendered voices, then, have much to teach us about the necessity of subjectivity and its contradictory epistemologies.

Juxtaposing films from the immediate post-war era with those produced between 1989 and 2005 with regard to issues of mourning, trauma, propaganda and history enables us to address the dynamics of post-memory – the experience of many children of Holocaust survivors, or others who grow up dominated by narratives that preceded their birth – in psychodynamic and representational terms. The past 15 years have witnessed the return of the history of Central European Jews to the screen through historical frescoes as well as intimate family narratives that encourage the intergenerational work of memory. But this post-socialist moment also raises perplexing questions about the silences and repression, the identification, shame and guilt that continue to haunt the victims, survivors and successor generations. For if the filmmakers' fantasy engages with history, so, too, does the external world intrude, often tragically, into the artistic work. It is, after all, primarily through interpretative strategies, which depend on such rhetorical devices as editing, narrative structure, camera work and the ultimately subjective decisions made behind the lens, that filmmakers invite us as spectators to participate in the communicative and critical possibilities of the cinematic experience.

As I hope to have suggested through these films, Jewish children, adolescents and adults in Central Europe during the war experienced the sudden transformation of their world from at least some degree of stability and security to utter chaos. Understanding the connection between death, loss and the often unconscious transmission of what they have witnessed lies at the heart of a historically responsible cinema, as much as that of psychoanalysis.

Notes

1 Michael Renov, lecture, film studies, University of Massachusetts, Amherst, 15 April 2005.
2 The 1993 release of Steven Spielberg's *Schindler's List* gave rise to bitter controversies and debates: perhaps especially in France, the film was regarded as transgressing boundaries of decency in Holocaust representation that had been rigorously promoted by filmmakers such as Claude Lanzmann, whose *Shoah* remains a landmark documentary film of the genre. Lanzmann and others accused Spielberg of humanizing the Holocaust using Hollywood techniques that made too approachable and ordinary what some critics judged sacred and therefore unrepresentable. The increase in the volume of production of films that reference the Holocaust may in part be attributable to the release of *Schindler's List*; among other factors, public debate surrounding the film led to the creation of Spielberg's 'Survivors of the Shoah Visual History Foundation', which has since become a major site of international archival, oral history, film, video and digital research and preservation.
3 This percentage corresponds to the number of Hungarian families in which a parental figure disappeared or was killed during the war. At one point, Takó's mother says: 'They wanted to kill us, too,' referring to the Arrow Cross (the political police) who targeted Jewish families.
4 The post-Communist era has opened new spaces for research on the history and status of the moving image: its construction, interpretation, ethical encounters and the multiple purposes of memory transmission. In the decade and a half since the fall of the Berlin Wall, a new generation of filmmakers has been engaging these issues in innovative film language that opens horizons for critical analysis in conversations that confront the contradictions and ambivalences characteristic of contemporary public and private Jewish identities. This transgenerational approach provides fresh angles of vision on assimilation (István Szabó's *Sunshine*, 1999; Péter Forgács's *Private Hungary*, 1989–2005 and Miklós Jancsó's ethnographic films on the lost Jews of Transylvania), religious affiliation (Judit Elek's *The Raftsmen*, 1989, Diana Gróo's documentary interviews of young Jews) and trans-national migration (Sandra Kogut's *Hungarian Passport*, 2003).
5 *Fateless* (*Sorstálanság*, Hungary/Germany/UK, 2005), directed by Lajos Koltai. Koltai was born in Budapest, where he has established himself as one of the world's most accomplished cinematographers. He has worked extensively as a collaborator on the films of István Szabó and, since 1987, on numerous American films. *Fateless* is his feature directorial debut.

References

Anthelme, R. (1990) *L'Espèce humaine*. Paris: Gallimard.
Brenner, I. and Kestenberg, J. (1996) *The Last Witness: Child Survivor of the Holocaust*. American Psychiatric Publishing.
Delbo, C. (1995) *Auschwitz and After*. New Haven, CT: Yale University Press.

Feldman, S. and Laub, D. (1992) *Testimony: Crises of Witnessing in Literature, Psychoanalysis and History*. New York: Routledge.

Friedlander, S. (1992) Trauma, transference, and 'working through' in writing the history of the Shoah, *History and Memory*, 4: 41.

Hartmann, G. (1996) *The Longest Shadow: In the Aftermath of the Holocaust*. New York: Palgrave Macmillan.

Kertész, I. (1975) *Fateless* (*Sorstálanság*). Evanston, IL: Northwestern University Press, 1992.

Kertész, I. (1993) 'In dark shadow', in *A holokauszt mint kultúra. Három elöadás* (*The Holocaust as Culture: Three Lectures*). Budapest: Századvég.

Langer, L.L. (1994) The literature of Auschwitz, in *Admitting the Holocaust: Collected Essays*. New York: Oxford University Press.

Levi, P. (1986) *The Drowned and the Saved*, trans. Raymond Rosenthal. New York: Vintage International, 1989.

Liebman, S. (1996) Lost and found: Wanda Jakubowska's 'The Last Stop', *Cineaste*, 22.

Portuges, C. (2001) Home Movies, found images, and 'amateur film' as a witness to history: Péter Forgács's 'Private Hungary', *The Moving Image*, Fall: 107–23.

Raczymow, H. (1979) *Contes d'exil et d'oubli*. Paris: Gallimard.

Renor, M. (2004) *The Subject of Documentary*. Minneapolis: University of Minnesota Press.

Rothberg, M. (2003) After the witness: a report from the Twentieth Anniversary Conference of the Fortunoff Video Archive for Holocaust Testimonies at Yale, *History & Memory*, 15(1): 85–96.

Suleiman, S.R. (2002) The 1.5 generation: thinking about child survivors and the Holocaust, *American Imago*, 59(3): 277–95.

8

CUT AND LACED
Traumatism and fetishism in Luis Buñuel's *Un Chien Andalou*
Andrew Webber

Un Chien Andalou (France, 1928)
Director: Luis Buñuel, with Salvador Dalí
Distributor: Kino Video

This chapter arises from work I did on city films in the context of a recent book project on the European avant-garde (Webber 2004: 103–66). The methodology for the project as a whole was based on a dialogue of tensions between political and psychoanalytic modes of critique, between Marx and Freud. The chapter on city cinema aimed to draw out the contradictory economies of much early avant-garde filmmaking by finding psychoanalytic purchase in revolutionary films and political tensions in those with a more psychical agenda. The bifocal logic of the psycho-political methodology in the avant-garde project meant looking for trespass into or spilling out of the interior in the politically driven films of early Soviet Russia and for the reaching of the more psychically driven films of surrealism or expressionism into more external, social-political spaces. *Un Chien Andalou* (1928), by Buñuel and Dalí, was a focal example of the latter, and what is proposed here is an amplification of the psychoanalytically disposed reading of that film's politics through close – perhaps fetishistic – analysis of a particular feature: its preoccupation with lace and lacemaking.

One of the key instances used to trace the dialectically complicated relationship between inside and out in films of the early avant-garde was window scenes. And the attachment to lace that is the focus of the present chapter relates intimately to the window as a symptomatic structure of framing and mediation for that dialectical model. In films by Eisenstein and Vertov, lace is exemplary of a fetishistic lure that diverts the camera from its proper place recording the public activity of the Soviet city and in through the window, both literally and metaphorically, onto more private viewing experiences. These are meant to be marked as ideologically suspect, associated, for example, with the female soldiers undressing in the counter-revolutionary space of the palace in Eisenstein's *October* (1927), with the accoutrements of the bourgeois furies who strip and beat the young Bolshevik in the same film, or with the young woman awakening into her commodified world at the beginning of Vertov's urban symphony *Man with a Movie Camera* (1929). Yet such lacy views recurrently draw the lingering aesthetic, and psychosexual, interest of these men with movie cameras. Lace here stands metonymically for the more general counter-revolutionary, scopophilic seductions of interiors and their fabrics: domestic, corporeal and psychical interiors that tease the camera away from its focus on the Soviet polity. Not for nothing does Barthes highlight the fetish value of Eisenstein's filmwork: 'isn't it said that in some *cinémathèque* or other a piece of film is missing from the copy of *Battleship Potemkin* – the scene with the baby's pram of course – it having been cut off and stolen lovingly like a lock of hair, a glove or an item of women's underwear?' (1977: 72). This fetish quality indicates that urban political filmmaking, as envisaged here in the epic scene on the Odessa steps, can be cut up and secreted away for more private purposes (the baby's pram sequence – of course – because it is a particularly individualized and identificatory part of the mass spectacle). And while a sequence in *Man with a Movie Camera* aligns the act of filmmaking with the production apparatus of the textile industry, Vertov's camera too is susceptible to consumerist pleasure, to the psycho-fetishistic and commodity fetishistic allure of lace.

Before turning to the laciness of *Un Chien Andalou*, a film with a more overt preoccupation with fetishism, it is worth considering the general disposition of lace as *viewing material*. Lace occupies a special sort of space between: between innocence and guile, sacred and profane, the infantile and the adult only, inside and out. Whether on bodies or buildings, it is a cover for intimacy. It is designed to be seen as well as to hide and, in many cases, be hidden, or at least partially so. Lace is a blocking structure, but one made of holes, indicating something of its kinkiness, its ambiguous constitution. In the case of the lace conventionally used on windows, it is designed to allow viewing one way and frustrate it the other. But as a cover, corporeal or architectural, it also draws attention to what is undercover: it is flat but indicates with its porosity the attraction of hidden depths. Lace is a lure, presenting a device amenable to both exhibitionist and voyeur, especially in conjunction with the right forms of lighting. And by drawing the viewer to it and into its ornamental fabrication, it is also the sort of viewing material that engages the visual into the haptic. It is tactile to the eye of the beholder, and if the lace at the window is to be seen through, it demands an intimate kind of physical proximity. It has a special quality of touchability, but also of touch taboo. This ambivalent tactility also indicates a more pathological aspect to lace. It has a certain relationship to gauze and so to the sort of netting material that is used to cover wounds. In terms of its function for film, this aspect of lace, as a fabric of open stitches, can usefully be understood as representing its relationship to the principle of suture. Suture is the process that, according to a psychoanalytic understanding of how film works, stitches the wounded subject into narrative structures, thereby at once offering a therapeutic fabric, a sustaining diversion from trauma, and representing a constraint on the satisfactions that a symbolic order like film will offer the subject. As a covering or edging material and as a fetish, lace is peculiarly ready to adopt the suturing function, drawing the viewing subject into the give-and-take of narrative, letting you see, but only ever see so much.

Lace can thus be seen as particularly appropriate viewing material for film, with a special relationship to the material conditions of the cinematic medium. An example would be the use of lace curtains as screen devices at the beginning of one of the most programmatically psychoanalytic of films, Pasolini's *Oedipus Rex* (1967). Here, one version of the sequence of primal scenes that open the Oedipal narrative of the film is enacted as projection on lace, as the infant Oedipus is first drawn to his bedroom window by the light and shadow falling on the lace curtain, then beholds the shadows of his parents dancing behind a lace curtain across the square. The translucent material of lace acts as a form of screen, offering the viewer a *screened* image, at once shown and hidden. The primal scene is thus enacted as a primitive form of cinematic viewing. And lace is no less material in the setting up of the primal scene of cinema that is the prologue of *Un Chien Andalou*, as a key part of the *mise-en-scène* for the at once iconic and iconoclastic assault upon the eye.

The infamous slitting of the eye acts as a multivalent icon or fetish, even as it seems to cut out such possibilities. It serves a sociopolitical purpose, demonstrating the need to see things in a radically different way from the conventions of bourgeois culture; it is aesthetically framed and sequenced, and so in readiness to become a cinematographic fetish; and it is, above all, one of cinema's foundational acts of psychic fantasy, enacting the primal cinematic trauma of a cut to the eye. It achieves in archetypal form the sort of extreme psychic shock to the eye that Artaud envisaged as the filmic counterpart to the theatre of cruelty: 'We must find a film with purely visual sensations the dramatic force of which springs from a shock to the eyes, drawn, one might say, from the very substance of the eye' (1964, vol. 3: 22). What Artaud proposes then, and what *Un Chien Andalou* enacts, is a drastic visual assault aimed at releasing psychic substance. It follows a mimetic logic, shocking the eye of the viewer and spilling its affective substance out of its conventional containment in the optical regime.

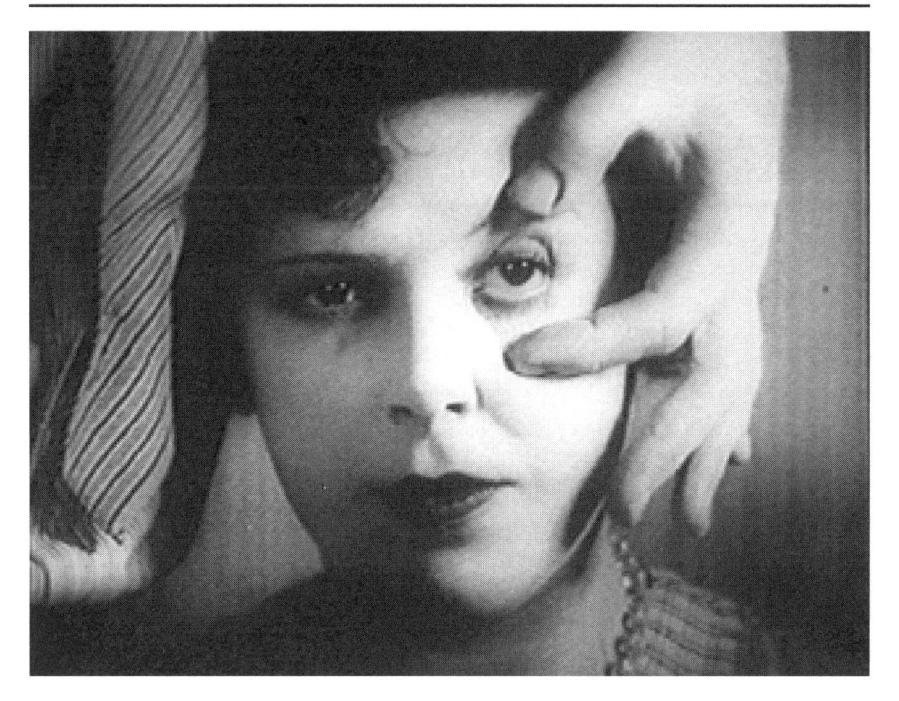

Simone Mareuil in *Un Chien Andalou*

This scene establishes the film then as psycho-drama, as film-theatre of cruelty. The prologue is as it were played out behind the scenes of that film-theatre, in the wardrobe or the cutting room. The female 'star' sits in costume, awaiting the 'director'. The male figure, a director-figure indeed, played by Buñuel himself, sharpens his razor. As has often been remarked, the prologue is a self-reflexive 'act'; the manual cutting of the eye stands for the director's editorial intervention in the material of the film, and for the need for both actors and spectators to be made to look different. It appears to refer, in particular, to the introductory sequence of the first explicitly psychoanalytic film, Pabst's *Secrets of a Soul* (1926), where the shaving of his wife's neck introduces the phobic case history of the protagonist. Here too, the shaving scene is intercut with the man with the razor drawn to look out of the window.

The director's preparatory work also appears to include an interfilmic citation of the iconic image of the woman with the wounded eye from Eisenstein's *Battleship Potemkin* (1925), one of Buñuel's favourite films, inflicted here in a controlled, interior space and in a hyberbolic, close-up form. These two interfilmic frames help to prepare for an image for which the audience can, however, never be prepared. Expectation is provided in its careful setting up: the sharpening of the razor, tested against the man's thumbnail, the visual anticipation in the slicing of the sliver of cloud across the moon, and the holding of the eye in readiness. It is clear that the director is not about to apply make-up here. All of this helps to make the actual act of slicing the eye unwatchable. The viewers are ready to avert their gaze from this unbearable sight and so not to see what actually happens: a brazen film trick. The eye of a dead animal, surrounded by unshaven facial hair, is substituted for that of the living woman. This is a cut that you're never ready to see and thus never see not happening. While the blinding of the eye seems to represent the end-point of cinematic possibility, it should in fact be seen as a limited form of *découpage*, the key aesthetic trope of cinema for Buñuel. As he defines it, the cut of *découpage* is also the hinge between images: 'Excising one thing to turn it into another' (1995: 131–2). The cutting of the woman's eye is also a cut to the other, animal eye, not the terminal elision of the viewing process, but a creative act of segmentation. It thus does not stop the film but leads into its montage-based narrative of cuttings and splicings.

The prologue can be understood, in an extension of the psychoanalytic sense, as a primal scene. The scene that we witness illicitly, behind the scenes of the film proper, a coming together of a male and a female figure that is traversed by a cut, a traumatic mark of separation, conforms to that model. Not for nothing does Linda Williams (1992), in her 'rhetorico-psychoanalytic' analysis of the film, read the cut as a figure of castration and then use this as a template for the sequential openings and closings of the film. The cut of castration can certainly be argued to mark the presence of what we are given to see here with traumatic absence, as Williams suggests. In conjunction with the model of *découpage* elaborated by Buñuel, it might be most appropriate to understand it as incorporated into a structure that psychoanalytic film theory would call suture. That is, the imaginary allure of self-sufficiency (imaged here in the specular gaze of the female figure) is subjected to a cut, but the symbolic order, the order of language, here construed as film language, intervenes to recover the cut, stitching it into the editorial fabric, the *fort-da* game, of cinematic narrative.[1] In Buñuel's terms, the excision of the *découpage* also turns the first thing into another. As Williams recognizes, the gaps or artificial orifices that are cut into the body are figures not just of absence, but of the desire that is provoked by absence. The hole or wound creates desire for an object to fill the gap, which, in turn, produces narrative development.

The film remains ambiguously cast between the potential for desire as a creative force arising out of the condition of absence and the darker, more perverse possibility that desire could in fact take absence, the cut, as its object. The first of these is particularly present in the form of the fetish, the items of clothing and other part objects that are subject to special cathectic investment by the characters. The second possibility, what we might term a traumato-philic attachment, is present in the recurrent mutilations, the fixture upon absence as much as on lacy aprons or other covers for absence that are configured with it.

The prologue of *Un Chien Andalou* establishes a relationship between visual desire, trauma and lace, one that is organized around the window as crux between interior and exterior. There is a correlation here between lace curtains and the lacy cloud that cuts over the moon, at once imitating and suturing the cut to the eye. It can be said to introduce into the film the principle of the fetish, at once a cover for, and also an intermediary representation of, the object of desire and loss. This principle is then maintained through the attention to lace and cognate materials that will serve to suture the recurrent woundings inflicted in the course of the film. By not so much slicing the moon as metaphorical eye as partially veiling it – how, after all, can lace or vapour inflict a cut? – the image establishes what we might call the *logic of lace* as a particular conjunction of showing/seeing and not showing/not seeing. The lace or vapour elements of the prologue to *Un Chien Andalou* both conspire in the act of blinding/castration and draw a veil over its effect. This logic of lace can be said to organize the successive scenarios of the film. From the substitutions of the prologue onwards, *Un Chien Andalou* is a masterpiece of strategic discontinuity editing, and the lace curtain that forms a key visual link between the prologue and the main narrative is used in both cases as an emblem of fixation upon, and discontinuity in, the act of viewing. The cutting of the eye is also prefigured by the cutting out of less evident elements in the visual frame, not least the lace curtain, which appears and disappears from the window-frame as the man sharpens the razor and goes out onto the balcony.

The prologue scene looks forward then to that near the start of the film's main narrative which features the view out of an apartment window onto the Parisian street. The male protagonist, cycling through the streets in his frilly maid's apparel, has an accident on the road beneath the apartment window, drawing the attention from within of the female protagonist. As she jumps up in apparent anticipation of his accidental arrival, the woman casts aside a book that re-opens at a reproduction of Vermeer's *The Lace-maker*, a female figure who wears a collar not unlike the cyclist's. While *Man with a Movie Camera* aligned the spooling, cutting, and splicing of the cine-eye machine with the spinning technology of the textile industry, this image indicates a different mode of production: a profoundly private act of visual concentration and manual fabrication, its eyes closed to the outside world. The figuration of the textile factory worker as a latter-day icon, superimposed upon a circle of spinning spools at the culmination of *Man with a Movie Camera*, contrasts with the more conventional, pre-industrial iconic image of the lace-maker. The Vermeer picture suggests a production of accessories that will bear a particular investment of personal meaning, ultimately in domestic forms of textile fetishism. The cyclist's costume accessories and the lace curtains at the window, through which these will be seen by the woman and later thrown out by the man's double, sustain that mode of production, one that focuses on the private, undercover pleasures of fetishism and voyeurism. It is through a private act of laying out the fetishistic clothing and of visual concentration that the woman as lace-maker achieves the recovery of her male counterpart in the following sequence. The elements of the costume come together and the man appears in apparently recovered form behind her. Lace-making stands here for an act of suture, a stitching together of the traumatically broken narrative by a recuperation of what is lost in a new form. But the texture is always already torn; the new form typically carries the incompletion of the old, as here in the hole in the man's hand that attracts the gaze of both figures. The hand that cuts new forms and works new textures for the eye, in textile or in film, here follows the eye in being cut open and exuding uncontrollable substances – there jelly, here the swarming ants.

Lace-making functions as a fetishistic cover, at once covering and indicating ambivalent objects which combine desire and trauma. And it extends from the costume and window accessories to other effects, reprising the metonymic associations with the cloud or the smoke that the man blows over his eyes in the prologue. In the main body of the film it is figured in the condensed breath of the man on the window as he watches the street-scene below with increasing scopophilic and traumatophilic excitement (this scene can be said to preview a tradition of filmic pleasure in the spectacle of accidents that is most explicitly formulated in Cronenberg's *Crash*, 1996). And in a more technical sense lace-making is imitated by the many dissolves that efface even as they mark the syncopated fabric of the film's montage, following the cinematographic trope of *découpage* as both a cut and a more fluid transformation. An exemplary case for my argument would be when the double goes over to the window to cast out the man's costume and is, as it were, cut into the lace curtain by such a blurred segmentation. This also correlates with the gauze shot that is used to soften the focus on the man's double as he executes him, applying as it were a lace curtain, or a vapour as the screenplay has it, to the lens. Lace and cognate materials and effects are thus bound ambivalently into the versions of the clinch between desire and trauma that make up the narrative.

The Lace-maker picture can be said to function as *mise-en-abyme*, an emblematic internal reflection of and upon the film's disposition. It is a picture which represents an ultimate form of interior focus, and yet one which breaches its apparent self-absorption. On the one hand it stitches or sutures and on the other is caught spilling out. Giuliana Bruno talks of how Vermeer configures his feminine interiors with cartography. This indicates, she argues, possibilities for these female subjects of following the model of Vermeer's male geographers and astronomers by engaging in virtual exploration. Their domestic activities of viewing and touching thus project them outside their domestic fixture into the city and beyond: 'Recurrently ... his female

Jan Vermeer's *The Lace-maker* (Musée du Louvre, Paris)

subjects are juxtaposed with wall maps . . . One wonders . . . if the women are honorary cartographers. Whichever the case, this reciprocal epistemic interplay renders a sense of intimate geographies. It even suggests that cartography is itself an intimate drafting – a liminal passage from private to social history' (2002: 415). *The Lace-maker*, however, might more appropriately be seen as producing another and less coordinated version of this idea of passage from inside to out. It presents an image of visual fabrication that at once displays an appearance of seamless containment in the form of an elaborate composition and shows a spilling out: where binding threads become fluid and unruly, and exquisite paintwork incontinent. This indicates its relationship to *Un Chien Andalou*, where the jelly that spills out of the eye, the ants that swarm out of the hand, or the hair that sprouts over the mouth and elsewhere, also relate to a fantasy idea of what might spill out of film when its pellicle is cut, its skin transgressed from within or without. These emblematic figures of breached body surfaces indicate a tension between containment and excrescence in the body of the film image.

To read the filmic motifs and rhetorical turns of *Un Chien Andalou* in this self-reflexive manner seems appropriate, given that the man who slits the eye in the prologue and watches the cloud lace through the moon is the film's director, responsible for the editorial cutting and lacing of its material, its traumatisms and fetishisms. And the images of spillage from Vermeer's sewing-cushion and Buñuel's eye, the one decorous the other drastic in appearance – and yet convergent in their respective compositions – in turn illustrate the sort of dialectic between meshing in and breaking out that the lace curtains of the film effect. Within the interiors of late seventeenth-century Delft and early twentieth-century Paris, behind their lace covers, there are ambiguous, if not perverse, substances looking to break out.

This same configuration also holds for the film that closes Buñuel's career in the cinema of fetishism and traumatism, *That Obscure Object of Desire* (1977).[2] In its closing scene, shot in Paris a half a century after *Un Chien Andalou*, Buñuel comes full circle by restaging the Vermeer picture as *mise-en-abyme*. The features of his cinematic primal scene, drawn from both the prologue and the main narrative of *Un Chien Andalou*, recur here. A woman is seen sewing lace in a shop window in a Paris arcade, enacting the iconography of *The Lace-maker as tableau vivant*. She is not making lace, however, but repairing it. The lace is bloodied, introducing the bleeding effect of the threads spilling out of Vermeer's cushion into the lacework. The woman's needle is doing reparative violence to a cut in the lace, one that imitates the shape of an eye and projects the gaze into the figure of the gaping wound, while also attending to its suturation. Outside the window, the male and female protagonists re-enact the viewing of the street accident from inside by the protagonists of *Un Chien Andalou*. They are caught in the attitude that Buñuel seems to want to establish as the primal scene of film viewing, with a window as screen-frame for the obscure object of cinematic desire,[3] and lace as its ambiguous, traumatically marked, fetishistic accoutrement. Where the first film started by opening up the eye in a violent act of blinding, the last finishes with a sudden explosion that inflicts a different kind of blinding violence on the viewer. The first, false ending – an overture to an eye-opening psycho-cinematic career – becomes a more truly terminal viewing moment at the end of the last film, albeit only because of the intervention of the director's death. In both the premature 'ending' of the cut in *Un Chien Andalou* and the ending proper of *That Obscure Object*, the allure of cinematic fetishism is bound, or sutured, into the apparently terminal threat of cinematic traumatism, but always under the productive sign of *découpage*: 'excising one thing to turn it into another'.

Notes

1. As Silverman notes, suture follows the stitching rhythm of exchange between absence and presence of the *fort-da* (1983: 200).
2. My argument here was animated by the discussion of *That Obscure Object of Desire* by my co-panellist at the *epff3*, Peter Evans, as well as comments from the floor.
3. Following Buñuel's description of the cinema screen as a 'marvellous window' (1995: 138).

References

Artaud, A. (1964) *Oeuvres complètes*. Paris: Gallimard.
Barthes, R. (1977) *Image – Music – Text*. London: Fontana.
Bruno, G. (2002) *Atlas of Emotions: Journeys in Art, Architecture, and Film*. New York: Verso.
Buñuel, L. (1995) *Unspeakable Betrayal: Selected Writings*. Berkeley, CA: University of California Press.
Silverman, K. (1983) *The Subject of Semiotics*. New York: Oxford University Press.
Webber, A.J. (2004) *The European Avant-garde: 1900–1940*. Cambridge: Polity.
Williams, L. (1992) *Figures of Desire: A Theory and Analysis of Surrealist Film*. Berkeley, CA: University of California Press.

9

TWO SHORT FILMS BY JAN SVANKMAJER
Jabberwocky and *Punch and Judy*

Helen Taylor Robinson

Zvahlav aneb Saticky Slameného Huberta (Jabberwocky) (Czech Republic, 1971)
Rakvickarna (Punch and Judy) (Czech Republic, 1966)
Director: Jan Svankmajer
Distributor: Krátky Film Praha

Jan Svankmajer was born in 1934 in Prague, in what is now the Czech Republic, and describes himself as a 'militant surrealist' who creates collages, tactile sculptures, surrealist objects and films. Thus he is not a film animator as such, but a complex manipulator of multiple forms in the film medium. He also writes eloquently: dreams, poems, short prose.

Svankmajer openly adheres to the writings of Freud – particularly on dreams, sexuality, the unconscious and free associations – as the sources, among others, for his and all art. His manner and style are deliberately and sophisticatedly contrived to create his effects, so that there is a great deal to absorb in the power and brevity of his work, which he continues to produce to the present day.

The title of *Jabberwocky* (1971) is a reference to the 'non-sense' poem by Lewis Carroll from his satire on childhood and adulthood, *Alice Through the Looking Glass* (Svankmajer also made a film called *Alice* in relation to *Alice in Wonderland*, Carroll's first work on the same subject). The title of his other short film, *Punch and Judy* (1966), of course refers to the age-old puppet characters, who traditionally fight: Punch in jealousy of the baby, killing it; Judy with Punch, for this outrage; Punch then killing Judy; and, finally, traditionally, and in triumph, Punch's survival, for he escapes prison, death and the very devil by his capacity to outwit them all. For Svankmajer, both these

Jabberwocky

deliberate literary and artistic allusions – like the audio-visual jokes, grotesqueries and satires that litter each shot of these films – and, indeed, each different musical and auditory intervention he chooses, are devices that deliver his meaning; nothing in these films is a matter of chance.

Although the films are narratives, in that they pass through our watching consciousness in a process of continuous time and would appear to be sequential, their main task, as part of the surrealist dictate, is to create a series of powerful overlapping and discordant images and sounds that are deliberately evocative of the stream of consciousness or dream-like experience. So, in this sense, there cannot be a synopsis, of an ordered or meaningful kind, in the traditional sense, for the reader of this text has had no access to the experience. If such a dreaming reality *can* be described at all, it falls within the constraints of this necessary paradox.

Thus, loosely speaking, but nevertheless cinematographically highly determined, the viewer of *Jabberwocky* sees a series of tableaux in rapid succession, as a child's voice speaks the opening stanzas of the nonsense poem by Carroll. These tableaux cease to have words eventually, as nonsense and childhood change into sense and adulthood, but they begin by focusing upon a cupboard set in a kind of child's playroom in which a number of childhood related experiences with a strong subversive element are made to come to life. Girls, boys, dollies, rocking horses, toy soldiers, feeding and cradling scenes, schoolrooms and desks, all appear in a deliberate challenge to the convention of conscious child development, set to the repetitive sound of a high-pitched female voice and a low bass male voice, operatically 'seeing to' (with a wordless la-la-la sound) and nonsensically authorizing this childhood from behind the scenes, as puppets may be made to dance to the tune of their creator. An increasing diminution of liveliness, instinctuality and pleasure (in the interests of control, education, indoctrination of ideas and a factory-like production line of childhood) is conveyed. The emphasis is, in particular, upon the little boy child, perhaps over and above the little girl, although a series of images of a sharp knife-like object dancing on its tip and causing lace to tear and blood to spill also suggests an image of the sharpest of little dancing females causing mayhem as another outcome of this mode of rearing; but it is the boy who looks to end up in the cupboard in a bleak black suit of adulthood, as the film closes. Svankmajer thus makes the final, provocative point to society at the end, in this intense and innovative collage of impressions. In significant moments in the film's rapid staccato imagery, a real full-size black cat knocks down the small playthings we watch, disturbingly, reminding us by his size and proportion of the scale of instinctual life in comparison with our playthings of culture and civilization. In the film's final moments, this cat is locked up in a small wire cage, at the base of the cupboard where a grey suit hangs. In the image of the cat struggling, helpless to get free, we are reminded by association of the child now 'hung' and 'stilled' in his adult cage, with the implication that the film has been creating all the wriggling and protest and the stance of assault on our mental reality (our small cupboard-minds) in challenge to the small cupboard of civilized reality we are forced to abide within.

In *Punch and Judy* similarly, scenes, or rather tableaux, of the industrialized and demonically relentless working lives of the people — comic-grotesque, wooden puppet figures in familiar day-to-day settings of life — are shown. These scenes of work and life lived at a crazy speed and ferocity point up 'the cradle to the grave' existence in all its emptiness. These then give way to a little play within this play, as if asking us to pause and reflect for a moment, as art conventionally allows us to do. A little puppet theatre where hands put on the puppet garments of Pulcinella and Harlequin sets itself in motion. A real creature, a small guinea-pig owned by Punch, and fed and stroked, at once seems to lead to an envious attack by Harlequin, emerging from his house, who wants to possess the living animal. This he tries to do using wealth, violence, cunning and other human attributes that lead to war and destruction. Scenes of repeated attack, and then recovery, occur (we are given many opportunities for change, but we still drive the nails down hard into our own little coffin-like sets of behaviours, so the images of hammering, nailing and pounding to death suggest), and finally the violent demise of both parties follows, set to absurd-sounding tunes, rhythms and percussion that have a merry-go-round quality. Images of skeletons, of famous moral satirists of the vices of civilization like Dickens, pass fleetingly by, but in the end the coffin encloses the little pair, the hands remove themselves from the puppets and the enactment of the ruination of life, by those whose instincts are at the service of their baser natures, is concluded. The guinea-pig shuffles off in abandonment of these absurd masters, and the nails in our coffins (for the subtitle of the film is *The Coffin Factory*) are left for us to contemplate.

Both these short, intensely emotional pieces have the effect of rendering absurd, yet making us feel disturbed and uncomfortable at an irrational level with, what passes before our eyes, in the tradition of satire within the surrealist convention. That convention has its sources in the use of 'the term Surrealist as applied only to those objects, however disquieting or unpleasant they may

Punch and Judy

be, that have the power to evoke sensations of psychic reality, of "another world", even though it be one', as the poet Paul Eluard noted, 'which is assuredly in this one' (Hamilton Heard 1973: 276). What we do not have a doubt of, when in the hands of an artist, is the value of the imagination as our mainstay against the pains, ills and suffering imposed by reality. When reality provides us with the best of its riches, we are fine. But for all the rest, and that is much of the time, great Art ministers to our needs, and heals wherever we seek for cure. That which imaginatively empowers us in this artist's work, his body of imagination, is his unremitting conviction of the energy of instinctual life in its endless and varied dialectic with all that dams, subverts, cages and destroys it. His capacity to laugh at, satirize and mock the oppressors of the instinctual adds even greater bite or strength to his conviction. He is not frightened of the enemy. He is a surrealist, in the way perhaps the psycho-analyst is an 'unconciousness-ist', to make the point with such an ungainly term. And he has the measure of his opponent, and can play and torment and tease him, thus making us, as participant viewers in the process, safe to relax, while this deadliest of games is being played out (Charlie Chaplin had the same insouciance in *The Great Dictator*, 1940).

Svankmajer's genius is in his particular use of the form in which he addresses this age-old theme of art and artists. This is through his use of artifice in opposition to life energy, the rigidified toys, dolls and puppets, or their moving representations such as dresses, suits and habits (to affirm the pun), and alongside them innumerable other artefacts and objects, the cupboards, for example, where we keep our idols secreted and hidden; and, I think, he draws us, with a tone of irreverence and a lightness of touch, into attendance on what I want to call the 'totemic' features of human civilization: the special and revered and sacred *versions* of the real that we worship in place of the real other world that we cannot easily tolerate – our totems, with all their fearful significance to the human tribe. These are the things that stand for what we value, only now derogated from their lively and dangerous forms into dead and vapid vessels, safe to handle, safe to push around even, yet always ready to terrify us back into a use of their power. And we watch, with all the fear and laughter associated with the breaking of all taboo, this artist's confident manipulation of these features, for we recognize their relationship to the real, and also run from such recognition with all haste. We are close to the world of fetish (large gloves eerily slide forward off Dolly's fingers in *Jabberwocky* . . .), the world of the special and the bizarre, of the zombie or automaton self, and its relations with the instinctual, in the process of mutation. All these circle around us in the atmosphere, or in the vicinity, of this filmic material, like the horrific toothy puppet monkeys who play their tune at the opening sequence of *Punch and Judy* . . . grotesques, caught between life and death, god-like, yet denigrated, instinctuality.

At the same time, by juxtaposing with these the living, breathing and natural objects also within each film – the black cat in *Jabberwocky* and the small snuffling guinea-pig in *Punch and Judy* – by setting these natural creatures, isolated, alone, and in contrast to this strange world of the human totemic paraphernalia, Svankmajer reminds us of the presence of ordinary instinctual reality prior to human interference, prior to the cult of controlling, worshipping, and thus subjugating the instincts; and he allows us to see the impulses to do this, all the more frighteningly at work. The black cat does end up, in the culmination of childhood, squashed and pulsating in a cage at the bottom of the cupboard, with the large black suit of manhood centre-stage, and the crumpled sailor-suit of childhood fantasies and wishes relinquished in the other corner in a small heap. The camera closes in on the button that now sits at the site of the genital area in the dark, black picture. From instincts to symbols of their repression, or the satire of the progress of civilization (in *Jabberwocky*). In *Punch and Judy* the guinea-pig, after a near miss, escapes decimation from the warring hammers of Harlequin and Pulcinella, and hobbles out through the gaping hole in the back curtain of the little playhouse, where a rent in our so called progress permits him to leave, this time, to survive another day. Nature, trying to hold her own, is radically outnumbered in the Svankmajer vision. Human beings are mocked, in the clowns' antics, for their apparent progress of civilizing of the instincts; for of course the clowns only unleash them, in their own distorted form, maiming and hacking as they do at each other. Jangling bells and vehement merry-go-round walz music and the clanking machines suggest the effective repetition of the same. We are all going nowhere, round and round, ever faster, in crushing instinctual life. Svankmajer is faithfully holding our faces to these truths imaginatively, while we might well wish to change perspective.

If you make the child, who is the repository of the instincts – the child, the baby, the adolescent – if you make him a totem (that is, you secretly castrate him of his joy and pain and pleasure and sadness, and substitute for it the convenient but dead alternatives that allow you to control, manipulate and groom him for civilization and its discontents, to coin a famous phrase, getting him to wear your black suit and dangle like a skeleton in the cupboard 'as if' he were a man); if you pretend, by your ludicrous operatic singing of high voice/mother and low voice/father, that you are doing all you can to love and care for him, while boiling, shredding, mincing and producing factory versions of the same for him or her to digest, and grow likewise; if you do all this, and revere it and totemize it and, in the process, you set the altar of the cupboard, the dolls' house, the school desk, to its veneration, then you deserve the scribble all over your sham idolatry that ends the *Jabberwocky* film, you deserve the mess that you produced, and you deserve the exposure of the sharp eye of this document recording your procedures.

Again, in the same way, if you make Nature a totem, and appear to value her, fight, kill, plunder, steal to possess her, and in the course of it forget what you were doing it for, if you show your utter contempt for Nature's instinctual forces by rubbing her protective fur (the guinea-pig's) the wrong way, and leaving her vulnerable features exposed, the eyes, ears and mouth of the little creature pulled about as if it were nothing less than a toy, and if you give it a token feed to represent care, then when you end up in the small narrow box, for all this activity, Nature, thus misused, turns her backside on you in disgust and, again, you deserve no better.

In our ritual substitutes for instinctual reality, we are always in danger of losing the very thing we are in awe of. And each new generation sees through the holes in this simulacrum of reality, and wants to tear the altar down, and start again. The artist, in Freud's terms, like each new generation of growing adolescents, hurls imaginative venom at the ageing and depleted primal father, and substitutes a new god in a new image. And this act of insurrection is life affirming, until it's time for another generation and another renewal. In Svankmajer's account, the battle for this new ground is depicted as a necessary and continual siege. Not a single screen second is diverted from this theme. Which is why I began by saying we feel safe in the power of his imagination. For his inventiveness and his vitality of imagery and metaphor in representing this are, each time, a war on sterility, ossification and the interment of anything that moves.

If we too, as viewers, can be chased around by the nightmare comedies of what Svankmajer gets to sprout, to unscrew, to metamorphose and set itself in motion, the whole instinctual unravelling that threatens from all manner of mysterious portals in his dream tales, then we might actually wake up and try and interpret our dream, as Freud suggested, instead of lying there quietly, soporifically, in our beds as if we never need to move. Any reification, any totemization – and cinema is the relatively new screen altar at which we worship and sacrifice our valued objects, just as psychoanalysis, too, can become a place for cult behaviour – any such rigidifying endangers what we have in the way of energy, vitality and creativity. We need all the help we can get from artistic innovation and insight to help us on our way.

References

Carroll, L. (1865) *Alice's Adventures in Wonderland*. London: Macmillan, 1963.
Carroll, L. (1872) *Through the Looking Glass and What Alice Found There*. London: Macmillan, 1963.
Hamilton Heard, G. (1973) *19th and 20th Century Art* ed. H.W. Hanson. New York: Abrams.

10

COMPILATION FILM AS 'DEFERRED ACTION'
Vincent Monnikendam's *Mother Dao, the Turtle-like*

Laura Mulvey

Moeder Dao, de Schildpadg elijkende (*Mother Dao, the Turtle-like*)
(The Netherlands, 1995)
Director: Vincent Monnikendam
Distributor: Nederlandse Programma Stichting

It sometimes seems as though the cinema's legacy has only recently acquired the status of serious and historical document. With the passing of time itself, the vast accumulation of film footage, that mirrors the twentieth century like a parallel universe, has inevitably attracted the attention of film and video artists as well as historians. However, from its earliest days, some pioneering film historians perceived that out of film's special relationship with reality, human culture had acquired a unique source of documentation. As early as 1898, the Polish photographer Boleslaw Matuszewski published a brochure suggesting that film would be 'A New Source for History', due to its ability to capture reality (Sjöberg 2001: 41). This relationship was subsequently realized, above all, in the compilation film. However, I would like to suggest in this chapter that, through the compilation film, a relationship might be forged not only between cinema and history, but also between cinema, history and psychoanalysis.

Compilation films are made from pre-existing footage. Once selections are made from the raw material, a new narrative and a new consciousness emerge out of the old footage. Due to this process of reassembling the old into the new, all compilation films have a double time structure; all consist of pre-existing material, which is then reassembled into a new film. As Jay Leyda (1964) put it: 'films beget films'. Although a relevance to history is easy to find in the compilation film, it is the double time structure that opens the door to psychoanalytic theory. The interweaving of a filmic past and present may not be as complex as the negotiation between the raw material of the unconscious and its later interpretation, but an enquiry into one structure, the cinematic, leads to the other, the psychoanalytic. This juxtaposition is one of analogy, not direct comparison, and emanates from the shared double temporal structure, that is, from form not content. However, from the point of view of content, a compilation film's raw material may bear witness to 'traumatic' events, suggesting the kind of link between history, memory and psychoanalysis that has recently been the subject of considerable academic research and theoretical debate. This short chapter, unable to engage with these debates, is intended simply to suggest that the cinema's specific and unique ability to record and preserve events and images from the past might place it on a cusp between structure and content, raw material and narrative, and between psychoanalysis and history.

One strand of compilation film, within the avant-garde tradition, recycles pre-existing material for political and aesthetic purposes. The long history of the compilation film as political commentary is evidenced, for instance, by Esther Shub's *Fall of the Romanov Dynasty* (USSR, 1927) or Alain Resnais' *Night and Fog* (France, 1955). Both films examine the past from a diametrically different perspective from that which the original material had been shot. Shub used documentary footage shot under the Russian tsars to celebrate the tenth anniversary of the 1917 Revolution; Resnais used Nazi film of Auschwitz to reveal the horrors of the concentration camps. Filmmakers are now turning more and more to archival material to bring images of the past into the present in such a way as to comment on the original and alter its meaning. It is this element of critique that differentiates films of this kind from the recent spate of television programmes, however illuminating and fascinating, that are compiled from historical footage.

I am using the film *Mother Dao, the Turtle-like* to explore an intersection between history, cinema and psychoanalysis through the compilation film. As a point of departure, *Mother Dao* is endowed with the genre's characteristic time structure. To create the new film, Vincent Monnikendam drew his raw material from more than 200 documentaries, mainly stored in the archive of the Netherlands Film Museum. These films had been commissioned by a number of institutional and industrial organizations, among others the Dutch-East Indian Oil Foundation, Netherlands-East Indian Railways, Mission of the Dutch Reformed Churches, Dutch Ministry of the Colonies. Most of the footage was shot between 1913 and 1930. From these disparate sources, a record of the colonization of the Dutch East Indies (now Indonesia), told essentially from the perspective of the colonizers, an alternative story has been extracted. The difference between the colonial perspective, imposed by and celebrating a position of power, and the indigenous people's experience of colonization as violent and repressive, forms a first layer of disjunction, one that is inherent in the film's raw material. The director's task has been to arrange the footage in such a way that the hidden story, invisible to colonizing powers but always there, becomes visible.

Monnikendam seems, by and large, to have worked along the same lines as Esther Shub. This is Shub's description of her process of selection and assemblage:

> In the montage, I tried to avoid looking at the newsreel footage for its own sake, and to maintain the principle of its documentary quality. All was subordinated to the theme. This gave me the possibility, in spite of the known limitations of the photographed events and facts, to link the meanings of the material so that it evoked the pre-revolutionary period and the February days.
>
> (Leyda 1964: 25)

Similarly, Monnikendam builds the story not through a linear narrative, but through an accumulation of images that illustrate the theme: the arrival of the colonial presence, the imposition of colonial projects and the effects on the people. In this sense, the images 'evoke' and 'link' to create, as it were, a historical tapestry with greater regard for the theme, the tragedy that overcame the people, than for the very varied cultures and geographical locations spread across the archipelago. Out of this reassembling and ordering of the raw material, *Mother Dao* forms the second layer of disjunction. The final film reflects back on the power relation inscribed in the original footage and returns the indigenous people to the centre of their history. In the process, however, the material but ghostly quality of film comes to the fore.

Mother Dao has no guiding voiceover; occasionally poems mourning the suffering of the people and the effects of colonization are read on the soundtrack. Sometimes, specific images are given relevant sounds – trains and factories, for instance. With the absence of verbal commentary, the film avoids any attempt to provide the colonized people with a retroactive, retrospective 'voice'. On the contrary, the absence of speech becomes an eloquent statement that bears witness to loss of control over meaning, or in Lacanian terms, a lost 'symbolic order' that characterizes colonial conditions. The absence of speech puts further weight on the images themselves, allowing them to 'speak' the past more vividly. However, in a short prologue Monnikendam introduces the myth of Mother Dao, creator of the earth, nature and mankind. With this residual trace of pre-colonial culture, the film creates a counterpoint, although on a small scale, to the film as a whole contributing to the sense of loss or mourning running through it. In its overall structure, the cultural space that the film offers the indigenous people is the silence of shock, trauma and loss.

The footage shows a process typical of colonization: destruction of nature, clearing of forests, penetration of missionaries. That is, the transformation of nature and the introduction of colonial culture are shown to be forces that detach, almost literally uproot, the indigenous people from their social and cultural traditions. This process represents an initial shock. But then the film simply assembles its raw material into sequences that show, alongside the evacuation of tradition, the shock of modernity. Colonization opens a space for the industrialization of agricultural production and the people are transformed into a labour force and subjected to the inexorable logic of capitalist exploitation. Typically, the colonial economy is concentrated on primary products that will be transformed into commodities abroad. Tobacco (an imported crop) plantations transform the land; small children wade along water-filled ditches to care for the plants. Workers are measured, weighed and their fingerprints recorded before they are collected into large processing camps.

Other sequences show workers tending the huge machines that prepare the tobacco crop for export. Each phase of the process is shown and filmed clearly with pride: the huge, modern machines dominate the workers while the colonial managers and administrators walk up and down a raised platform in their white suits. Furthermore, recurring shots of the railway, the steam ship, the motor car and the aeroplane demonstrate the power of the colonizing force over the primitive conditions of the indigenous people and

People are measured

Compilation film as 'deferred action'

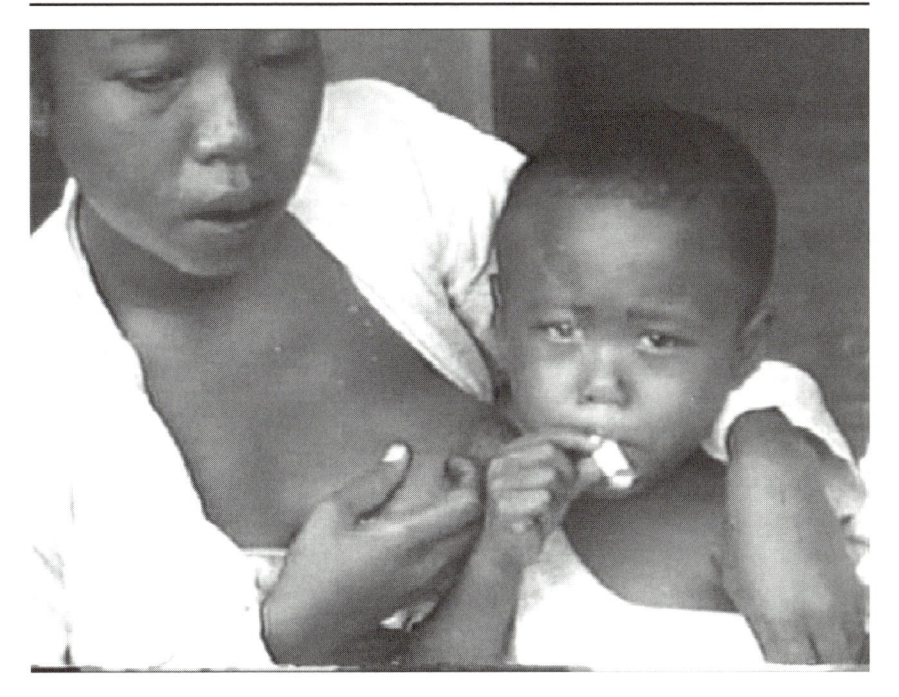

Smoking at the breast

confirm the integral part that these machines play in imposing a new order. The factory scenes are framed on the scale of the machine rather than the worker, and tracking shots celebrate the camera as yet another site of mechanical and social power. As tobacco transforms the economy, it also invades the culture. Everyone smokes. At one point the camera dwells on a child at the breast, alternating its mother's milk with a puff on a primitive cigarette.

This material was, of course, filmed with the complacency, celebration and self-congratulation of the masters. But the colonial ideology is displaced by the startlingly raw reality of the events taking place before the camera. The passing of time itself, combined with the filmmaker's own political understanding of the material, has transformed celebration into a disturbing reflection on colonial power. These traces, that preserve a historical moment in the past into the present, reveal the colonial process in a light that is at odds with its self-image. It is this encounter, between raw material that records and marks a moment of historical trauma, and its later reorganization and revision, that sets up a possible meeting point between psychoanalytic thought and historical thought through the medium of film. Clearly, psychoanalysis has, by and large, been concerned with the study of the individual psyche, while history, on the other hand, studies collective, generalized experience. But, equally clearly, both are absorbed in excavating and questioning the past.

While psychoanalysts actively decipher the legacy of past events on the subject's psyche, historians, whatever their interpretation of the legacy of events across time, transform the raw material of the past into narrative for the present and the future. It is possibly here that the temporality of film, and particularly the double temporality of compilation film, might form a bridge between the two, if only by analogy and within a limited framework. *Mother Dao* maps out this kind of terrain.

In the first instance, the photographic medium (its indexicality, in semiotic terms) is embedded in time. At the moment when a camera's shutter opens, light inscribes an image onto photosensitive material. That instant of exposure fixes the object's image (its shadow, as it were) on the celluloid. As the image is registered in an instant, that moment is henceforth suspended and preserved across time and into multiple futures. It is these qualities, a unique moment of time held still but persistent, the impact of reality left as a mark or trace, that suggest an analogy with Freud's visualization of trauma. An event that cannot be absorbed into consciousness leaves a mark or trace on the psyche in which the moment, a present, is fossilized and carried forward, as though indexically, into the future. In *Mother Dao*, consciousness of the material nature of the photographic image (the fossilization of a present moment, the inscription of the camera's reality) is accentuated by the spectator's consciousness of the compilation film's 'self-referentiality'. Awareness of the medium flows over onto the images on the screen as the living presence of this past. These aesthetic factors, in turn, flow over onto the traumatic nature of the events taking place on the screen, as it were, 'doubly' inscribing their reality. The first layer of 'photographic' temporality reinforces the next, recorded moments of the past preserved, the 'raw material' of history. This second layer introduces the content of the film: a record of the experience of colonization as a traumatic event that left its mark on both individuals and the collective, inwardly and outwardly. Although the theory of trauma was developed for the individual psyche, this kind of experience suggests the extension of the theory to collective experience. As unspeakable and inassimilable events take place within the external, social and historical world, they evade history and challenge psychoanalytic theory. *Mother Dao* demonstrates over and over again the porous nature of the boundary between the individual and the collective. As a photograph cannot generalize, each individual who appears in front of the camera silently conjures up a missing story. But each individual subject is locked into the collective story: the child workers seemingly 3 or 4 years old, the women struggling and suffocating among swirling cotton, the workers subordinated to the rhythm of their machines. All are incorporated into an exploitative and repressive economic and social system imposed by invasion and ruled from far away.

Freud suggests that trauma brings with it a sense of 'helplessness' in the face of conditions that cannot be controlled or internalized by the psyche.

Helplessness pervades the images in *Mother Dao*, both those of individuals and of the collective. One key aspect of film's significance as a historical document is precisely its ability to record the individual within the general. To pause the film image on one person is to see his or her specificity and then the incorporation of a living body and individuality into the gestures and way of life demanded by the colonial system. This pause for thought leads back into the material nature of the film image: the presence of a historical moment suspended in time and the embalmed presence of a nameless worker whose otherwise unmarked history has been recorded, if only for a fleeting instant. The pause also, of course, leads out of the specific image into a wider reflection on the history of colonialism and its legacy of damage.

Mother Dao presents a record of the process of colonization in which pain and trauma have been preserved on film and now appear on the screen. The shock of colonization, regimentation, exploitation and the multiple brutalities and humiliations associated with the colonial regime find a realization, of a kind, through the language of cinema itself. Here, a clear division opens up between the colonizers and the colonized. The camera's gaze represents the gaze of power. These films, made to celebrate the Dutch achievements in the colony, not only function as a triumphal record of the process (for both local and Colonial Office consumption) but also inscribe the reality of colonial power into the very moment of filming. The camera's gaze solicits participation from its equals. The white people acknowledge its presence: families stand facing the camera for a traditional portrait, white-suited functionaries and factory managers 'perform' their roles. Towards the end, three functionaries start to ham for the camera. As they move towards it, their gestures become increasingly ridiculous and excessive, and the camera, with characteristic relentlessness, captures and exposes their arrogance and vanity.

The indigenous people, on the other hand, are the objects of the camera's gaze and its very presence asserts the superiority of the colonial regime. The indigenous people can neither return its look nor acknowledge its presence. They work continuously, their hurried movements very often driven by the pace of a machine. The camera sometimes takes up a distant position to emphasize the large space and the impressive dimensions of the machines. The camera's celebration of the grandiose dimensions of the factory space not only gives a telling visual image of the workers' powerlessness but also seems to inscribe, through its own mastery of space, the power of ideology and the immaterial forces to which these people are subordinated. In the first instance, the camera's presence, its imposition of power in filming, represents, as a metonymy, the gaze of the regime, that is, a discourse of politics. On the other hand, as the camera subordinates each individual worker to its gaze, its significance shifts toward metaphor. The worker's averted look, visibly inscribed in the process of filming, evokes the camera's easy transformation of the relations of power into the hidden drives of voyeurism and sadism. As the camera

The returned look

asserts its 'will to power', it introduces the discourse of psychoanalysis. Throughout the film, the rare glances that the workers give the camera stand out, almost like moments of defiance.

All these aspects of the colonial power structure are premised, needless to say, on the process of revision that the raw material has undergone. The filmmaker has selected fragments from a vast archive to give visibility to a historical 'truth' (to risk using the word) that lies hidden in the records of Dutch colonialism. More than half a century lies between the films shot in the Dutch East Indies and their re-assemblage. During this time political and ideological changes have affected the meaning of the footage and its re-presentation in revised form suggests a further analogy with the psycho-analytic theory of trauma. With the concept of *Nachtraglichkeit*, Freud directly addressed the question of psychical temporality indicating that certain past events are subject to revision. As defined by Jean Laplanche and Jean-Baptiste Pontalis, 'deferred action' (as Strachey translated the term) implies that 'experiences, impressions and memory traces may be revised at a later date to fit in with fresh experiences or with the attainment of a new stage of development. They may in that event be endowed not only with a new meaning but also with psychical effectiveness' (Laplanche and Pontalis 1967: 111).

There are suggestive points of intersection between this definition of a psychic process and the double temporality of the compilation film.

Laplanche and Pontalis point out that the memory traces are a residue of trauma, the legacy of material that surpassed the subject's understanding at the time of the original event. The confusion of photographic time, the imprint of a present moment that persists into the future, may be compared to the confusion of the time of trauma. For Roland Barthes (1981), a photograph may suddenly arouse in the viewer an involuntary experience of time in which the past and present oscillate (one aspect of the *punctum*). In keeping with the structure of trauma, this confusing sensation of the persistence of the past into the present cannot be easily or logically assimilated into consciousness. With film, the confusion of time is further complicated by its duration, the very 'liveness' of these inhabitants of history. Although the reordering of found footage in *Mother Dao* offers a 'revision' of past events within the context of an altered consciousness, the new narrative does not completely dissolve the impact of the inassimilable presence of the past. The effect may be compared, perhaps, to an unresolved, incomplete, deferred action. Laplanche expanded his thoughts on *Nachtraglichkeit* with a new translation of the word as 'afterwardsness'. He argues that hidden in these kinds of memory traces is 'a message from the other':

> Even if we concentrate all our attention on the retroactive temporal direction, in the sense that someone reinterprets their past, this past cannot be a purely factual one, an unprocessed or raw given. It is impossible therefore to put forward a purely hermeneutic position on this – that is to say, that everyone interprets their past according to their present – because the past already has something deposited within it that demands to be deciphered, which is the message of the other person. But does not modern hermeneutics forget its very beginning, when it was – in the religious interpretation of sacred texts – a hermeneutic of the message?
>
> (Laplanche 1999: 265)

To adapt Laplanche, the revision of the original archive footage that represented the Dutch colonial vision and understanding of the indigenous people reveals 'something deposited within it that demands to be deciphered': the traces of the trauma of colonial experience. *Mother Dao* suggests that cinema has a unique ability to bear witness to the past, to visualize the 'message' and carry forward its 'demand'. But the reordering and rearticulation of the footage stops short of a coherent narrative, and reaches out, by analogy, to history and psychoanalysis, as though these two disciplines might address the task of decipherment and a response to the 'message'.

Lacan (1953) uses metaphors taken from the traces of history to evoke the way in which the individual psyche is marked by the past. The metaphors suggest, again by analogy, a reverse process in which the individual psychic experience might become a metaphor for the collective. Throughout the series of metaphors runs the theme of translation: how the marks of the past may be transformed by means of speech into an acceptable exegesis. In the context of my argument, Lacan's statement triggers a parallel between the unconscious and the erasure of history under, for instance, a colonial regime and its hope for recovery: 'The unconscious is that chapter of my history that is marked by a blank or occupied by a falsehood: it is the censored chapter. But the truth can be rediscovered; usually it has already been written down elsewhere' (Lacan 1953: 51). Lacan goes on to use metaphors of storage which have kept the past alive: monuments as hysterical symptoms, archival documents as childhood memories, a semantic evolution corresponding to a particular vocabulary, and legends bearing 'my history'. Finally, he sums up: 'and lastly, in the traces that are inevitably preserved by the distortions necessitated by the linking of the adulterated chapter to the chapters surrounding it, and whose meaning will be re-established by my exegesis'.

The cinema gathers into itself: monumentality, the archive, semantics and legends, shifting between, on the one hand, a similar rootedness in the past as trace, and, on the other, a unique ability to preserve a reality, not the trace, of the past into the future. Once again, the adulterated chapter will only find meaning ultimately in its 'exegesis'.

Acknowledgements

For Rachel Moore, with gratitude for first introducing me to *Mother Dao, the Turtle-like*. And with many thanks to Mark Hobart and Ni Madé Pujawati for discussing the film with me in the light of their intimate knowledge of Indonesia.

References

Barthes, R. (1981) *Camera Lucida: Reflections on Photography*. New York: Hills & Wang.
Lacan, J. (1953) The function and field of speech and language in psychoanalysis, in *Ecrits*. London: Tavistock Publications, 1977.
Laplanche, J. (1999). Notes on afterwardsness, in *Essays on Otherness*. London: Routledge.
Laplanche, J. and Pontalis J. B. (1967) *The Language of Psychoanalysis*. London: Hogarth Press, 1973.
Leyda, J. (1964) *Film Begets Film*. London: George Allen & Unwin.
Sjöberg, P. (2001) *The World in Pieces: A Study of the Compilation Film*. Stockholm: Aura forlag.

11

MOVING BEYOND THE CONSTRAINTS OF THE MORTAL SELF
Universal images of narcissism in Jan Troell's *The Flight of the Eagle*

Lissa Weinstein

Ingenjör Andreées luftärd (*The Flight of the Eagle*) (Sweden, 1982)
Director: Jan Troell
Distributor: Summit

Introduction

Long before the film's title materializes, stark white letters, **A TRUE STORY** appear, followed by an image of an austere, endless horizon, a *ganzfeld* where land is scarcely delineated from sea or sky. Black and white photos follow, articulated only as the camera zooms in. With mounting terror, the viewer recognizes a blackened skeleton, its mouth open in horror, wide pits for eyes. These macabre photos, the remains of the ill-fated 1897 Polar expedition of August Salomon Andrée, are the ending of the 'true' story that forms the basis for Jan Troell's mystically beautiful film *The Flight of the Eagle* (1982).

The film documents a failed attempt by three men to fly over the North Pole in a hydrogen gas balloon in order to plant the Swedish flag. Andrée, the expedition's leader, was a driven and obsessive civil servant who, despite the passion for fame which eventuated in this mad quest, had spent most of his career sequestered in a patent office in Stockholm. Although known as an aeronaut, he had never taken a balloon flight of more than three hours. Nils Strindberg, an impressionable young physicist and musician, was chosen both for his scientific skills and photographic abilities. He planned to record their historic findings. Knut Fraenkel, an engineer, adventurer and avid gymnast, impulsively joined the expedition after one of the original members left because of doubts about its scientific feasibility and safety. The men hoped simultaneously to celebrate Sweden's glory and to secure their place in history. After floating aimlessly for nearly three days, the balloon, burdened with ice, fell to the frozen sea below. The explorers then set off on foot, walking in one direction while the ice drifted in another. Their bodies were found 33 years later, along with their diaries and Strindberg's photographic record of their trek. The film intersperses the recovered photographs with an imaginative reconstruction of the men's phenomenological experience, focusing on the affective underpinnings that drove their desire for recognition. As the diaries were quite sparse, the film is 'true' only in the sense that a feeling of reality in a dream points to an especially close connection to the latent thoughts (Freud 1900). Although the film presents a discursive, sequential story, associated elements of the latent narrative are connected through repetitive images, musical themes and alterations in the colour palette.

Multiple interpretations of this complex film are possible: it can be read as a parable of man's relationship to nature, or seen in the historical context of polar exploration. However, unlike *Shackleton's Legendary Antarctic Adventure* (Butler, 2000), a recent and in many ways comparable example of the polar exploration film genre, the struggle in *The Flight of the Eagle* is not, as it may appear on the surface, man against nature. Rather, the expedition's catastrophic failures evolve within the context of Andrée's internal conflicts. The film captures both the descent of the balloon and the psychological descent of the protagonist from the perverse excitement of grandiose wishes to an awareness of the body's frailty and the depth of loneliness when ties to human objects are severed.

At the same time that the film brilliantly depicts narcissistic fantasies and the conflicts they stimulate, the inclusion of the photographs induces a parallel set of conflicts in the viewer. Both the content of the film and its structure force the audience to attend to the problems inherent in a driven quest for renown as a maladaptive solution to the dilemma of ageing. While these two aspects of the film are inextricably intertwined, for heuristic purposes they will be discussed separately. The film's depiction of narcissistic conflict will be explicated, focusing particularly on the character of Andrée, and then followed by a discussion of structure, audience effect and cultural considerations.

Narcissistic fantasies: moving beyond the constraints of the mortal self

The film opens with Andrée as a child, capturing a bird in his net. Ecstatic, he tries to hold the trapped bird. The bird escapes into the air, while Andrée remains tethered to the earth, throwing his net pointlessly skyward. The image condenses his unattainable wish to fly, the pain of separation and the death of the self fantasy, a parallel to the Myth of The Fall (Thompson 1955) where the child's all powerful oneness with nature is suddenly challenged. The image reoccurs at several points in the film, representing the breakdown of Andrée's omnipotence and momentarily allowing fears of failure into consciousness before he shunts them aside. The ropes surrounding the balloon will later reprise the image of the netting in which the bird was trapped; the ice that forms on the ropes will eventually bring the balloon down to earth.

The formal narrative begins with Andrée's humiliation a year prior to the actual expedition. Originally scheduled for 1896, the flight was postponed due to inauspicious weather. Asked if he is disappointed, Andrée replies that 'he must learn to live with his failures until he can overcome them'. Small and powerless against the capricious winds, the camera views him at a distance, a minuscule figure watching as the enormous balloon sadly deflates in its housing. We next see Andrée, a man inspired only by his dream, staring out the window of his patent office in Stockholm. Figures in the street below appear to move robotically; looking at them through his eyes, the viewer senses his emotional disconnection from everyday life. The sounds of a clock ticking accompany his musings, reminding him of time's relentless passage.

Andrée's wish to remain permanently filled by the admiration of others provokes a loss of reality sense. Narcissistic fantasies engender conflict with the categories of reality that form the backdrop of the superego, rather than the moral constraints of the superego itself (Bach 1977a). Their presence is marked by the existence of concurrent knowledge and simultaneous denial. The omnipotence of thought defends against recognition of weakness; words are used not to communicate but to soothe, placate and elevate self-esteem. Andrée ignores scientific fact, as well as his own limited aeronautic experience, as he gathers support for his expedition. When his former protégé challenges him in a public forum, noting that the balloon leaks too much gas and they can no longer be sure of the fivefold safety margin on which they had counted, Andrée replies, 'Fivefold, why not sixfold? Or sevenfold? ... What are safety margins compared to Sweden's glory?' His reply is met by thunderous applause, as rational calculations prove no match for Andrée's charismatic ability to seduce others into identifying with his desire for success.

The unconscious phallic content of Andrée's wishes is highlighted when he demonstrates the device which will shoot up a Swedish flag in instantaneous erection upon implanting in the soil of the North Pole. In a more metaphorical expression of the desire for potency, physical actions are used to demonstrate the body's ability to surpass gravity as the men train for their expedition in a gym. The repetitive back and forth rhythm of the men's movements indicates the masturbatory nature of their fantasy of transcendence, as the sound of clocks ticking again makes clear their altered, regressed relation to time – time measured in relation to affective necessities rather than impersonal reality.

Andrée's need to maintain an illusion of self-sufficiency and deny dependency (Modell 1975) precludes an ongoing relationship with a woman other than his mother, with whom he remains emotionally involved. The necessity of the appreciative gaze of strangers supersedes his desire for intimacy, and he cannot reciprocate his mistress's passion. After the initial failed attempt, he rebuffs her excitement at his return, telling her he must try again and stating: 'I am the expedition'. Love, to Andrée, is 'congruency – two figures that completely cover each other', more a description of a wished-for mirror than a love relationship. True genitality eludes him as he believes that sexuality and attachment will leave him weak; his mistress's desire is a weight, to be thrown off like the ballast that hampers the ascent of the balloon.

Prior to the expedition setting off, the men go to Paris to be outfitted and to check on the balloon's construction. These events were not described in the diaries; their inclusion in the film forms part of the latent narrative that depicts the men's idealized version of themselves as perceptual reality. The extended sequence offers a tapestry whose bright threads function to hide to any rents in the fabric of denial. The overly intense hue in which the sequence is painted underlines its fantastical quality. These hues will later be repeated when the men, lost in the grey white of frozen ice, try to recapture in fantasy images of the women they have left behind. While in Paris, their practice flights show them floating gracefully above the city, able to masterfully control the balloon merely by dropping a few grains of sand from between their fingers. All three men are elegantly attired, young, clean-shaven and virile. Typical of narcissistic fantasy, desire rules sense. The subjective experience, for both viewer and protagonists, is of being carried along by the action, rather than being its author (Kohut 1971; Bach 1977a). As the men watch a performance of the cancan, Fraenkel grabs one of the dancers using the ceremonial scarf made for his presentation to the czar after the successful conclusion of the expedition. His companion urges him to go to her and 'make the supreme sacrifice'. As the dancer leans over him, her face appears macabre and cadaverous, suggesting a tie between his giddy excitement and their ultimate downfall.

While in Paris, the men are sculpted in wax for museum viewing, literally creating doubles of themselves. The resulting simulacra are eerie recreations without the affects and blemishes that make one human, 'doubles' (Von Kleist 1810; Lacan 1949; Nelson 2002) that serve as a concrete manifestation of the infatuation with one's own image, as well as a defence against narcissistic vulnerabilities, especially those of imperfection, ageing and death (Rank 1925). Andrée presents his mother with his life-size wax head, complete with the facial hair appropriate for a Polar explorer. When she disapproves of the beard, Andrée dutifully picks out the whiskers, hoping that his idealized twin will more closely approximate the image she desires. As he works, she says: 'If I'm no longer here when you return, you mustn't get the idea that your grand expedition had something to do with me going the way, with me going the way of all worldly things . . . Everyone has to face it. It's the only thing that's certain in this life.' His mother's disapproval and subtle contempt for his ambition, alongside her threatened abandonment should he attempt to separate from her, suggest another force driving Andrée onward – the need to seek his mother's admiring gaze.

Inevitably, denial breaks down, as the reality it seeks to avoid impinges, leading to a subsequent failure in the synthetic function of the ego (Freud 1940). Andrée is plagued by three repetitive images that he attempts to immediately brush aside, much as we, the film viewers, try to forget the photographic images that cut into our complacency and remind us of the terror of the men's ultimate death. These intrusive images include the earlier sequence of Andrée as a boy trying to recapture the bird in flight, a vision of a barren land and the sound of a clock ticking. The images underline his need to 'avoid withering away amidst all the papers on my desk' as they point to the failures of development that have driven him forward – the sudden deflation of grandiosity, the inability to bask in a perpetually admiring gaze and his ultimate inconsequentiality before the passage of time. They appear as he stares at a precariously balanced house of cards in his study, at a ceremonial dinner in Paris, on the way to visit his mother prior to departure, and when he orders the dismantling of the balloon house. Together, they insinuate that Andrée is at least partially aware of the folly of his venture, but proceeds nonetheless.

For a second year, the men return amidst great fanfare to the balloon house on Dane Island to wait for a favourable wind, while the balloon inflates. The balloon, a highly condensed, multiply determined symbol, is nearly a film character in its own right (Kael 1983). Its size ('14 kilometers of material, 7 million stitches') is noted repeatedly. In addition to its phallic significance, its black colour and the haunting music that accompanies it subliminally suggest death. Aloft, the balloon represents another universal narcissistic fantasy – the 'rope to another world' (Eliade 1965, cited in Bach 1977b) that would allow privileged beings to climb to heaven. Womb as well as coffin, the balloon is also maternal; the men call it 'Mother Balloon', an alternative to Mother Earth, who will one day claim us all. Prior to their departure, Andrée literally enters the balloon and stands momentarily inside it. Returning to an intrauterine-like environment, he makes manifest the connection between the words gravity, gravid and grave, noted by Wolff (1982) in his paper on the unconscious meanings of flying. By conquering gravity, Andrée hopes to soar above the constraints of the mortal self.

Despite questionable weather and the knowledge that the balloon will leak more gas than is safe, the men convince each other to begin their ascent. Unable to disappoint the admiring gazes of their onlookers, their faces betray the fear underneath a showy bravado. The expedition nearly crashes into the sea at its start, yet the men make a disastrous decision not to abort while still in sight of land. Once aloft, having thrown out most of their ballast and lost the guide ropes that would have allowed them to steer, the men momentarily rejoice in their new-found position above the earth, as they imagine that, Godlike, they are forcing the earth to rotate beneath them. Andre writes in his diary:

> It is not a little strange to be floating here above the Polar Sea. To be the first that have floated here in a balloon. How soon, I wonder, shall we have successors . . . I cannot deny that all three of us are dominated by a feeling of pride. We think we can well face death, having done what we have done. Isn't it all, perhaps the expression of an extremely strong sense of individuality which cannot bear the thought of living and dying like a man in the ranks, forgotten by coming generations?
>
> (Ray 1930: 308)

Their pleasure is short-lived as the balloon is soon becalmed and burdened with ice. Forced to land on an ice floe, Andrée remarks on the balloon's similarity to a cadaver as he watches it deflate. As the men take photos of their landing, Nils Strindberg's camera, a second powerful inanimate presence in the film, offers the viewer the peculiar perspective of watching pictures being taken of people who are already dead. Despite what should be the obvious danger of their situation, the men cheerfully plot their course and tie on their sledges to begin their trek. Andrée, fulfilling his idealized role as explorer and scientist, obsessively documents his findings.

In the undifferentiated, unforgiving landscape, the developing homoerotic intimacy between the three men offers the only haven. Close-ups bring the viewer into their tent; we come to share both their denial and the dire nature of the plight. They are forced to share clothing and sleep in a single sleeping bag, finding themselves curled into one another in the night. Trading details of their histories while they darn socks, they groom each other and tolerate an unbidden awareness of each other's anal bodily functions after infected bear meat they eat makes it impossible for them to control their bowels. In an extravagant, absurd scene, Knut and Nils dance together on the ice after discovering that their arduous trek has been fruitless, as the ice is drifting more rapidly than they can walk in the opposite direction. The dance exemplifies their retrenchment into perverse, yet sustaining, homoerotic ties. On the

The *Eagle* has landed

soundtrack, the music that accompanies their dance is the one used for the cancan prior to their departure. Once the sounds celebrated their triumph, now the music attends their demise on the ice, offering a prudent note to those heeding the seduction of immortality.

As in the relative isolation of the emotionally permissive analytic setting when transference love recruits similar affective experiences, Andrée begins to review and revisit images of his mistress and hallucinates her voice in the frozen emptiness. In the context of his newly-found shared intimacies, Andrée reconstructs his memories, authoring a scene where he is belatedly able to admit his love. The camera views them from above, standing like figures on a giant frozen wedding cake, combining an image of the snow that will kill them with an icon of earthly desire.

Eventually the floe reaches an uninhabited glacier. In a true example of the uncanny (Freud 1919) where what is *unheimlich* (unfamiliar) was once *heimlich* (familiar or known), the barren land that Andrée relentlessly pursued is identical to the inhospitable *ganzfeld* that existed all along in his imagination. While Knut likens the glacier to Neifheimland, 'the barren hell of the Norse gods', Andrée asks if it would be all right to name the glacier Minna Andrée's Place, after his mother. His journey of discovery, driven by the repetition compulsion, has paradoxically led him back to the trauma of his mother's disapproval. Naming the glacier after her implies that it was her desolate gaze that brought about the inner emptiness and resulting grandiose self-inflation, body narcissism and cravings for admiration through which he attempted to repair damage done to his self-representation (Reich 1960), as well as his inability to transmute these needs into ego abilities.

The men prepare their camp for the winter, continuing to age before our eyes. Nearly indistinguishable, they have truly become self-objects for each other. Their previously hairless visages are covered in stubble; their unwashed faces are increasingly lined. When a mirror is discovered among their possessions, they are initially eager to see themselves and then horrified by their appearance. Knut sadly remarks that you can't see much of yourself without a mirror, but then attempts to observe himself without reflection and concludes: 'You see chest, stomach, legs, arms, hands, shoulder, back – a little. Quite a bit when you think about it.' Knut's statement about knowing the self in the absence of a reflected gaze will come to have profound meaning for Andrée when he is finally left alone. The struggle to attain an objective view of the self while continuing to affirm one's subjective experience is the ultimate resolution of the narcissistic dilemma, as it is only through this confluence of perspectives that the knowledge of separation, castration and death becomes tolerable (Bach 1977b).

Andrée remains consciously unaware of the nearness of death, despite numerous portents in his fantasies. Nils, physically the weakest of the three, dies first, as he remembers swimming in a warm summer lake with his fiancée. His memory reproduces the scene in luminous greens, gold and reds reminiscent of a Renoir. In sharp contrast to his burning memory, his body lies

Lost in an ice desert

frozen in the ice, while his camera, standing behind him, records his death. Shocked by his young friend's wasteful end, Knut confronts Andrée in the film's climactic scene:

> *Knut:* Why did you write that in your diary? . . . I cannot deny that the three of us are overwhelmed by a feeling of great pride. You have been struck by a feeling that overwhelms us, all three. You knew the whole time that we would fail. We feel we are ready to accept death now that we have done what we have done. You knew it. You knew it the whole time.
>
> *Andrée:* Forgive me, I had no choice.

Unable to tame the strong horse of his ambition, Andrée realizes he has been subject to a will he experienced as outside himself. Yet Frankl offers Andrée a profound acceptance of his failing. He joins him, stroking his hair and saying: 'We had no choice,' mirroring Andrée's affect, accepting and containing his self-destruction. He provides, inadvertently, the developmental experience that Andrée has lacked from his cold mother.

Soon after, Knut is fatally attacked by a bear. Too late to save him, Andrée begs, with almost unbearable passion, 'You mustn't die because you have to stay with me.' As Andrée prepares to bury Knut in the ceremonial scarf chosen for their triumphant return, he sheds a tear – the ice inside him truly unfrozen. At last, Andrée is able to accept the dependence that is often the greatest fear of the narcissist (Kernberg 1970).

Unfortunately, it is too late. In the film's final scene, Andrée attempts to view his own body. Without the contact of another voice to sustain him, alone in the frozen hell, he attempts desperately to mimic Knut's bodily postures as he tried to look at himself without the aid of a mirror. Unable to bear the unending solitude, and shut out of the symbolic order that language represents, Andrée seeks to maintain a tie to his object in the only way available to him, a mute imitative form. The accompanying violin music underscores Andrée's desire for his lost object, as it reprises the tune Nils played on the eve of their departure, as he thought of the fiancée whom he had left behind.

Like Icarus, who also lost his way trying to fly too high, Andrée has fallen to earth, placed finally between sky and land. The narcissistic solution he sought had left him unable to locate himself, as it is only in reference to others that the self finds its definition. By pursuing goals which attempted to supersede mortality, and by disconnecting from the intimate objects that bind the energy of the death instinct, Andrée evoked his own destruction.

The film suggests that the successful resolution of the inevitable narcissistic conflicts of midlife requires the integration of two bifurcated self-representations, simultaneously grounding the self in pleasurable and timeless relations to internal objects and reconnecting with a rich and powerful, sexually variegated, fantasy life, while also allowing an objective consciousness of the transient nature of individual existence. A failure to transmute the gaze internally leads to an insatiable hunger for external recognition. Whether recognition takes the historical forms of the audience of God or the audience of history (Braudy 1997) or, as in today's culture, the more palpable and immediate 'audience for performance' where renown itself is the goal, an achievement that is separated from internally generated motivations, and which substitutes for one's ties to objects, is inevitably empty.

Historical film, created film, audience response

If Jan Troell had achieved nothing more than a rich and complex portrait of a flawed man riddled with narcissistic conflicts, *The Flight of the Eagle* would still be a remarkable film. However, by including the historical photographs and by providing the tragic conclusion at the outset of the film, Troell created a multitextured narrative that induces a dichotomy in the viewer's state of consciousness, forcing a contrapuntal interpretation of the film (Pick and Mulvey 2005). The black and white images offer historical certainty, a *memento mori* (Kael 1983) which serves as an encapsulated reminder of the irrevocable character of death. In contrast, the intense colour of the created film, like a screen memory, functions to obscure the truth of the protagonists' powerlessness before the forces of time and nature. As the film progresses toward the men's death, the bright palette gradually fades, morphing into the browns, greys and white of the photographs, as the wished-for truth becomes the historical actuality.

Drawn into a web of denial while sharing the men's experience and hopes for the future, the insertion of the photographs cuts into the viewer's complacency, forcing one to confront the 'fundamental lack' (Comolli, cited in Silverman 1988) that is central to cinematic representation. Even when history is as carefully recreated as in *The Flight of the Eagle*, actual reality and film reality are in fundamental opposition. Troell's near perfect reproductions of the photographic images in the created film only serve to heighten any awareness of artifice. The photographs repeatedly sever the cord between image and actuality, making one aware that what is being seen, what is believed, is not real. The photographs, as well as the presence of Strindberg's anthropomorphized camera, remind the viewers that the camera, not their perceptual apparatus, is creating the film. Further, the presentation of the men's remains at the beginning makes the viewer aware of their powerlessness to intervene in a series of events that they know will end in death. This awareness is jarring, leaving the spectator in a state that is not fully 'whole'.

Thus, the viewer is forced into a parallel experience to that of Andrée, who is plagued by repetitive images suggesting his potential failure. The interspersed photographs make it possible to see the men's death foretold as, for example, when the eerie percussive sound that accompanies the film's titles is interspersed with music at a party prior to the men's departure, or when in the midst of a sexually titillating scene, the face of a cancan dancer appears macabre and cadaverous. At the same time, the film is so intimate, particularly in the scenes on the ice, that one critic commented: 'the austere restraint with which the most heart-rending scenes are presented, with camera placements and movements that, without calling attention to themselves [is] nevertheless so apt as to make even a crusty old skeptic like me forget he is watching a movie' (Simon 1983). The viewer exists simultaneously as an observer of a historical event, and as a participant in the expedition, left to continually consider the relationship between two sets of data – film as history and film as creation. Like Andrée, the viewer becomes momentarily aware of struggling to believe something that is false, and like Andrée the viewer is powerless to stop the progression of events.

Such powerlessness is present, to some degree, in the viewing of every film. Authorship always exists elsewhere. However, the photographs at the beginning heighten the viewer's consciousness of their impotence, made all the more painful by the stunning artistry of the film. By including universal symbols of narcissism (Bach 1977b) such as the wish to transcend gravity, the fantasy of the 'double' and the death of the self-fantasy, Troell erases any distance between the viewer and the Victorian explorers. Thus, one wants to tell them to abandon the mission at its catastrophic beginning, or later to yell: 'No, you will die!' when they decide not to take the shortest route so that they can make a scientific contribution. This profound loss of potency leaves the viewer uneasy, engendering a narcissistic injury which serves to deepen the identification with Andrée's struggle.

Finally, by depicting the historical end point, Troell grounds the viewer, cautioning him about the dangers of the quest for immortality while simultaneously making the seductive elements of such fantasies comprehensible. It is the inclusion of the dual perspective that transforms *The Flight of the Eagle* from a genre film into a far more profound work of art, a moral film that provides a cautionary statement about the danger of abandoning one's objects in search of immortality. It underlines the inescapable limitations of the physical body, the reality of man's powerlessness before the forces of time, and the necessity of embracing the limiting conditions that form the core of an adjustment to reality.

When the remains of the expedition were found, Andrée achieved his dream of immortality. The men's bodies were returned to Sweden amidst great fanfare. The right to reproduce the diaries under the name *Andrée's Story* was the bidding war of the 1930's publishing industry. A fictionalized account of the expedition was written in 1967 by Per Olof Sundman, and the current film was nominated for an Oscar in 1982. Yet despite universal critical acclaim, the film never found a wide audience in America.

If popular films offer a privileged window into the dominant unconscious fantasies and tensions of their culture (Ray 1985), then the commercial failure of an excellent film also informs us about the interaction of culture and underlying fantasy. Perhaps in a country that reveres the narcissistic quest – a country founded on the fallacy of endless opportunity and limitless self-recreation – the sobering message of *The Flight of the Eagle*, tragic in the truest sense of the word, had little chance of commercial success.

References

Bach, S. (1977a) On the narcissistic state of consciousness, *International Journal of Psychoanalysis*, 58: 209–30.

Bach, S. (1977b) On narcissistic fantasies, *International Review of Psychoanalysis*, 4: 281–93.

Braudy, L. (1997) *The Frenzy of Renown: Fame and Its History*. New York: Random House.

Freud, S. (1900) The interpretation of dreams, *Standard Edition*, Vol. V. London: Hogarth Press.

Freud, S. (1919) The uncanny, *Standard Edition*, Vol. V. London: Hogarth Press.

Freud, S. (1940) On the splitting of the ego in defence, *Standard Edition*, Vol. XXIII. London: Hogarth Press.

Kael, P. (1983) Gents and hicks, *The New Yorker*, 16 May.

Kernberg, O. (1970) Factors in the psychoanalytic treatment of narcissistic personalities, *Journal of the American Psychoanalytic Association*, 18: 51–85.

Kohut, H. (1971) *The Analysis of the Self: A Systematic Approach to the Psychoanalytic Treatment of Narcissistic Personality Disorders*. New York: International Universities Press.

Lacan, J. (1949) The mirror stage as formative of the function of the I as revealed in psychoanalytic experience, *Ecrits: A Selection* New York: W.W. Norton.

Modell, A. (1975) A narcissistic defense against affects and the illusion of self sufficiency, *International Journal of Psychoanalysis*, 56: 275–82.

Nelson, V. (2002) *The Secret Life of Puppets: Tracing the Curious Reversing Roles of Art and Religion by Surveying the History of Simulacra as Players and Holy Objects in Western Culture*. Cambridge, MA: Harvard University Press.

Pick, D. and Mulvey, L. (2005) *Mother Dao*. Paper presented at the 3rd European Psychoanalytic Film Festival, November.

Rank, O. (1925) *The Double: A Psychoanalytic Study*. Chapel Hill, NC: University of North Carolina Press, 1971.

Ray, E. (1930) *Andrée's Story: The Complete Record of His Polar Flight, 1897*. New York: Viking Press.

Ray, R. B. (1985) *A Certain Tendency of the Hollywood Cinema, 1930–1980*. Princeton, NJ: Princeton University Press.

Reich, A. (1960) Pathological forms of self-esteem regulation, *Psychoanalytic Study of the Child*, 15: 215–32.

Simon, J. (1983) Men in white, *National Review*, 702–5.
Silverman, K. (1988) *The Acoustic Mirror*. Bloomington, IN: Indiana University Press.
Sundman, P.O. (1967/1970) *The Flight of the Eagle*. New York: Random House.
Thompson, S. (1955) *Motif-Index of Folk Literature*. Bloomington, IN: Indiana University Press.
Von Kleist, H. (1810) Uber das Marionetten Theater (On the marionette theatre), *Berliner Abendblatter*, 12–15 December.
Wolff, E. (1982) Flying – some psychoanalytic observations and considerations, *Psychoanalytic Study of the Child*, 37: 461–83.

12

TRICYCLES, BICYCLES, LIFE CYCLES
Psychoanalytic perspectives on childhood loss and transgenerational parenting in Sylvain Chômet's *Belleville Rendez-Vous*[1]

Alexander Stein

Les triplettes de Belleville (*Belleville Rendez-Vous* or *The Triplets of Belleville*)
(France, Canada, 2003)
Director: Sylvain Chômet
Distributor: Celluloid Dreams

Belleville Rendez-Vous (known in the United States as *The Triplets of Belleville*) by Sylvain Chômet (2003) is a work of whimsical originality, and a tour de force of feature-length animated filmmaking. Chômet's cinematic palette interweaves audio-visual and narrative inventiveness with technical bravura. Together, these elements are informed by a wide range of sociohistorical, cultural and aesthetic influences, as various as Betty Boop, Jacques Tati and European comic books, the classic Hanna-Barbera cartoons of Tex Avery and Chuck Jones, the early animation pioneer Winsor McCay, Disney, Czech animator Karel Zeman, Terry Gilliam, Nick Park, as well as musical referents including Mozart, J.S. Bach, Django Reinhardt, the Andrews Sisters, Fred Astaire and Josephine Baker.

Many interpretive avenues are suggested by the phantasmagorical kaleidoscope of sights, sounds, characters and implausible events. This ambiguity is amplified by a lack of dialogue, and the medium of animation itself, which by its nature lends itself to depictions of sur- and hyper-reality. Film in general, but animation in particular, is uniquely felicitous in visually representing distortions of time, the attendant effects of the ageing process and behavior or actions otherwise physically impossible. *Belleville Rendez-Vous* exaggerates and parodies conventions of masculinity and femininity: in this world, men are presented mostly as simpering, ineffectual fops, who are also either submissive and impotent, or aggressive and domineering louts. Women, conversely, are mostly idealized, larger-than-life, seemingly all-powerful and indomitable. This could be superficially understood on the level of social commentary, addressing caricatures of culture, class, ageism, gender and Franco-American nationalism. As becomes discernible, however, these are distorted and attenuated renderings, core characteristics which have been hyperbolized, as in many dreams, in the service of a wish or some other intrapsychic motive.

It is from the perspective of a dream, where entwining themes unfold and events occur in ways possible only in the unconscious, that the film can be most profitably approached. I will utilize the idea of film-as-dream to shed light on what I view as the primary theme here: the impact of loss and affiliated concerns of mourning and melancholia on developmental processes at varying stages in the life cycle. These are elaborated here in the context of a work of animated cinema and its fictional characterizations, rather than clinical case material.

When considered as multiply condensed, distorted and intersecting overlays of the wishes, fantasies, strivings and conflicts of the main protagonists, a larger mosaic emerges in which component themes of loss, longing, growth, development, decay and reparation emerge. No single voice is dominant – there is a near absence of spoken language and only a few snippets of barely intelligible dialogue. As in fathoming the latent content of any dream, we are not confined to representations of any single personage, gender, time, place or even species. The surreal narrative of the film qua dream work is conveyed by fantastical imagery, symbolic allusion and non-verbal signifiers.

First, a brief synopsis – the manifest material. An orphaned boy named Champion is raised by his grandmother, Madame Souza. Her gift of a tricycle catalyses a passion for cycle-racing that becomes the centerpiece of their life together. Fast-forwarding to early adulthood, and after years of relentless training – throughout which the elderly, astigmatic and club-footed Grandma improbably serves as her grandson's trainer – Champion comes into his name and becomes a world-class bike racer. When he and a pair of other top competitors are abducted by a pair of sinister thugs during the Tour de France, Mme Souza sets off to rescue her beloved grandson with the help of Bruno, their fat old dog. They pursue Champion across the ocean in a rented pedal-boat, and arrive in the corpulently capitalist megalopolis of Belleville. Lost, confused and penniless in the gargantuan city, Grandma and dog are taken in by a trio of decrepit women – the eponymous triplets – a glamorous close-harmony singing act in their youth who now live in poverty and obscurity. They subsist monotonously on a diet of frogs harvested through acts of wildly overzealous violence, and make infectious music with household appliances. Bruno's keen nose eventually leads them to the hapless Champion, held captive by the Mafia Godfather in a cycle-racing betting parlour. In a balletic Sergio Leone-like final sequence, Mme Souza, Bruno, and the triplets unleash an outlandish scheme to liberate Champion using musical prowess, feminine wile and brute force. Propelled by Champion's thoroughbred quadriceps, they ride off together, disappearing over the horizon and into the silver screen.[2]

Of the cast of main characters – Mme Souza, Champion, Bruno the dog, the triplets and various Mafiosi – all, in my view, are reducible to two: grandmother and boy. Each symbolically condenses antipodal facets of the ageing process. Depending, then, on whom we take as the dreamer, the material presented by each is uniquely interpretable, as will be the potential meaning of any of the other figures and ancillary components.

This allows a stereoscopically complementary interpretation, one view focusing on issues concerning the grandmother and the other on the boy. Within this scheme, I will interweave the issues and interpretations relevant to each, rather than present them separately. I have in mind in adopting this approach Freud's proposal that a dreamer in his relation to his dream-wishes can only be compared to an amalgamation of two separate people who are linked by some important common element (1900: 581, n. 1).

The common element that links the boy and his grandmother here is profound loss; everything extends from the central premise that each suffers developmental deformations occasioned by the absence (which we can reasonably assume as death) of the boy's parents. Whether Mme Souza is the maternal or paternal grandmother is of minor consequence, bearing only on her having lost a son or a daughter (as well as son-in-law or daughter-in-law). Of greater import, given that she is also alone (again, assuming she is a widow), is the dynamic familial disequilibrium created in this vacuum, wherein a young family of husband, wife and child, together with a husband and wife from the prior generation – the grandparents – is tragically reconfigured to just grandmother and grandson. Their respective social roles, psychical positions and developmental trajectories are thrown asunder. For each of them, the common trauma of primary object loss constitutes a serious developmental interference (Nagera 1970), the repercussions of which manifest in responsive asynchronous patterns of mourning, or failure to mourn, and distortions to growth and the achievement of developmental tasks, each in accordance with their phase-particular needs (Bowlby 1963).

In what follows, I elaborate these ideas guided by two central premises. The first is that both Grandma Souza and young Champion are contending with the cardinal features of pathological mourning – the repression of yearning

Champion with Bruno the dog

for the lost objects and the unconscious urge to recover them, displacement of reproaches against them, projective identification and the defensive function of care of a vicarious figure as a composite of aggressive and reparative wishes toward the lost objects. The second, directly following from this, is that each of them is attempting to reorganize reality and reverse or repair their respective developmental interferences through fantasy formations and pathogenic sublimatory enactments.

Considered in this light, Mme Souza can be seen in one regard as a paradigmatic older woman, contending with a welter of issues specific to late adulthood, notably: confrontation with the ageing process and concomitant alterations to psychic organization; self-image; self-identity; sexuality; agency; power; social and family position; as well as recalibrated experience of time sense, with related appraisals of past, present and future. But also implicated, particular to her heartbreaking circumstances, are developmental crises of transgenerational attachment involving herself, as a grandmother, as double parental surrogate, primary generative force and presence, and object for identification and internalization by a grandchild psychologically disfigured by the devastating early loss of his parents; together with the diminution or deprivation of typical end of life and grandparenthood functions.

In the background are many important additional symbols: vehicles (bikes, trains, boats and cars); locations (the house that Grandma, Champion and Bruno share, and its blighted, exurban environs; the triplets' dismal flat; the Mafia lair; and Belleville itself); and landscapes or terrains (the ocean, mountains and cities). Each of these conjures some affect-laden sensation (Mme

Souza's house is as bleak and isolated as a crypt, the ocean is menacing and vast, the mountains simmering, arid and steep, the Mafia fortress is sinister and fetid as an old spittoon, the city-scapes inhospitably vertiginous, the triplets' flat as dilapidated as their old bodies). Innumerable, incessant noises pervade; music is ever present. There are dreams aplenty, with Bruno the dog clearly the dreamer, which feature the recurrent central image of a train.

Perhaps most important are the various representations of time – in motion, travel, the compressed depiction of time's passage, music and sounds, the use of moving pictures (film and television) and in the animated characterizations themselves. Regarding telling a story without spoken dialogue, Chômet indicates: 'that moment when you see the drawings move, that's a really magic moment, and there is no sound to it . . . an animation without the constraints of spoken words is stronger. If you have to fit everything to the words, all the gestural movement revolves around the mouth. Without it, you are much freer to . . . talk through animation itself' (Moins 2003: 28).

Many years elapse from the beginning of the film to its end – in a prologue, the triplets are shown in their youthful prime, but are already elderly once Champion is introduced and the story proper has commenced – and nearly two decades pass documenting Champion's growth from young boy to young man. Despite these reality-based chronological transformations, Mme Souza appears unchanged. From the start, she is an old woman – a woman of a certain age, as is euphemistically said, whose precise age is uncertain. She is manifestly infirm: one leg is shorter than the other and she wears an impressive platform shoe as compensation. Her body is stumpy and solid, her breasts abundant and pendulous; she is unequivocally matronly. Her eyes are greatly magnified by thick glasses which constantly slip down her broad nose and which she is incessantly flicking back in place, an idiosyncratic tic suggestive of her uncomfortable struggle to take her relational world in, see what to do or where to go.

Significantly, Champion as a boy appears more like a portly if unnaturally innocent old man, who, as he ages and physically develops, takes on the characteristic features of a gaunt, malnourished child possessed of disproportionately large legs and an enormous beak of a nose.

This grotesque external reversal and distortion can be understood as reflective of Champion's inner world. His developmental processes have been deformed by the precipitous loss of his parents. Significant life changes typically occur within normative timeframes. When these come off schedule, the transition from one phase to the next along the developmental continuum is more difficult (Robinson 1989). In certain instances, it may be derailed altogether. Among a host of consequent issues, several appear most evidently. As we first observe Champion, he is withdrawn, depressed and psychologically inert. He appears not to be thriving and is disinterested in activities and interactions. In short, Champion displays classic symptoms of a child whose

Tricycles, bicycles, life cycles

Grandma Souza

internal milieu has been profoundly disrupted by early separation from his parents, the permanence of which would be incomprehensible for him until much later.

An additional feature in this imagery is the fantasy of reversal of generations. In this, a child becomes in his imagination the parent of his parent, that is, the equivalent of his own grandparent. The influence of grandparents on character formation is significant, whether or not one, some or all of a child's grandparents predecease his birth. As progenitors to the child's parents, whose influence is everything, grandparents represent a backwards telescoping of the gamut of characteristic fantasies, symptoms and values which shape successive generations. Grandparents also serve numerous important intrapsychic and developmental functions, among them a comforting presence that, as Erikson suggests, assures the young that 'in the long run, people turn out okay' (1950, cited in Robinson 1989: 485). This is a handicapped proposition for an orphaned child whose first experience of life ratifies the opposite. It simultaneously encapsulates a false hope for the future as well as generates a grandiose reparative fantasy in which becoming one's own grandparent hopes to avoid the calamity of parental loss to come. Grandma and Champion, then, cling to reciprocal investments in the other as stalwarts against the threat of death. As it is not uncommon for survivors of traumatic loss to assume vacated roles, there will be developmental confusion for boy and grandmother as each attempts to reconcile his or her psychological place within their transgenerational dyad. This presents additional complexities in the light of the typical child's transformation in fantasy of the grandparent into an infant, a magical notion enhanced both by the elder's physical shrinkage and the universal denial of death (Rappaport 1958).

In all of this, which speaks ineluctably to the issue of time, perhaps the most overdetermined and highly condensed symbolic motif is movement. There are few scenes which are not kinetic. Even when one character is still, another is in motion (e.g. Champion and Mme Souza watching images moving on the television, or Bruno's obsessional preoccupation with passing trains). Throughout, Mme Souza, Champion, or Bruno are on or in some vehicle, in pursuit of someone or watching others travelling. This kineticism firstly and overarchingly signifies the search for the lost object which typifies early phase mourning. The principal dramatic propellant is a hybridization of movements, at first impinged – Champion's kidnapping and imprisonment – then unbridled – the ensuing chase and liberation. This trope of transformative, expansive motion is recurrent: Grandma and Champion start as static objects, listless and withdrawn, only gradually progressing toward animation. It is in this confluence of the meanings of animation – as artistic medium and a literal enlivening – that form and content assume synthesized aesthetic, affective and conceptual resonance.

Perhaps encumbered by her own fractured mourning, an attuned, effective response to young Champion's depressive collapse at first eludes Grandma. We see them sitting together in front of the television, and then drearily playing with a train set; they mope. After a time, she introduces him to an old piano in the hope of arousing his desire to play music – itself representational of her attempt to enable Champion's giving expressive sound and voice to his muzzled grief – but her clumsy and unmelodious pecking – a sonic extension of her own internal world – proves uninspiring. Grandma's inability to use the piano as an instrument for communicating with young Champion is especially interesting in the light of her later musical improvisatory adroitness with the triplets following her separation from Champion. This apparent contradiction – or, in any case, discrepancy – is suggestive of the primarily non-verbal and non-linguistic mode of communication between infants and care-giving adults, and the failures in this family to properly cultivate proto-language into mature discourse. The dearth of language permeates the relational landscape here, calling to mind the possibility that Mme Souza might never have been satisfactorily able to communicate with children – perhaps her own child, Champion's father or mother, included – and is only now in old age, spurred by traumatic circumstances, working to more fully develop her maternal competence. As music ultimately serves as the medium for salvation and working through – the final concert is a highly orchestrated aural sortie designed to facilitate Champion's liberation – these visual images of music and music making can be understood as illustrative of Grandma and Champion's dual, if asynchronous, developmental lines toward the capacity

Tricycles, bicycles, life cycles

for symbolization and the communication of previously unspeakable affect states.

Finally, with the introduction of new life – Bruno as a puppy – all of them seem at least temporarily on the road to resuscitation. Once Champion is given the tricycle, he too seems to start to move, although, meaningfully, only in constrained circles in the garden. He is as yet unable to escape the binding gravitational force of grief.

As time passes, Grandma and Champion begin to move in tandem. Eventually, as a late adolescent, Champion's fantasy-based identification with the photograph hanging over his little boy bed of his parents with a bicycle consolidates into a wish-suffused pursuit: cycling becomes the obsessionally dominant focus of existence. With this photo in mind, the bicycle can be understood as the nodal hub from which all other spokes of the dreamwork (symbolic instantiations of affect and ideation) derive. We can, firstly, imagine that Champion links the image of bicycle with his missing parents, giving rise to the formulation of a fantasy conjoining them. Grandma's gift of the tricycle could only thus enliven Champion, functioning as the symbolic equivalent of his being reunited with his parents. Cycling must be admired as an elegant device of the dream process, making the primary ideational vehicle an object which in reality only moves forward by which to disguise the unconscious wish to stall or reverse the flow of time. Linguistically, *cycle*, a word referring to the sporting activity and its instrument, incorporates the mental preoccupation with issues regarding the life cycle. Lastly, cycle racing is entirely preoccupied with time. It is measured in the rhythms of the body, inhalation and

Champion dreaming to be a champion

exhalation, muscle twitch, contraction and extension, oxygen and lactic acid burn rates; revolutions and ratios; distances and velocities. It can thus be taken as a developmental allusion to the 'cradle' of time sense (Rappaport 1951, cited in Colarusso 1998), the homeostatic regulatory mechanisms and sensations, and physiological rhythmicity of gratification and frustration in infancy.

There is an important prolonged sequence depicting the ritual of post-training meals and accompanying activities. Manifestly understandable for an athlete in training, it is more representationally overdetermined and conjoins multiple meanings for grandmother and child. The primary signification is orality, in particular, the condensation of necessity and pleasure in feeding which is both a central constituent of the mother–infant bond, and kinesthetic foundation to the establishment of time sense. These ideas are symbolized through images showing Grandma's precise monitoring and management of Champion's weight intake with scales and clocks and her truing his wheel rims with wrenches and tuning forks. Each is a multiply functioning allusion to the balancing and attunement between mother and infant which '[in] the frequent repetition of the hunger-satiation cycle . . . makes feeding the major time-related instinctual experience of early infancy . . . mother becomes the conveyor of time. Through her power to relieve hunger and pain, [mother] gives and controls time' (Colarusso 1998: 114).

Also included here is Bruno's salivating wait for Champion's leftovers. The melding and interweaving of Bruno's and Champion's points of view suggest they are symbolic Janus-faced extensions of each other. Another of Bruno's dreams is produced at this point in which the train, appearing as a peculiar nineteenth-century contraption, part steam-engine, part tuktuk, which is dragged by Champion yoked to it like a work-ox, has Bruno imperiously seated astride the phallus-shaped engine pulling Champion's reins. Coming as it does in a state of hungry dependence, this imagery can be understood as a sadomasochistic fantasy about primary narcissistic needs and desires, involving the interplay of domination and subjugation, and oscillating reversals of oral dependency with anal aggression. This also more generally renders the leitmotif of the train – in all other instances an object conveying others as it passes by, never stopping, never present or accessibly boardable – as an allusion to the absence of a protective masculine figure, and the profound yearning to hold and harness a father to balance the surfeit of women and help pull the family into the larger community.

Pertinently, each appearance of Bruno and train – whether in a dream or not – includes the auditory component of Bruno's barking. Especially when considered in the context of a world largely without spoken words, all sound must be heard as having special semiotic and paralinguistic significance. Here, we may take the barking of a dog as expressions beyond that: signifying utterances in a different language or some quasi-musical register displaced from those whom we expect to be able to use words. Another layer of understanding of Bruno's constant barking at passing trains, then, would be as an audible signal, akin to crying, meant to loudly enunciate the family's longing, but inability, to integrate and move forward, either within itself or the external world.

During the post-workout massage, involving an egg-beater and vacuum (devices which return later, in Belleville, as musical instruments), we see how Grandma's rhapsodic attention to her grandson's body and bodily needs transcends her role as hyperinvolved coach. Her exquisite ministrations – the worshipful caress of his engorged phallic legs, her conveying his limp, exhausted and satiated body, almost post-prandially, up the rickety stairs to tuck him into bed – evoke simultaneously a mother's devotional care of her infant and a fervent sexuality unavailable for expression in her present reality.

While digesting his food, Champion rides a stationary training bike, which also manually powers a record player. His exertions literally make their own music, suggesting his deeply held psychic position that he alone must bear the work and responsibility for being sung to, an allusion to the lullabies of childhood of which he was originally, and largely still, deprived. This, I believe, points to another facet of his rigorously focused pursuit of athletic excellence, and concerns more than sublimation. One segment is reaction formation, a redirection of hostile and aggressive impulses into their ostensible opposite. Another is the internal conscription of trauma-based longing as the impetus for accomplishment, a transformation of the feelings of loss, worthlessness, rage, guilt and bewilderment into an activity of restitution, control and eminence, in the attempt to master or vanquish the precipitating feelings (Eisendtadt *et al.* 1989, reviewed in Singer 1992). Orphans frequently feel abandoned. They are prone to fantasies of reunion with the dead parents and have an inability to accept death as final. They often also assume responsibility and feel guilt for the parents' death, since Oedipal triumph reinforces both the conviction of the power of evil thoughts and fears of confrontation with vengeful ghosts (Singer 1992). Attempts to overcome this typically involve an internalization of idealized part objects, and motivate pursuits designed to resurrect, such as through artistic creations, or to achieve, as a posthumous gift.

It is not insignificant that Champion goes nowhere during these rides. This image links back to his boyhood circumnavigations around the garden on his tricycle, and forward to his imprisonment in the Mafia betting parlour where, as nothing more than a magnificent carousel horse, he is pitted against his former Tour de France competitors to ride literally for their lives and others' profit while immobily chasing images of the countryside projected on to a movie screen. In symbolic terms, this frenetic motionlessness can be understood to illustrate the circularity and inescapable limitations of his straightjacketed Oedipal strivings and his attempts toward individuation. In the sense that Champion is developmentally arrested, he cannot move by himself; motility, to say nothing of separation, has not been achieved. We can imagine that he rides with his elderly trainer-cum-maternal object's coaching whistle rhythmically shrilling in his mind's ear. His appearance as self-propelled as a professional cyclist would be a projection of his ideal self, a fantasy extension of the image of his father and his father's surrogates, the admired icons and champions of cycle racing whose photos also adorn his bedroom wall. But he is always ferried or carried by others. The Mafia thugs' sweep wagon or his ocean voyage in the bowels of the great steamship are in this view like prams or parents' arms. In children's perceptions, and in the adult's fantastical reconstruction of childhood experiences, the world of adults is enormous and the grown-ups in it omnipotent and infallible. For a bereaved and traumatized child like Champion, it would also be sinister, thus making understandable images which synthesize these qualities in two-dimensional terms: the adults in Champion's world are for him either all good or all bad.

Grandma Souza, by contrast, appears as a veritable superwoman. There seems to be no law of physics or process of physical decline to which she is susceptible. This nature of fantasy is as characteristic of cartoons as of dreams. As the incarnation of an idealized fantasy persona, she would be as much a concoction of the orphaned boy, desperate to encounter in his grandmother an indestructible substitute mother, as of Mme Souza herself, instantiating herself both as an object for idealization and internalization by her grandson-child and, narcissistically, as a figure representing the domination and revocation of the ravages of her own ageing process.

The composite figure of the triplets can be similarly understood, that is, as symbolic condensations of these central preoccupations. The difficulties of the triplets' present-day circumstances notwithstanding, they are endowed with an array of idealized attributes, ranging from their romanticized, sophisticated and successful past, to their life together now, still connected by the bonds of life and love. Complex aspects of the end of life phase include loss of community, the disappearance of linkages to a shared history and consequent feelings of isolation. As depicted in the image of Mme Souza sleeping on the triplets' couch while they laugh together in bed in a separate room while watching old movie reels of their younger selves, we can perceive both Mme Souza's wish to reclaim that sphere of connectedness and vitality as well as her realistic appraisal of solitude.

Of course, beneath the admirable veneer of resourcefulness, perseverance and cohesion – primarily an idealizing construction – they are all trapped in an attenuated repetition compulsion, living a marginalized, lonely and threadbare existence which for all intents and purposes remains fixed in a lost past. It is only by the catalyst of another, present loss – Champion's abduction – that the women are able to disengage themselves from their obsessive ruminating and animate themselves to action.

In the end, as in all fairy-tale dreams with happy endings, Champion is freed and the evildoers get their comeuppance. Toward that goal, Grandma,

Tricycles, bicycles, life cycles

The triplets of Belleville on stage

the triplets and Bruno form a strategic alliance where each comes to life and can excel independently. Thus do an old woman disguised as a diminutive immigrant mechanic, and a torch-song performance using an empty refrigerator, a vacuum cleaner, an old newspaper and a bicycle wheel give rise to an orgy of violence and destruction in the service of a regenerative fantasy – that the bonds of love and the power of fantasy qua cinema are able to conquer evil, right wrongs, and restore loss. While Champion cannot liberate himself alone, his strengths as a man-cyclist are now brought to bear with potent results. As the stationary racing platform becomes unmoored and crashes through the walls of the Mafia fortress, we are given to understand that, finally, there is forward movement. The characters collaborate and comingle their resources, suggesting the possibility for an integration of part objects, a consolidation of object-relatedness, and a capacity to more healthily reconcile projections of an idealized environment with aspects of a cherished past.

One cycle is broken, another is complete, another begins.

Notes

1 A version of this chapter has been previously published in *The International Journal of Psychoanalysis*, 87(4): 1125–34.
2 It is important to underscore that this précis is unavoidably inadequate to the task of conveying the sensorial and aesthetic experience of the film. While a prior viewing of the film is not essential to understanding this chapter, my commentary will necessarily take on greater resonance to the reader who is familiar with the cinematic referents.

References

Bowlby, J. (1963) Pathological mourning and childhood mourning, *Journal of the American Psychoanalytic Association*, 11: 500–41.

Colarusso, C.A. (1998) A developmental line of time sense: in late adulthood and throughout the life cycle, *Psychoanalitic Study of the Child*, 53: 113–40.

Freud, S. (1900) *The interpretation of dreams*, part II, in *Standard Edition*, Vol. V. London: Hogarth Press.

Moins, P. (2003) Sylvain Chômet: Animation is like a manifesto, *Animation World Magazine*, 8: 26–30. Available from mag.awn.com/index.php?article_no=1923.

Nagera, H. (1970) Children's reactions to the death of important objects – a developmental approach, *Psychoanalitic Study of the Child*, 25: 360–400.

Rappaport, E.A. (1958) The grandparent syndrome, *Psychoanalytic Quarterly*, 27: 518–38.

Robinson, L.H. (1989) Grandparenting, *Journal of the American Academy of Psychoanalysis*, 17: 483–91.

Singer, M. (1992). Eisenstadt, M., Haynal, A., Rentchnick, P., de Senarclens, P. (1989) *Parental Loss and Achievement* (review), *Psychoanalytic Quarterly*, 61: 270–4.

13

LOSS, MOURNING AND DESIRE IN MIDLIFE
François Ozon's *Under the Sand* and *Swimming Pool*

Diana Diamond

Sous le sable (*Under the Sand*) (France, 2000)
Director: François Ozon
Distributor: Winstar Cinema

Swimming Pool (France, 2003)
Director: François Ozon
Distributor: Universal Cinemas

I will begin by describing two clips from François Ozon's film, *Swimming Pool*. In the first the camera pans sensuously over the body of a young woman, Julie, as she lies sprawled in the sun. It then turns upward to reveal a man gazing lustfully down at her. The two begin to masturbate in synchrony. The image of a middle-aged woman waking up at the end of this sequence suggests these shots represent her erotic dream. In a later parallel sequence, the camera similarly pans over the body of this mature woman, Sarah, a writer of mystery novels, who is sharing a house with Julie while on holiday in the south of France. This time, the shot dead ends not in a scene of voyeuristic passion, but in the static image of the diminutive, withered figure of the property's caretaker. Ozon stated in an interview 'I wanted this mature body to seem desirable ... the main point was that I wanted Sarah and Julie's bodies to affect one another' (2003: 2). Indeed, the sequence ends with mutual gaze between the two women.

In these scenes François Ozon, 'mounts the camera on an everyday body' (Deleuze 1989: 189) to comment on the problematic of desire and desirability in midlife. These two shots introduce us to Ozon's cinematic aesthetic which

Julie (Ludivine Sagnier)

Sarah (Charlotte Rampling)

both celebrates the eroticism and desirability of the mature woman, and vamps on the prevailing youth-centered airbrushed images of cinematic beauty. The lingering movement of the camera evokes desire mediated through the gaze, as does the positioning of the characters at right angles to each other (Schiller 2005).

In *Swimming Pool* and *Under the Sand* the camera showcases a mature actress's (Charlotte Rampling's) face and body with rare candor and detail, and in so doing reveals what is concealed from thought – the complex web of desire, loss and mourning in midlife. Eliot Jaques defined midlife as a time of psychic upheaval and transformation when infantile anxieties around love and hate, destructiveness and death, suppressed in early adulthood in the interests of occupational advancement and procreation, resurface and are reworked as the individual faces the inherent limitations of mortality. It is also a time when the prolific and often prodigious, but largely unconscious, white-hot creativity of youth is replaced by a more contemplative and sculpted vision that emerges from the recognition that 'inherent goodness is accompanied by hate and destructive forces within, which contribute to man's own misery and tragedy' (Jaques 1965: 505). Under the best of circumstances the reintegration of hate under the domain of love allows one to contemplate death with tranquillity rather than bitterness, and to confront one's own and others' destructiveness, without descent into persecutory anxieties.

Under the Sand and *Swimming Pool* depict women in the throes of midlife transitions, which are clearly of central concern to Ozon, whose preoccupation with issues of loss and mortality is evident in a recent interview in which he said, quoting Montaigne: 'You have to think about death every day in order to tame it . . . maybe that's what I'm doing' (Ozon, in Johnston 2001: 13). These anxieties are expressed through his female characters – as Ozon himself said: 'I find that as a man, sometimes it's easier to talk about yourself through the opposite sex . . . I think I have the soul of Pygmalion. Women characters in the cinema are more interesting because women show their emotions more' (in Hohenadel 2002: 23).

While these quotes suggest that *Under the Sand* and *Swimming Pool* reflect aspects of Ozon's subjectivity, this chapter primarily explores the ways in which Ozon's films reflect a universal developmental crisis or phase that is 'vicariously experienced by the audience' (Gabbard 2001: 7). In mapping the interior landscape of midlife, Ozon addresses a ubiquitous, but often invisible, reality in that age cuts across our lives and bodies in a way that other differences do not, but remains under-theorized and under-represented in the popular imagination. The narrative structures of both *Under the Sand* and *Swimming Pool* evoke some of the core developmental issues of midlife, including the complexities and reversals of the gaze and spectatorship.

In both these films, the rip-tides of ageing and death carry the central characters into psychic undertows in which fantasy and reality, creativity and perversion, even sanity and madness, are confounded. The films represent two diametrically opposed resolutions of the midlife crisis, with its resuscitation of infantile and depressive anxieties around love, hate, destructiveness and reparation. While Jaques hypothesizes that midlife inevitably is a time of psychic upheaval, it is important to note that the two female characters represent the pathological end of adaptation to the inexorable turmoil of midlife. They epitomize in different ways how an expectable developmental life crisis may evoke or dovetail with individual psychopathology. In *Under the Sand*, a middle-aged English professor drifts further and further into manic denial and narcissistic encapsulation as she struggles to accept the death of her spouse, who mysteriously vanishes on the beach at the start of their summer vacation. Although increasingly presented with evidence that he has drowned, including the viewing of his remains, she continues their relationship as though he were still alive, leading to a split in the ego (Freud 1938) with its bifurcated experience of reality. In *Swimming Pool*, by contrast, a dour British mystery writer, who has channelled her passion into her stereotyped if popular thrillers to the impoverishment of her emotional and erotic life, finds her limited adaptation challenged when she becomes paralysed by writer's block. She retreats to her publisher's country house in France for inspiration but is only able to discover a more vibrant plot after her own unconscious erotic and aggressive impulses are re-encountered when she becomes embroiled in a perverse voyeuristic relationship with her publisher's illegitimate French teenage daughter. At first viewing these films appear radically disparate, but as Bach (1989) has observed, perversion has its roots in failed mourning, and the inability to mourn losses and limitations may itself lead to perverse resolutions.

Both *Under the Sand* and *Swimming Pool* may be viewed as parables of midlife. Its potential resuscitation of infantile persecutory and depressive anxieties has often evoked the language of myths and fairy tales. Dante, for example, wrote that in the middle of life, 'I came to myself within a dark wood where the straight way was lost. Ah how hard it is to tell of that wood, savage and harsh and dense, the thought of which renews my fear . . . so bitter it is that death is hardly more . . .' (quoted in Jaques 1965: 503). Recently, Shine compared middle age to 'a deep dark forest full of howling wolves, wicked spells, ogres and witches, castles and enchanted gardens' (2005: 4). Ozon, who was influenced by Bettelheim's psychoanalytic study of fairy tales, has compared his filmic narratives, which explore the unconscious, to fairy tales which act as catalysts for the expression and containment of primitive anxieties. In giving imaginative expression to such impulses and anxieties, Ozon's films, like fairy tales, ameliorate the anguish that they may evoke. '*Ce que j'aime est commun aux contes et au cinema . . . . ils sont palliatif à une certaine sufferance*', stated Ozon (1999: 1).[1] The parallel between his films and fairy tales accounts for some of the more enigmatic aspects of Ozon's oeuvre that have remained somewhat opaque. Both *Under the Sand* and *Swimming Pool* violate narrative norms of time, space and causality; the spectator is often left wondering which events and/or characters are the products of dreams, reverie or the creative imagination. Ozon (2000: 126) himself said that he wanted his films to be open and ambiguous: 'I'm most excited by films where the signifiers are unclear and destabilized'.

Under the Sand gives voice to the unconscious wish that ageing and loss may be subverted, that eroticism and bodily perfection may persist undiminished in midlife, and that the reality of death may be overshadowed by fantasies of magic immortality (Frankiel 2002). In the beginning of the film Marie Drillion (Charlotte Rampling), a lecturer in English, and her husband of 25 years, Jean (Bruno Cremer), travel to their country house for an extended summer holiday in near wordless harmony. As we view the couple going about their daily life, stopping at a motorway café for coffee, opening the house, sharing a meal, we do not know if their silence bespeaks a marriage that is perfectly attuned or stale and dead. At first the couple seems complementary, with the phlegmatic and taciturn, if quietly accommodating, Jean balancing the vibrant and energetic, if somewhat relentlessly cheerful, Marie; but the filmic images are designed to suggest a certain ambiguity or to make the spectator feel 'both things at once' (Ozon, in Johnston 2001: 13). Jean's expressions alternate between affection, deadness and anguish, and his apathetic movements suggest lethargy and demoralization. The image of Jean turning over a log to find ants swarming beneath on the night he arrives at his country house strikes an ominous note and presages the dreadful events to come. Ozon also suggests that Marie's blissful insouciance obscures an underlying dread when we see her anxiously perusing her face in the mirror for signs of ageing, the camera playing over its lines and shadows. This scene reveals Marie's intense self-absorption and extreme narcissistic vulnerability. Subsequently Marie approaches Jean sexually, perhaps to reassure herself of her own attractiveness, but is subtly rebuffed by her weary husband. Through such images Ozon writes the grammar for his cinema of the body in which the 'physics of the body reveals the eidetic of the spirit' (Deleuze 1989: 204).

The following day Jean announces that he is going for a swim. After giving Marie one last pensive look, he simply vanishes on the beach. At first Marie, aided by authorities, searches frantically for Jean, and then spends the rest of her vacation alone, anxiously anticipating his return with every noise. Marie responds with shocked denial to enquiries about Jean's state of mind and potential for suicide, refusing to acknowledge the possibility of her husband's death, or the depression that might have led to it. Ozon foreshadows the meaning of her denial when he juxtaposes an image of a ravaged and haggard Marie with that of a statue of the naked Aphrodite, an image of female perfection and invulnerability that Marie cannot bear to relinquish.

Marie's inability to acknowledge the loss of her husband bifurcates her existence. Back in Paris, she goes to dinner parties alone, but talks about Jean as though he was still with her. She shops for clothes and buys a tie for Jean, but finds that she can't pay for them because her bank account is frozen as a result of his disappearance. When told by her lawyer to cut back her spending, she insists that she will discuss it with Jean who is travelling and will take care of the problem when he returns. She begins an affair with a publisher named Vincent (Jacques Nolot), but shares the details of this relationship with her husband who remains a ubiquitous, if illusory, presence in her life. When she finally makes love to Vincent, she tells him that this is the first time she has ever cheated on Jean. Finally, when she masturbates in a now celebrated scene of midlife female autoeroticism after a date with her lover, she imagines being caressed by two pairs of hands, those of Vincent and those of her husband.

Marie's initial denial of the loss, particularly in the face of the ambiguity of Jean's disappearance, even her hallucinating his presence, are not atypical in the early stages of mourning (Bowlby 1980; Parkes 1986; Frankiel 2002). However, the persistent duality of her existence suggests ego splitting in the face of pathological mourning (Freud 1938; Bowlby 1963; Blum 1983, 2003). This internal split is reflected in the dual worlds depicted by the filmmaker – one of consensual reality in which Marie goes on with her work and social life, and one in which she continues an illusory relationship with her husband. Cinematic techniques, such as making the husband's ghostly presence real to the spectator and magnifying Marie's face in close-up in almost every scene, with the background always a bit out of focus, highlight Marie's dual mode of thinking and experiencing. Indeed, in this film Ozon shows 'an imaginary world in as realistic a way as possible – flat so that reality and fantasy are shown as equivalents' (2003: 2).

We soon realize that Marie's denial of Jean's death is not an isolated event, but a consequence of chronic patterns of denial, self-deception and narcissistic self-absorption (Frankiel 2002). Her seeming devotion obscures their lack of genuine intimacy, as evidenced by her ignorance of his depression and dissatisfaction with the marriage. In the sphere of idealized fantasy in which Marie continues their relationship, Jean presents as more affectionate, available and attentive than he was prior to his disappearance, which clearly protects Marie from her underlying narcissistic vulnerability. Young-Breuhl has observed that 'Ego instinctually rooted idealizations of loved ones and of their cherishing love can function to protect us from any feeling we have that we are unlovable which is a source of shame' (2003: 287). Bach has similarly linked idealization and failed mourning with perversion: 'Thus instead of mourning we find a split in the ego and instead of separation through painful detachment and symbolic internalizations, we find repeated attempts at reunion ... through the false game of the idealized self and object' (1989: 21).

The extent to which Marie has organized her life around this idealized fantasy is evident when she tells Vincent that, although she adores teaching, she has limited her investment in her career: 'When I started teaching I had lots of plans, specialized research projects on exciting subjects, but in time I let them all go ... My relationship with Jean has always been my priority'. Marie has projected so much of herself into her fantasy of a perfect union with Jean that his disappearance threatens a catastrophic loss of self. Steiner observes that in situations where overidealization of the other compensates for an underlying hollowness in the self, the loss of the other may cause the individual to

Loss, mourning and desire in midlife

'panic and cling onto the object and deny the loss, as if he [she] can that way prevent his [her] own death' (1993: 63).

That her refusal to accept the loss of Jean is tied up with Marie's fear of her own ageing and death is conveyed imagistically throughout the film. Marie reads to Vincent from Virginia Woolf's suicide note to her husband in which she celebrates their perfect union even while she states that she intends to drown herself because she cannot bear to spoil his happiness with her encroaching madness – perhaps an unconscious acknowledgement about the despair that might have led to Jean's suicide. Tellingly, she teaches Virginia Woolf's novel, *The Waves*, about four friends mourning the death of one of them. As she reads a passage from *The Waves* to her class, which includes the incantation 'over and done with, over and done with', she becomes panic-stricken and ends the class abruptly on the sentence 'What have I lost . . . my youth is gone.' After receiving a phone call telling her that a body which fits Jean's description has been found in a fisherman's net, she rushes into the bedroom calling for her husband, but for the first time fails to conjure him up, meeting only her own reflection in the mirror.

Rather than responding to the coroner's ominous message, she makes love to Vincent, only achieving orgasm when she sees Jean lurking in the shadows. Afterwards she flees to sleep in his study where everything is as he left it, including his jacket slung over his desk chair. When Vincent follows her, gently telling her that he wants to help her face the reality of her husband's death, she attacks him viciously, saying, 'Who are you to help me?', and

Under the Sand

ruthlessly devalues him saying: 'The truth is you don't measure up.' To give up her idealization or to acknowledge Jean's death threatens her with psychic catastrophe. Indeed, she collapses after she realizes that the bedroom window of an apartment that she is considering renting looks over a cemetery.

When she inadvertently learns that Jean was being treated for depression, the reality of her husband's death begins to encroach on Marie. The derailment of her dual existence leads to the upsurge of persecutory anxieties that erupt during her visit to her mother-in-law. Confronted with the new evidence about Jean's disappearance, her mother-in-law replies: 'There are no suicides in the Drillion family', and vituperatively adds: 'The truth is more cruel . . . he disappeared because he was bored with you. Anyway you weren't able to give him a family.' When Marie tells her that a body matching Jean's description has been found in a fisherman's net her mother-in-law states, nonsensically, 'he loved fishing'. Marie responds that her mother-in-law must be mad to make such a comment and belongs in an insane asylum, to which she counters: 'you'll be there before me'. This bitter and rivalrous exchange shows that both women would rather retreat into madness than confront the reality of Jean's death.

Ultimately the split in the ego which prevents Marie from acknowledging and mourning the loss of her husband leads to a repudiation and hatred of reality itself (Steiner 1993). She returns to Les Landes to identify Jean's body at the morgue, insisting on seeing the corpse even after being told it is grotesquely mutilated and unrecognizable. The unimaginable sight is registered for the viewer by the focus on Marie's reflexive recoil and expression of horror, but she ultimately denies that the body is Jean's, despite being presented with conclusive genetic and forensic evidence. In the film's final scene she returns to the beach where Jean vanished and collapses with grief, sobbing uncontrollably for the first time. For a moment we believe that she has returned to her initial place of yearning and searching to complete her process of interrupted mourning, but when she sees a figure that resembles Jean in the distance, her face is suffused with joy and hope, and she runs frantically towards him. In this final scene, the trajectory of the filmic narrative comes full circle, taking us towards the possibility that Marie will at last mourn her husband's death and reconstitute her split inner world. But the final shot of Marie chasing an insubstantial figure in an ever-receding horizon epitomizes the perverse scenarios attendant on failed mourning with their 'repeated attempts at reunion' (Bach 1989: 21) with an idealized lost object. The futility and circularity of Marie's emotional trajectory is highlighted at the end by a reversion to the long take – a technique evident in the first part of the film prior to Jean's disappearance. Ozon reports that he shot the film in two parts, the open seaside shots in long takes in 35mm and the second part after Jean's death, when Marie is back in Paris, in 26mm, primarily with close-ups which feature Rampling in almost every shot. The two parts of the film vary in terms of tones and colour, as well as technique. The first part is noticeably brighter, but shot objectively like a 'news report', while the second part, with its close-ups and slightly out of focus background, helps to focus on the interiority of the character, to give the illusion of being 'inside a woman's head' (Ozon, in Johnston 2001: 13).

In fact the film represents a mélange of both Ozon's and Rampling's own experiences, and was not only shot but also conceived in two separate parts, with the first part done by Ozon alone and the second in collaboration with Rampling and three female scriptors (Elley 2000). The inspiration for the first part came from a childhood experience of Ozon's in which he witnessed a woman losing her husband in a manner similar to that which occurs in the film during a seaside holiday in Les Landes, at the age of 10 with his parents. He recalls the lifeguard and a helicopter arriving to search for the missing husband, and the wife finally taking his belongings home. 'It was a traumatic thing for a child to witness,' Ozon commented (in Johnston 2001: 12). When he approached Rampling about the film he had only conceptualized the first 20 minutes; the second part was inspired by Rampling's own experiences of loss and bereavement – her divorce from her husband of many years (Jean Michel Jarre) and the death of her sister. 'She'd been through a lot in terms of mourning and romantic separation,' the filmmaker writes (Ozon, in Johnston 2001: 12–13). 'She could nourish Marie and gave a lot of herself in the film, at moments the character and the actress merge together. You could say this is Charlotte's story.'

Under the Sand thus explores the stunting of emotional and creative powers that results when mourning fails and the realities of human destructiveness, hate and death are avoided through restitutive omnipotent fantasies. In contrast *Swimming Pool* portrays the deepened experience of reality, expanded creativity and enhanced capacity to cherish and mourn lost objects and experiences, rather than to idealize or reify them, that comes with a full awareness and acceptance of loss and death (Jaques 1965). While *Under the Sand* situates the heroine's internal world of wish, fantasy and desire within a somewhat linear, if subjective, cinematic narrative, in *Swimming Pool* we have teenage daughters who appear out of nowhere, metamorphosing into nymphets and then back into slightly gawky pubescent girls with braces; wizened dwarfs who reveal old secrets about murders and deaths that may or may not have happened; novels and bodies that vanish and reappear. The somewhat labyrinthine cinematic narrative is punctuated at crucial points by the characters sealing themselves off into sleep and then later waking with a start, so that we can never be quite sure which aspects of the ongoing events transpired in a dream state and which are meant to represent consensual reality. In fact, the film has the structure of a manifest dream which offers a surface coherence; but a a richer understanding becomes possible if the film is interpreted as a series of images, some of which plunge the viewer into somewhat discrete, if overlapping, domains of impulse, wish and fantasy. The incidents of voyeurism, fetishism and flashing in a terrain adjacent to the ruined castle of the Marquis de Sade lend a perverse dimension to the film (Ozon 2000).

Sarah Morton, a dour British mystery writer, is suddenly paralysed with writer's block after a long, successful career as a writer of thrillers. The main character of her mysteries, Inspector Dorwell, functions as an alter ego and foil for her sadomasochistic, perverse fantasy life and androgynous, but sexually inhibited, presentation. We first encounter Sarah when she is recognized on the subway by a loyal fan whom she rebuffs with the statement: 'You have mistaken me for someone else . . . I'm not the person you think I am.' These initial scenes establish Sarah as a woman whose rigid schizoid defense functions to protect her from any emotional engagement beyond caring for her aged father, with whom she remains mired in an Oedipal relationship, and churning out bestsellers for her publisher John Bosload (Charles Dance) with whom she appears to have had a long liaison. At the beginning of the film, Sarah seems to have reached the end of the gratification to be obtained from her manic productivity, involving the rigid sublimation of all aggression and desire in her mystery plots for the approval of her publisher/father figure. She castigates Bosload for not looking after her any more, and turns to him for solace and inspiration. At the same time she reveals in this initial encounter the perverse retreat into anality that both fuels and inhibit her talent and keeps her from the fully engaged relationship for which she longs (Schiller 2005). She confides to John that she is 'fed up with murders and investigations', that she doesn't 'give a damn about the money and success'. He suggests that she is in search of 'an inspiring plot', and offers her a sojourn at his house in France to jump-start her stalled creativity. When she asks him whether he will visit her there, John makes unconvincing promises to join her later, stating that he has his daughter to care for.

Sarah retreats to John's country house where she tries to overcome her creative and emotional paralysis. She works in a desultory way on a new novel, entitled *Inspector Dorwell on Holiday*, and flirts with a handsome waiter, Franck. When she peeks under the cover of the swimming pool on the property and recoils from the brackish water, we see her desire and dread of peering deeper into her own experience. The swimming pool functions 'like a movie-screen against which images are projected and into which a character penetrates' (Ozon 2003: 3).

The screen of Sarah's unconscious is suddenly illuminated by the unexpected arrival in the middle of the night of Julie (Ludivine Sagnier), John's illegitimate daughter, heretofore unbeknownst to Sarah. That Sarah's life is about to enter another dimension is anticipated in a scene where she opens the window of her bedroom and peers into the woods. The camera

Sarah (Charlotte Rampling)

zooms deeper into the darkness, suddenly illuminating the trees, vines and shadows of the forest, which assume a sinister and fanciful quality. Sarah confronts the split off, repressed and perverse aspects of herself in her encounters with Julie, her counterpoint as well as Oedipal rival for John's affection. When she first arrives, Julie taunts Sarah by asking: 'Are you my father's latest conquest?' Julie immediately plunges into the swimming pool, which Sarah has called a cesspool teeming with bacteria, and lounges by it topless, marking the swimming pool as the scene of a series of erotic encounters. Sarah treats Julie as an interloper into her work space and her relationship with John, whom she castigates for failing to tell her about his love child. The two women's interest and involvement with each other is sparked by their mutual connection to the elusive John, now a disembodied third presence heard only on the phone. Sarah explodes at Julie: 'I just want to work in peace,' even while she surreptitiously eats Julie's food, drinks her wine and watches her from the shadows.

Witnessing the teenage girl's sexual antics helps unleash the mature novelist's smoldering sexuality, while being confronted by Julie's emotional vulnerability evokes Sarah's maternal and generative longings. Sarah surreptitiously observes and listens to Julie's sexual exploits with mixed pleasure and contempt, and Julie meets her gaze head on in perverse scenarios in which voyeurism and exhibitionism, homoeroticism and hetereoeroticism converge. Sarah's voyeuristic and exhibitionistic activities provide a route to renewed sexual and creative engagement, functioning in Ozon's words as 'proof of attachment and concern' (2000: 126), even while they preserve her need for distance to protect against her envy, aggression and inhibited sexual longings. The triangular primal scene scenarios suggest Sarah's perversions express a retreat from a genital sexual intimacy which unconsciously replicates an

Oedipal situation that she has not resolved (Meyers 1992; Kernberg 1995). The triangulation of Sarah, John and Julie is a central aspect of the film as it allows Sarah to emerge from an Oedipal situation in which she has been trapped, while for Julie, Sarah's presence brings in her absent father and the dead mother, recreating the developmental possibilities of an Oedipal situation.

Sarah's voyeuristic activities represent furtive enactments of, and forays out of, her world of perverse fantasy, previously contained within her mystery plots (Meyers 1992). Through these scenarios, with their residues of infantile sexuality and the primal scene, Ozon reminds us that 'the undifferentiated sexual dispositions of the child' (Freud 1905: 50) persist in the adult as a wellspring for creative activities (Widlocher 2002). Indeed Sarah embodies Freud's notion that in gifted individuals, perversion, neurosis and creativity coexist. As Chasseguet-Smirgel has observed, 'the same individual might show a perverse area where pregenital instincts would be released into sexual activity, a neurotic area where they would undergo repression, and a third area where they would be sublimated' (1984: 90).

That Sarah moves fluidly between perversion and creativity is evident when she opens another file on her computer, called 'Julie', and immerses herself in a new narrative. Her face takes on a fresh luminosity, intensity and focus, as a molten creativity begins to stir within. Ozon portrays her sexual awakening along with the thawing of her frozen creativity as two sides of a midlife transition involving re-emergence and reintegration of infantile anxieties and impulses, with freer interaction between internal and external, conscious and unconscious domains. This integration engenders a new plot that breaks the mould of her formulaic thrillers with their rigid sadomasochistic themes, and takes her into an exploration of tragic themes involving love and hate, loss and betrayal, death and redemption, based on her encounters with Julie.

Sarah reads Julie's diary and transcribes it verbatim into her new novel, making it and Julie's confidences about her mother the basis for her new book. Julie tells Sarah that her mother also wrote a novel – a love story with a happy ending – which she burned when John Bosload told her it was 'awful', thus establishing both a parallel and a contrast between Sarah and her mother. 'He wants blood, sex and money . . . that's what you give him, isn't it?' Julie says, to which Sarah replies: 'But I like all that too . . .', showing an acknowledgement of the unconscious fantasies that have fuelled her mystery plots. The multiple shots in the film of Sarah writing, reflected in a mirror which itself is enclosed within another mirror, suggest that she is delving into layers of her internal world in ways that are reconfiguring her self-representation. Sarah's immersion in her new plot is followed by her plunging into the pool for the first time, and sunbathing sensuously beside it, after Julie. Through the medium of the swimming pool, Ozon states that there is 'an exchange of fluids' between the two women (2003: 2), implying that the eroticized and aggressivized interactions have rekindled Sarah's desire and creativity (Schiller 2005).

Reality and reverie converge when, after surreptitiously reading Sarah's new novel and realizing that it is based on her own history, Julie wreaks her revenge by bringing home Franck, the waiter with whom Sarah had flirted. The ensuing triangular dynamics catalyse the plot's conclusion. Sarah competes with Julie for Franck's attentions, dancing provocatively with him in front of Julie. Ultimately Sarah withdraws from the competition, as Julie, jealous of her conquest of Franck, acidly wishes her 'sweet dreams'. Here the film's narrative converges with Sarah's dream and imaginative life. Sarah retreats to her room and frantically records this latest chapter of the saga. Lured to her balcony by the sounds of a sexual encounter between Julie and Franck at the pool, she interrupts their tryst by tossing a rock into the water. She sequesters herself in sleep, but wakes up with a start bathed in sweat, deepening the ambiguity about the extent to which these events actually happened or were simply a frightening erotic dream.

The ensuing scenes of murder, seduction and exhibitionism take the characters deeper into perversion, involving a denial of the differences and boundaries between the generations and between real and fictional characters, the analization of bodies which are seen as disposable objects to be eliminated, and the idealization of part objects (Chasseguet-Smirgel 1984). Julie confuses Sarah with her dead mother, and tells Sarah that she thinks she has murdered Franck, 'for you, for the book'. Sarah improbably flashes her bare breasts at Marcel, the caretaker, luring him into an unlikely and perverse sexual encounter to distract him from seeing the fresh dirt over the grave in which Julie and Sarah have buried Franck's body.

However, here perversion functions in the service of reparation and creativity. Julie kills Franck to advance Sarah's book, and Sarah seduces Marcel to save Julie from detection. Julie departs, leaving Sarah with a copy of her mother's novel which was preserved even though the original burned. She tells her to take it and 'steal it', if the book inspires her, saying that perhaps if she gives Sarah these pages she might 'bring her mother back to life'. Sarah uses the purloined novel as a basis for finishing her own book, which she entitles *Swimming Pool*. Sarah's identification with Julie and her mother creates a scaffold to a more 'sculpted creativity' (Jaques 1965) that encompasses tragic themes around love and hate, loss and reparation, destructiveness and eroticism. Their detour into perversion allowed both Sarah's and Julie's development to be set back on track – Sarah was able to embrace the identity of mother with its implication of generativity, and Julie was able to reconnect with her preadolescent, child past.

Sarah's and Julie's transformation is evident in the film's final scenes. Sarah, whose sensual and playful presentation is a stark contrast to her earlier inhibited stance, presents her novel to John Bosload. When he tells her that writing about feelings is not her 'strong suit', she counters: 'I think it's the finest bloody piece of work I've done in a long time.' She tells him that she had anticipated his rejection of her novel with its echoes of his disclaimed wife and daughter, and that she has already found a new publisher who loved the book. She presents him with a signed copy and says ironically, 'Keep the book; it's inscribed to your daughter.' As she bids a final farewell to John, she encounters his daughter, now a slightly gawky pubescent girl with braces, who bears only passing resemblance to Julie. Once again Sarah observes John's daughter through a window, but this time with an expression of maternal warmth and tenderness rather than prurient curiosity.

In the last scene, Sarah is magically transported to Luberon where she re-encounters Julie and bids her a final farewell. As Julie waves to Sarah from the pool's edge, she is metamorphosed into the gawky adolescent girl and then back into Julie, the nymphet. Ozon ends his mercurial film with this final protean image, in which, like the midlife passage itself, identifications are in flux and the signifiers are destabilized in the face of fantasies and actions that are perverse, transgressive and ultimately transformative.

In both *Swimming Pool* and *Under the Sand*, Ozon plunges the spectator into radical uncertainty about the validity of the filmic events, so that fantasy and reality, past and present, even life and death, are confounded. Perhaps in so scrambling the signifiers, Ozon derails the spectators from their initial social construction of the film in the hope of catapulting them into a deeper engagement with the anxieties and enchantments of midlife, and perhaps even with the dilemmas and delights of viewing cinema itself. In Ozon's films, the anxieties of midlife are not eradicated, but they do lead us to a kind of enchantment.

Acknowledgements

I would like to express my gratitude to Lissa Weinstein, Alexander Stein and Andrea Sabbadini, each of whom contributed substantially to the development of this chapter and to my ongoing work in the area of film and psychoanalysis.

Note

1 'That which I love is common to fairy tales and cinema. They are a palliative for a certain kind of suffering.'

References

Bach, S. (1989) On sadomasochistic object relations, in G. Fogel and W. Myers (eds) *Perversions and Near Perversions in Clinical Practice*. New Haven, CT: Yale University Press.

Blum, H.P. (1983) Splitting of the ego and its relation to parent loss, *Journal of the American Psychoanalytic Association*, 31: 301–24.

Blum, H.P. (2003) Psychic trauma and traumatic object loss, *Journal of the American Psychoanalytic Association*, 51: 415–31.

Bowlby, J. (1963) Pathological mourning and childhood mourning, in R. Frankiel (ed.) *Essential Papers on Object Loss*. New York: New York University Press, 1994.

Bowlby, J. (1980) *Attachment and Loss. Vol. 3: Loss: Sadness and Depression*. New York: Basic Books.

Chasseguet-Smirgel, J. (1984) *Creativity and Perversion*. London: Free Association Books.

Deleuze, G. (1989) *Cinema 2*. Minneapolis, MN: University of Minnesota Press.

Elley, D. (2000) Film reviews: Toronto: 'Under the Sand', *Variety*, 380(6): 63.

Frankiel, R. (2002) Film review essay: *Sous le Sable* (*Under the Sand*), *International Journal of Psychoanalysis*, 83: 313–17.

Freud, S. (1905) Three essays on the theory of sexuality, *Standard Edition*, Vol. VII. London: Hogarth Press.

Freud, S. (1938) Splitting of the ego in the process of defence, *Standard Edition*. London: Hogarth Press.

Gabbard, G. (ed.) (2001) *Psychoanalysis and Film*. London: Karnac.

Hohenadel, K. (2002) Corralling eight egos by letting them run, *New York Times*, 22 September, Section 2: 23.

Jaques, E. (1965) Death and the mid-life crisis, *International Journal of Psychoanalysis*, 46: 502–14.

Johnston, S. (2001) Death every day, *Sight and Sound*, 11 April: 12–13.

Kernberg, O. (1995) *Love Relations*. New Haven, CT: Yale University Press.

Meyers, H.C. (1992) Perversion in everyday life, *Issues in Ego Psychology*, 15(1): 9–17.

Ozon, F. (1999) François Ozon fait des histoires, *L'Humanité*, 19 August.

Ozon, F. (2000) François Ozon, *Cahiers du Cinema*, 542: 126.

Ozon, F. (2003) François Ozon, interview from *Swimming Pool* press kit, www.François-ozon.com/anglais/ozon.entretiens03html.

Parkes, C.M. (1986) *Bereavement: Studies of Grief in Adult Life*, 2nd edn. Madison, CT: IUP.

Schiller, B.M. (2005) On the threshold of the creative imagination: *Swimming Pool* (2003), *International Journal of Psychoanalysis*, 86: 557–66.

Shine, C. (2005) The Witches of Corinth, *New York Review of Books*, 52(18): 13–14, 17 November. Reviews the book 'Truth and Consequences' by Alison Lurie.

Steiner, J. (1993) *Psychic Retreats: Pathological Organizations in Psychotic, Neurotic and Borderline Patients*. London: Routledge.

Widlocher, D. (2002) *Infantile Sexuality and Attachment*. New York: Other Press.

Young-Breuhl, E. (2003) Where do we fall when we fall in love? *Journal for the Psychoanalysis of Culture and Society*, 8: 279–88.

14

THREE SISTERS
Sibling knots in Bergman's *Cries and Whispers*[1]
Andrea Sabbadini

Viskningar och rop (*Cries and Whispers*) (Sweden, 1972)
Director: Ingmar Bergman
Distributor: New World Pictures

A father proudly shows a newly-born baby brother to his little 2-year-old girl, expecting her to rejoice. Instead, she asks: 'When will he die again?' Reporting this story, Anna Freud comments that children's jealousy should be taken seriously and attributes its origin to the relationship of the child to the mother: 'This wish for his brothers and sisters to be dead is thoroughly natural on the part of the child . . . An emotional conflict arises within him only when he realizes that his mother . . . demands that he give up these evil wishes, and even love [his siblings]. Here is the starting point of all the difficulties in the emotional relations among children within a family' (1930: 84–5).

With the exception of cursory references to 'sibling rivalry', psychoanalytic writings about brothers and sisters have been scanty, the main emphasis having been on the child's Oedipal relationship with parental figures. However, a number of recent publications (Bank and Kahn 1997; Volkan and Ast 1997; Mitchell 2000, 2003; Coles 2003, 2006) have given relationships among siblings a new prominence in our understanding of development. For instance, stressing the *lateral* relationships of siblings (and, later, of peers and affines) rather than the more conventional *vertical*, generational ones between children and parents, Mitchell challenges the psychogenesis of the Oedipal complex. 'In Freud's account,' she states, 'love and hate derive from the parental relationship and are subsequently transferred to siblings. I read these events the other way around: faced with a sibling, the child regresses to its wish for infantile unity with the mother; it is then that it finds the father in the way ... Feelings for siblings and peers cast their shadow over relations with parents' (2000: 23). While not necessarily sharing these rather extreme views, other authors also suggest that 'sibling relationships form a vital and lively part of the internal world and provide a blueprint in which an individual thinks about, creates and sustains relationships' (Silverstone 2006: 244).

With these psychoanalytic considerations in mind, let us now look at the 'treatment' of the relationship among sisters by Ingmar Bergman, a filmmaker especially sensitive to the minutest details of his characters' complex psychologies; here, in the devastatingly painful soul-searching description of their conflicting longings, frustrations, hopes and guilt, we discover the power of great cinema.[2]

Three sisters, like on Anton Chekhov's stage and Woody Allen's set, dominate the screen of *Cries and Whispers*, one of Bergman's masterpieces. This film is a powerful exploration of one of those deep-rooted family knots where love is inextricably (con)fused with cruelty, and neediness with anguish. The Swedish director's women – Agnes, Karin and Maria, and the wonderful actors playing them – Harriet Andersson, Ingrid Thulin and Liv Ullmann, respectively – are entrapped inside an even bleaker universe of suffering, emotional no less than physical, than that of either the Russian playwright or the New York comedian.

The sisters' agonizing pains – their cries and their whispers,[3] no less than their secrets and their lies – are inside them. Agnes' body is devastated by the cancer from which she is dying. Maria's mind is troubled by her neurotic compulsion to manipulate and exploit those nearest to her for her own selfish gratification. Karin's disordered personality is affected by such a paralysing coldness of heart that it deprives her of any capacity for humane gestures or words of comfort, a 'kind of rigid inflexibility and aversion to intimacy that can only come from being irreparably emotionally wounded' (Berardinelli 2002). Their dramas unfold within their family home, the luxurious version of a Vermeer interior, with its closely observed everyday-life little objects, such as the *memento mori* of a gilded clock on which the camera enjoys resting its eye. As the narrative unfolds, this mansion, no longer large enough to contain the sisters' suffering, fills itself with the sort of memories that make it almost claustrophobically suffocating. What allows us, the film spectators, to survive the experience of watching these women's agony being dissected in front of our eyes is the messianic function of the mother-earthly housekeeper, Anna (Kari Sylwan). This fourth woman, by reminding us of humankind's potential for compassion, comes to rescue us with her faith when our despair has almost reached the edge of the precipice.

In contrast to Anna, the sisters are sick, though each in different compartments of their selves. If their personalities are too complex to fit into easy

Karin (Ingrid Thulin), Anna (Kari Sylwan) and Maria (Liv Ullmann)

pathological categories, our analytical understanding of psychological problems still entitles us to suspect that they, while remaining responsible for their present circumstances, are also likely to have been the victims during childhood of considerable emotional, if not also physical, abuse. Bergman only hints at a few details about their upbringing; but the fact, for instance, that nothing at all is revealed about their father suggests that he was as absent from the girls' early life as he is from the film, and this fact alone must be of great importance. Bruce Sklarew (1987) convincingly argues that, in this film, 'Bergman reveals how difficult it is for each sister to establish intimacy, a cohesive self, and mature feminine identity *because of preoedipal struggles* to survive an inconsistent, narcissistic mother' (p. 169, my emphasis). I would add that unresolved Oedipal issues must also have played a significant role, as indicated by the sisters' problems in establishing and sustaining satisfactory relationships with their husbands and with each other, free from severely neurotic, perverse, reparatory or conflictual connotations.

We watch them interact with one another at the dramatic juncture in their lives – that of Agnes' last days on earth – on which Bergman focuses his slowly-moving camera, transformed into a magnifying lens for the observation of the human soul. This cinematic scrutiny is not, as it may at first appear, a morbidly voyeuristic or even sadistic operation, but the documentaristic (if also dreamlike and lyrical) equivalent of our own psychoanalytic work of uncovering the uncomfortable truths buried inside our patients' unconscious – not to cause them unnecessary suffering, embarrassment or guilt, but to help them come to terms with themselves. Some filmmakers, Bergman *in primis*, may be keen to distance themselves from psychoanalysis; yet, the sincerity and depth of their explorations of unreachable corners of the human mind have much in common with our own analytic endeavours.

Occasionally, even Karin and Maria can show genuine affection, for instance when they wash Agnes, change her nightshirt, comb her hair, read to her from a novel. But to truly emerge from their emotionally deprived selves, sisters Karin and Maria would have to develop a capacity to accept themselves and others, and to experience empathy for their predicaments, as Anna does. It is indeed in their final insensitivity to the maid who for 12 years has cared for Agnes, better than they could have ever done themselves, that Karin and Maria, together with their husbands, show the worst side of their characters, dismissing her with hardly a word of thanks. An important ingredient in what makes us all human, the capacity to feel gratitude, is missing in them, and one wonders if anybody – a friend, a therapist or a pastor (such as Bergman's own father, a Lutheran minister) – could ever break through their indifference and reach their hearts. For them life, as Karin exclaims several times, 'is nothing but a tissue of lies'. Nor is there much hope that the death of their sister would represent one of those epiphanic events that could transform their existences. Their bitterness and cynicism, as they become evident in the second half of

Agnes (Harriett Andersson)

the film, are far too deeply embedded in their souls to allow them to experience true grief for their loss. The only tangible manifestation that Maria and Karin are undergoing a process of mourning at all can perhaps be found in their attempt, aborted but nevertheless significant, to relate differently to one another and to overcome what must be their long-standing and extreme form of sibling rivalry.

Because of the narrative centre-stage position of Agnes' overwhelming distress and her eventual passing away, two other losses in the film risk going almost unnoticed; yet their psychological function is important to our understanding of some of the existential, personal and interpersonal dynamics of all the main *dramatis personae*. The first one is the death of a child, Anna's daughter. We learn about it early in the film when we are shown the housekeeper praying to the Lord to have angels guard her little girl in the heavens, as the camera focuses on a photograph of the two of them together. Later we meet this child herself, in a flashback sequence, when we are introduced to the doctor who is visiting the sisters' home to care for the sick young girl. We could suggest that such a traumatic loss as that of a child may have contributed to Anna's sensitivity to Agnes' suffering, as if by helping and comforting her charge she could also, through the unconscious mechanism of displacement, still be of help and comfort to her own deceased girl. The other crucial loss in *Cries and Whispers* is that of the sisters' mother, described as a beautiful, narcissistic woman, dead for 20 years but still in Agnes' thoughts 'almost every day' even if 'she could be cold and playfully cruel'. We meet her in a flashback scene when Agnes, as a child, usually feeling left out and jealous of her mother's favourite Maria (a point emphasized by the fact that both are played by the same actress, Liv Ullmann), remembers a rare occasion when she was, for once, accepted rather than scolded. 'I almost burst into tears,' Agnes recalls. 'I put my hand to her cheek. We were very close at that moment.' I may add that, in that memory, it is Agnes who ends up comforting her mother once she notices her sorrowful look. Here, their functions are reversed, with Agnes mothering her own mother: a situation we frequently come across in our work with analysands who were neglected as children.

I will now offer a few words about the intense sensual connotations of *Cries and Whispers*, not surprisingly perhaps in an *auteur* so influenced by Ibsen's and Strindberg's dramas, and most specifically by their austerely Nordic version of the Romantic association of death with sexuality. The screen, far from being silver, is dotted here with moving black or white images in a crimson interior environment. Red, the colour of passion, sin and blood, but also a colour which, as Bergman stated, 'represents for me the interior of the soul', seems to flood everything, sparing only a few brief, more peaceful scenes in the garden. On this crimson background, erotically-charged scenes abound, such as Maria's artful seduction of the doctor, who is weak, as are all the other men in the film: the first time (in flashback) when he comes to treat

Anna's dying child, and again a few years later when his patient is Agnes, dying in the bedroom next door. Infused with sensuality is also the sequence when Anna, responding to Agnes' panicked request for physical closeness to assuage her suffering, offers her the only form of human contact which could still give the dying woman some relief. We watch Anna unbutton her night-dress, caress and kiss Agnes, talk reassuringly to her, and gently guide Agnes's face, no longer twisted now with pain and fear, on her generous naked breasts. As she holds her there for a long quiet moment, Anna almost looks like a *mater dolorosa* in a Renaissance statue of the *pietà*. In contrast, following the long ceremony of Karin's undressing for the night and getting into bedclothes with Anna's help, we are presented with the shockingly erotic violence of Karin's deliberate self-harming gesture of inserting a shard of wine glass between her legs. Her initial masochistically ecstatic reaction to pain is complemented by her grotesquely spiteful grin of sadistic satisfaction as she smears blood from her genitals over her mouth in front of her bewildered husband.[4]

Perhaps more intensely sensual than all, if less manifestly so, are those instances in the days following Agnes' death, inhibited but not for that reason less intimate, when Maria tries to find access to her sister Karin's heart through physical contact with her body. In those touching (in both meanings of the word) moments when they attempt to discover a sense of closeness between them — responding to a longing which must exist somewhere in the depth of their beings, yet remains seemingly inaccessible — we watch them struggle with their feelings, from hatred to tenderness, from greed to suicidal rage, and hurt themselves in the process no less than they torture each other. Here are some extracts from those excruciating scenes, with Ullmann and Thulin shot in merciless close-ups, mostly on a red background.

Maria asks, 'Karin, why won't you be my friend? . . . We could embrace each other . . . Karin, couldn't we use these days in getting to know one another? Karin! I can't stand distance and silence . . .' Karin gets up and walks away from her. Maria follows her towards the door, tries to reach her, pleads with her: 'Have I said something to hurt you?' As Karin doesn't answer her and goes next door to read from Agnes' diary, Maria approaches her again and tries to caress her sister's face. Karin turns away and screams at her (with as much anguish as anger in her voice): 'Don't touch me! Don't come near me. I hate any sort of contact!' Then she seems to allow Maria to get closer, to hug, stroke and nearly kiss her . . . though at the same time Karin also begs her not to be kind to her. Then, suddenly, she burst into tears and turns her face to the wall; as she turns around again towards Maria, overwhelmed by her own inner conflicts, she cries (or are they whispers?): 'I can't! I can't! It's constant misery and torment, it's like in hell. I can't breathe any more because of the guilt . . . Leave me alone! Don't touch me!'

Later Karin, having hurt her sister again with hateful, unforgiving words in a scene around the dinner table, apologizes: 'Maria, forgive me. Perhaps you mean well. Perhaps you just want to get to know me . . .', and we see them for the first time touch and embrace and caress each other with what appears to be true reciprocal warmth. They even smile at each other for a moment, and talk – their words now inaudible to us as they are covered by the sombre notes of Bach's Saraband for cello.

Later yet, as they part after Agnes's funeral and abandon their house, Karin, the older sister who was throughout the film the harsher of the two, tells Maria: 'You touched me. Remember?', hoping perhaps for a final reconciliation. But Maria retorts, cold as ice: 'I can't remember every silly thing, or be made to answer for them.'

As the end-titles of Bergman's drama run across the screen and the projector finally switches off, the cinema still for a minute in the dark, we are left meditating on our own existential condition of ultimate solitude, and wondering whether any brothers or sisters will ever come to our recue . . . By then the last cries and whispers have become almost inaudible.

Notes

1 A shorter version of this chapter has been previously published in *Projections 51*, 16(3): 58–63 (2006).
2 Of the countless films centered around sibling relationships, and also relevant to a psychoanalytic discourse, I shall limit myself to mention Hitchcock's *The Shadow of a Doubt* (1943), Siodmak's *Dark Mirror* (1946), Visconti's *Rocco and His Brothers* (1960), Truffaut's *Anne and Muriel* (1971), Allen's *Hannah and Her Sisters* (1986) and Levinson's *Rain Man* (1988).
3 'The "cries" for help express the yearning for closeness and attachment, for intimacy. The "whispers" are the torment of the frustrated longings, the hovering unattainable fulfillment' (Sklarew 1987: 175).
4 A similar scene can be found in Michael Haneke's *La pianiste* (*The Piano Teacher*) (2001), where the sexually repressed musician Erika (Isabelle Huppert) inserts a razor blade inside her vagina.

References

Bank, S.P. and Kahn, M.D. (1997) *The Sibling Bond*. New York: Basic Books.
Berardinelli, J. (2002) Review: *Cries and Whispers*, http://movie-reviews.colossus.net.
Coles, P. (2003) *The Importance of Sibling Relationships in Psychoanalysis*. London: Karnac.
Coles, P. (ed) (2006) *Sibling Relationships*. London: Karnac.
Freud, A. (1930) Four lectures on psychoanalysis for teachers and parents, in *Introduction to Psychoanalysis, 1922–1935*. London: Hogarth Press, 1974.
Mitchell, J. (2000) *Mad Men and Medusas. Reclaiming Hysteria and the Effects of Sibling Relations on the Human Condition*. Harmondsworth: Penguin.
Mitchell, J. (2003) *Siblings: Sex and Violence*. Oxford: Polity.
Silverstone, J. (2006) Siblings, in P. Coles (ed.) *Sibling Relationships*. London: Karnac.

Sklarew, B.H. (1987) Ingmar Bergman's *Cries and Whispers*: the consequences of pre-oedipal developmental disturbances, in J.H. Smith and W. Kerrigan (eds) *Images in Our Souls: Cavell, Psychoanalysis, and Cinema*. Baltimore, MD: Johns Hopkins University Press.

Volkan, V.A. and Ast, G. (1997) *Siblings in the Unconscious and Psychopathology*. New York: International Universities Press.

15

TIME REGAINED
The complex magic of reverse motion
Ian Christie

> What, then, is time? If no one asks me, I know; if I wish to explain it to one who asks, I know not.
>
> St. Augustine (*Confessions*, XI, xiv)

Reverse motion – action seeming to run backwards in time – is probably the most magical of all filmic devices. Like slowed or accelerated motion, and time-lapse photography, it exploits film's sequential structure. But unlike these, it offers a spectacle which is 'impossible', yet wholly realistic. The demolished wall that miraculously rebuilds itself, the diver who rises from the water to regain precisely the end of the diving board – no matter that we know how easy the effect is to achieve, by simply running the filmstrip backwards, the experience remains in some sense magical.

Of course the larger fact of moving, or as they were often known, 'living' pictures was also magical for the first spectators, as accounts from the 1890s attest.[1] But if the first successful moving picture demonstrations of Edison, Lumière and Paul impressed by their lifelike recording of normal movement, almost immediately viewers were equally intrigued by the *ab*normal movement of reverse motion. There are reliable accounts of at least one early Lumière film being run backwards as well as forwards.[2] *Demolition of a Wall* may have been the most popular choice for this treatment because its subject – workmen under the supervision of Auguste Lumière knocking down the remains of a stone wall – produced the specific effect of chaos seeming to revert to order. Some early posters announcing film programmes advertised that certain subjects would be 'reversed', indicating that this was an established attraction by 1896–7; and around 1900 there is a variation on Lumière's *Train*

Arriving at the Station, in which the action of the first part, a crowded platform with passengers colliding, is reversed in the second half of the film, so that all the events already seen unroll backwards, making the film an exact palindrome.[3]

However, this use of reverse motion had become rare by 1900 and the reverse filming that continued to be used by the makers of trick films up to about 1908 was usually 'disguised'.[4] When a structure of children's nursery bricks appears to 'jump up' by means of reversal in Pathé's *Japonaiserie* (Velle, 1904), this was intended to be 'magical' in the context of a performance carried out by two oriental conjurors.[5] A special case would be the popular multi-part 'life of Christ' series, in which reverse motion was used to portray miracles. Otherwise, stage-based trick films, in which the familiar logic of causality and continuity is confounded, would themselves become unfashionable after 1908, as cinema began to leave its novelty phase and veer emphatically towards extended spectacle and narrative.

Virginia Woolf recalled this early period in a 1926 essay on cinema, suggesting that philosophers who proclaim the 'fag-end of civilization' have forgotten 'the savages of the twentieth century watching the pictures'. Woolf's position is both complex and ambivalent. She evokes the seemingly simple early art of cinema, with its actualities of the king shaking hands with a football team and other sporting events, only to suggest that such images 'have taken on a quality which does not belong to the simple photograph of real life', and to find in these an eerie record of 'life as it is when we have no part in it'.[6] Woolf's critique of the cinema of realist narrative and literary adaptation aligned her with the European avant-gardes that were also calling for its liberation in order to become a medium capable of conveying 'visual emotion'. Some, like her, saw abstraction as the most promising direction, but might we not speculate that cinema had, in effect, repressed its infantile traits, including reversing and other disruptive tropes, in order to institutionalize its newly achieved 'reality effect'?

Part of the evidence for this would come from considering how the avant-garde filmmakers of Europe turned to such long-banished features of early cinema in order to challenge and disrupt the tranquil course of bourgeois realism. And reversing, when it reappeared, did not become exclusively associated with the left- or the right-leaning avant-gardes. One of the earliest examples occurs in Dziga Vertov's *Kino Eye* (*Kino glaz*, 1925), planned to promote his revolutionary use of cinema to 'decode' reality and exhort fellow Soviet citizens to greater zeal. Here, in a sequence devoted to healthy recreation contrasted with the plight of drinkers and antisocial elements, a diver rises gracefully out of the water onto a diving board – as if to suggest that the new Soviet man or woman could achieve the seemingly impossible.[7] Later, in another manifesto film, *Man with a Movie Camera* (1929), Vertov would again interrupt the transparency of filmic representation in a sequence that shows the image being 'frozen', then strips of film being selected for editing, and finally their images set in motion again after they have 'joined' the film proper.

Vertov's contemporary and rival within the first generation of Soviet filmmakers, Sergei Eisenstein, would initially eschew reverse motion, using instead rhythmic editing and startling juxtapositions of subject and scale in *The Strike* (1925) and in his breakthrough film *The Battleship Potemkin* (1926). But as his interest in the syntax and structure of cinema deepened, he included a spectacular reverse motion sequence in *October* (1928), a commemorative film commissioned to mark the tenth anniversary of the Bolshevik revolution. Early in the film, a giant statue of the enthroned tsar, Alexander III, is shown being dismembered by insurgent workers; then later, as the fate of the revolutionary process hangs in the balance, between February and October, the same statue is seen apparently reassembling itself, with throne, limbs and crowned head all returning to their former seamless unity. Rarely, if ever, has reverse motion been used as tellingly for ideological purposes, posing the counterfactual possibility of restoration, while also creating a visual metaphor for the 'reversal' of the revolution. To underline further its significance, Eisenstein envisaged carrying the same procedure into the accompanying score, asking his composer, Edmund Meisel, to write the music for the original scene in reverse for this sequence.[8]

Within the context of a film devoted to exploring the meaning of revolution on a symbolic as well as a political level, Eisenstein had found a remarkable use for reverse motion as a 'device', in the sense proposed by formalist critics such as Viktor Shklovsky.[9] One of Shklovsky's favourite examples of literary devices 'laid bare' was the range of unusual typographic features included in Lawrence Sterne's novel *Tristram Shandy* (1759–66), where two completely black pages mark the death of a character, a serpentine squiggle represents another's gesture with a stick and five diagrammatic lines condense the narratives followed in each volumes, complete with digressions. *October* offers a similarly Shandean gamut of devices that rupture its realist chronicle of 1917, to which the visual simile of statue belongs, suggesting not only the fragility of the February Revolution, but perhaps also that what had been achieved by deposing Tsar Nicholas could be as easily repaired as a child's toy, unless Kerensky's regime was replaced by the Bolsheviks.

The avant-gardism of *October* disconcerted many who had expected a reverent commemoration of the Revolution, but reverse motion continued to play a limited role within avowed avant-garde films of the 1920s until Jean Cocteau used it extensively in *The Blood of a Poet* (*Le Sang d'un Poète*) (1930). Cocteau (1889–63) was already famously versatile as a poet, novelist, dramatist and painter before he turned to cinema, to make the first of four widely-spaced feature-length films. Three of these offer allegories of the poet's life

The Blood of a Poet

and vocation, and in all of them Cocteau gave full rein to his delight in cinema's primitive magic as a means of astonishing the audience.

In *The Blood of a Poet* he used sets built in false perspective combined with reverse filming in slow motion to create a dreamlike state. In the episode 'Do Walls Have Ears?' Cocteau's alter ego, the poet (played by Enrique Rivero), witnesses a series of bizarre tableaux through the keyholes of rooms while seeming to float along a corridor. The keyhole device was another trope associated with early cinema, having been used to connect a series of tableaux in such films as Pathé's *Scenes on Every Floor* (1904) and Hepworth's *The Inquisitive Boots* (1905), and its use by Cocteau formed part of the widespread return to anti-naturalistic devices and 'primitive' forms by the avant-garde filmmakers of the 1920s. René Clair and Francis Picabia's *Entr'acte* (1924) used both fast and slow motion as well as the slapstick chase form; while Fernand Léger and Dudley Murphy's *Le Ballet Mécanique* (1924) includes among its many kaleidoscopic editing effects a shot of an elderly washerwoman climbing stairs which is repeated so often, joined with an 'invisible' edit, that it becomes not only an ironic modernized image of Sysiphus, the mythological figure condemned to carry his burden eternally, but also a modernist sculptural object – equivalent in its repetition of seemingly banal elements to Constantin Brancusi's 'Endless Column' series (1926–38). (By contrast, Luis Buñuel and Salvador Dali's *Un Chien Andalou* relies mostly on 'irrational' matching of disparate images, with some use of slow motion, to achieve its celebrated evocation of dreams' disconcerting illogicality.)

Among these, however, only *Le Sang d'un Poète* makes extensive use of reverse motion and this seems to be closely linked with Cocteau's personal mythology of the poet as an archaic figure in the modern world, invested with supernatural powers which are in effect made visible by means of 'magical' filmic effects. In the corridor sequence, as in Cocteau's later films *Orphée* (1950) and *Le Testament d'Orphée* (1960) the actor must perform so that his actions will appear relatively normal when shown 'forward' – in effect 'acting in reverse' to produce a subtly unrealistic effect when finally projected on the screen.

In his farewell to cinema, *Le Testament d'Orphée*, Cocteau himself appears as the poet being called to account for his life, and making very deliberate use of reverse and stop motion effects. One of these shows a flower being 'reassembled' petal by petal (after its destruction had no doubt been filmed with the camera upside down) in a virtuoso display of cinema's long-banished power of enchantment – a gesture that may also have been encouraged by the formal experimentation that had been unleashed by the French *nouvelle vague* at the turn of the decade, following the release of Alain Resnais' *Hiroshima mon Amour* (1959) and *L'Année dernière à Marienbad* (1961).

Le Testament d'Orphée

Time regained

Both of these films contributed to a new sense of the plasticity of time in cinema: the one by allowing a repressed past, which focused on a forbidden love affair between a French girl and a German soldier, to erupt in jagged flashbacks into the present of another affair in contemporary Hiroshima; and the other by creating a 'hypothetical' past which is evoked in a dreamlike spa hotel where time seems almost to stand still. However, in spite of Resnais' and others' continued experimentation with the representation of filmic time during the 1960s, actual reverse motion would scarcely reappear until Elem Klimov used it for the climax of his harrowing recreation of the German invasion of Belorussia in *Come and See* (1985). This film follows a young boy who sees his village sacked by the invading German army, and who joins the partisans in the forest, witnessing a seemingly endless catalogue of brutality and sadism. In a partisan counter-attack, he confronts a German soldier begging for mercy, at which point the films enters a kind of fugue, with rapidly cut images of German twentieth-century history running backwards towards the figure of Hitler as a youth and ultimately a baby.

The traumatized youth finds he cannot shoot, although his prematurely aged face is almost paralysed by the accumulation of horror he has seen. Here reverse motion serves an altogether more 'serious' purpose than in any film since *October*. Indeed, it has to bear much of the weight of our exposure to an

Come and See

unparalleled display of savagery on the part of the invading German army – as if asking us whether the history that led to Hitler and the invasion of Russia could have been different. Or whether we can attribute all the blame for the Nazi terror to this Adolf Hitler, who was once an innocent baby. The film offers no unequivocal interpretation of its most surprising trope – except that this rupture in an otherwise relentlessly first-person adoption of the boy's point of view is precisely a break, a way of stepping outside the brutal causality of his limited perception of this corner of the war. It may be worth noting a parallel, and equally rare, use of reverse narration in literary fiction. Martin Amis' novel *Time's Arrow* also deals with the brutality of the Nazi regime, narrating first the later life in America of Dr Tod T. Friendly, which turns out to be the afterlife of a German who was a doctor in Auschwitz.[10] Here, as in Klimov's film, the shock value of reverse narration seems to be an attempt to counteract conventional responses to the numbingly familiar narrative of the concentration camp.[11] While both of these instances are clearly motivated in the first instance by an urgent desire to 'refresh' perception of the otherwise unbearable, what remains unclear is whether the authors also intend a more fundamental reflection on historical causality – on the contingency of the Nazi catastrophe.

At a simple perceptual level, filmic reverse motion produces a paradoxical sense of inevitability: the wall and the diver both rise, defying gravity, *because they have already fallen*. Does this sense of inevitability transfer to the use of reverse narration on a larger scale, when a story is told 'backwards' from its ending? The most common instances of this are probably fictional narratives cast in the form of memoirs or letters, which are 'introduced' by their authors in the guise of chroniclers – as in the opening of R.L. Stevenson's *Treasure Island*.[12] Here, the narrative's conclusion may serve as its point of departure, even if the rest of the story follows normal chronology. Similarly, much detective and crime fiction starts from the aftermath of a crime and effectively consists of a reconstruction of what led up to that event, creating a double movement of discovery and revelation. Films based on such fiction may also begin with the crime or its discovery, towards which the rest of the narrative will 'return', while typically maintaining normal chronology in what has come to be known as a 'flashback'.

But what of films that eschew such conventions and use reverse narration throughout? Three European examples will serve to demonstrate why this remains a rare and disconcerting strategy, but also one that offers an intriguing counterpoint to the normal experience of narrative.[13] *Betrayal* (David Jones, 1983) and *5 × 2* (François Ozon, 2004) both narrate the history of a relationship from its collapse to its beginning. David Jones' film derives from Harold Pinter's earlier play and tells the story of an extramarital affair between two worldly middle-class Londoners, Emma and Jerry (Patricia Hodge and Jeremy Irons), backwards from its delayed consequence, the break-up of Emma's marriage to Robert (Ben Kingsley), to the lovers' first attraction at a party some seven years earlier. In a series of scenes that are each dated in relation to the preceding one ('one year earlier', etc.), the pair move from recrimination and disenchantment 'back' to the shared excitement of the shabby flat where they meet after their affair begins.[14] The trajectory of François Ozon's film is similar, opening with the divorce of Marion (Valeria Bruni Tedeschi) and Gilles (Stéphane Freiss) which is followed by a near-rape as the pair make love for the last time. Subsequently, four sequences cover a late stage in their disintegrating relationship, the birth of their child, their wedding and their first meeting while on holiday in Italy.

What these have in common, despite their very different milieux, is the effect of making us increasingly conflicted spectators of the relationships. Knowing the indifference and the rage respectively in which they have ended inevitably colours our engagement with the earlier (but for us later) scenes of attraction and seduction. In *Betrayal*, where the relationship is clandestine and carried on under the nose of Emma's husband, Robert, who publishes one of Jerry's clients, we are drawn into the subterfuge of concealment even after we know that the husband already knows about the affair. Somewhat like the audience of a classic *film noir* such as *Double Indemnity*, we know from the start that these relationships are doomed to failure.[15] All of the main characters, except perhaps the wife in *5 × 2*, have behaved badly at some point, have lied or misrepresented their true feelings. As we watch the start of their relationships we 'know' enough to be judgemental; whereas at the outset of our acquaintance with them we know too little to understand why things have reached such a painful conclusion.

Two related questions arise at this point. First, is this how I would describe a more conventionally narrated film about the disintegration of a relationship, a film such as the epic *Scenes from a Marriage* (Ingmar Bergman, 1973)? And is my account of *Betrayal* and *5 × 2* being skewed by the psychoanalytic context of writing? If I answer both in the negative, this may clarify why reverse narration seems to offer an experience of some analytic interest. We cannot, I suggest, simply describe 'what happens' in these films, but must necessarily describe *how* we experience them and how they set up a kind of narrative-emotional dissonance within the normal viewing process. The fact that one is a richly-written story of highly articulate people, making full use of Pinter's ability to convey menace and fear beneath banality, and the other in part a story of non-communication, is less important than the realization that both films offer a disconcerting encounter with narrative and causality. As with reverse motion, our familiar expectations are challenged. With reverse narration, we know both too little and then too much about the characters and their relationships, having been granted an 'impossible' perspective.

And of course these narratives have been constructed deliberately to run in reverse.[16] We sense that they are offered as exemplary, or tutelary: through

5 × 2

them we understand, if only by analogy, what it would be like to know the future – to foresee the consequences of casual actions and chance encounters. Another way of describing this might be in terms of the analyst's experience of what patients present. Any film can convey a sense of control over the flux of events, as a life is compressed into a brief span of screen time. But in reverse narration, the magical quality of this overview is emphasized: we feel a sense of *omnipotence* as outcomes are traced back to their sources, as the very process of diagnosis or interpretation is dramatized.

Two further recent examples of reverse narration and motion demand consideration, since these demonstrate that the trope is far from exhausted in its capacity to disturb the conventional equilibrium of fiction cinema. Gaspar Noé's *Irréversible* (France, 2002) was a highly controversial film for reasons other than its structure, which tells a confusing and deeply shocking story of rape and bloody revenge in contemporary Paris in reverse order. It starts, therefore, with the aftermath of a savage fight in a gay nightclub, and proceeds back through the events that led to this assault, as a woman's boyfriend (Vincent Cassel) seeks to avenge her brutal rape in a subway; and only towards the end of the film do we discover that Alex (Monica Bellucci) is in fact pregnant and looking forward to the birth of her child. Much of the controversy surrounding the film was generated by its use of a hand-held camera moving violently in close-up and low light in the opening scenes, and also by the almost unbearably extended rape, shot with an icily detached static camera. Reverse narrative seemed to many a gratuitous addition, giving the film an intellectual alibi for its shock tactics.

For others, however, including this writer, the structure is a vital part of the film's assault on the very voyeurism that lies at the heart of the cinema experience. We cannot sympathize with or vicariously enjoy Marcus' (Vincent Cassel) revenge because we don't understand what is happening at this stage of the narrative. Likewise, our pain and embarrassment at being forced to witness Bellucci's sadistic rape gives way to sympathy and pity as we move 'back' to her unsuspecting life before the attack. In the simplest terms, Noé is engaged in intensifying our perception of what cinema often cosmeticizes; and in refreshing the sense of contingency that traditional narrative cannot help but subordinate to its causal patterning. Beyond this, the film's title, together with an epigraph – 'time destroys everything' – and a brief allusion to a 1920s book *An Experiment With Time*, suggest that Noé wants to engage us in thinking about cinema itself as an apparatus that can 'reverse' time, or create the illusion of doing so.[17] If the film begins as an assault on the audience, then its movement back towards a serene Edenic image of Bellucci

Irréversible

is experienced as therapeutic – a startling postmodern version of catharsis that purges us of the night's horrors.[18]

Equally challenging, though to less immediately visceral effect, is the use of reverse motion in Michael Haneke's *Caché* (*Hidden*) (2005), already hailed as one of the most profoundly unsettling films of recent years. Its first appearance comes when a shot of a quiet street in Paris is suddenly disturbed, then runs backwards – thus revealing that it is in fact a videotape, which we discover is being watched by the film's central characters, a fashionable couple who work in television and the media. Surveillance cameras and monitors have become increasingly common in films during recent decades, all offering the possibility of 'time revisited' within a present narrative, but here the lack of any apparatus or indeed visible agency in the stalking of Georges and Anne gives the exterior image of their house, which they watch within, a veritable edge of metaphysical dread. As in Haneke's earlier work, notably *Funny Games* (1997; being remade in 2006) and *La Pianiste* (*The Piano Teacher*) (2001), the extreme unease verging on terror suffered by the characters is conveyed to the spectator by avoiding any 'framing' effect of distanciation; so that in *Caché*, we experience some of the couple's shock when the tranquil, unexplained image we are watching suddenly reveals its instability by going into fast-forward and backward mode.

From this early point onwards, as we follow Georges' own hesitant self-examination, struggling with the childhood memory of cruelty towards an

Caché

Arab boy that he has repressed, we experience a more or less constant uncertainty as to the *status* of the images we are watching. Are they first-order narrative, memory or fantasy, or possibly the creation of an unseen second narrator? By the end of the film, and especially in its enigmatic final sequence, we have irretrievably lost any security of point of view; and the malleability of the video image, here incorporated full-frame into the film's own image discourse, plays a vital part in this destabilization, making *Caché* not only a disturbing exposé of French attitudes towards its former colonial peoples, but a more profound meditation on bad faith and anxiety in the age of omnipresent media surveillance.

This chapter has examined a number of purposeful uses of reverse motion and reverse narration which suggest that these remain potent devices within the expressive resources of cinema, even if they remain marginal – and even subversive of cinema's underlying 'reality effect'.[19] Can we perhaps look to psychoanalysis for help with theorizing these devices and their affective power? One possible line of exploration would look to D.W. Winnicott's (1971) account of play as a basis for considering the 'infantile' or ludic aspect of, at least, reverse motion. If this always declares the filmmaker's wish to undermine or interrupt operational realism, then it may also be considered a denial of cinema's foundational 'reality principle' – and as such it may function in the cases we have noted as a kind of reverse 'transitional object', linking the normal reality of cinema back to its magical origins as a machine for simulating life. In this sense, its intrinsic *playfulness* can also be related to Winnicott's more general account of creativity arising from the early experience of play.[20] But we might also go back to Freud's discussion of magic and omnipotence in *Totem and Taboo* (1913) and later in 'The "Uncanny"' (1919), and explain what I have described as the conflicted pleasure of 'reversing' (we '*know* it is not real') as a reminder of the animism of cinema's infancy, or primitive period – yet another 'return of the (incompletely) repressed'. In the dawning age of widespread digital recording and storage, with its near-unlimited potential to recall and reconfigure the past, might we not expect that 'time's arrow' will be as often reversed as aimed forward, to create new ways of engaging our senses of simultaneity, connection and causation? We have hardly begun to come to terms with the implications of digitality being inherently non-linear and 'non-directional'.

Notes

1 For a selection of early reactions, see Harding and Popple, (eds) (1996) Chapter 1.
2 *The Demolition of a Wall* (*L'Ecroulement d'un mur*) shown forwards and then backwards was described in 1896 in a text quoted by Jacques and Marie André (1987) as 'a marvel of photography and of cinematography' (p. 85).

3 This film, otherwise unidentified but apparently French and probably by Pathé, was discovered during research for the BBC television series *The Last Machine* and included in the first programme, *The Time and Space Machine*. See Christie (1994: 32).
4 Filmmakers could shoot in reverse by turning the camera upside down, so that when the resulting film is shown normally it runs backwards – an easier practice before the filmstrip became asymmetrical with the addition of a soundtrack area.
5 The film was known in English as *Magic Bricks* and appears on the British Film Institute video compilation, *Early Cinema*. For a description, see Hammond (1981).
6 For a discussion of how cinema may have helped to shape Woolf's own writing of fiction, see Trotter (2005).
7 Also to advance Vertov's programme of demystifying cinema and revealing how its effects are achieved, as he would do in *Man with a Movie Camera* (1929).
8 In his posthumous memoirs, Eisenstein (1995: 545–6) explained how the sequence was filmed and confirmed its intended meaning, noting that reverse filming is always effective, 'as in the old comic films'.
9 Viktor Shklovsky (1893–1984) was the leading theorist of the Russian 'formalist' school of literary theory, which flourished between c.1915–28, after which it fell into official disfavour. In his book, *The Theory of Prose* (1925), Shklovsky devoted one chapter to *Tristram Shandy*, under the title, 'The Novel as Parody'. Arguing that it is 'the most typical novel in the world', he delighted in Sterne's literal use of graphic and other devices – so that the novel is, in effect, about its own construction and a parody of naturalistic novels.
10 As well as telling Tod/Odilo's life backwards from death to birth, Amis tries to reproduce the effect of reverse motion minutely in the text – as in, for instance, 'He jumped the queue at the ticket counter – his stub realised $18 – but he went on standing in line' (1991: 75); or 'picture me now in the operating theatre . . . spooning tumour into the human body' (p. 99).
11 In an afterword, Amis explains how he brought together the idea of 'telling the story of a man's life backwards in time' with both historical material and memoir literature on the camps.
12 Stevenson writes as the character Jim Hawkins: 'Squire Trelawney, Dr Livesey and the rest of these gentlemen having asked me to write down the whole particulars about Treasure Island . . . I take up my pen.'
13 Outside European cinema, the most notable examples of reverse narrative have been *Memento* (Nolan, 2000) and *Eternal Sunshine of the Spotless Mind* (Gondry, 2004) – the former a crime mystery with a hero suffering from long-term memory loss as its premise, and the latter a variation on the screwball romantic comedy, with a 'memory-removal' device to justify its temporal fragmentation.
14 The film's chronology is not actually linear, but opens with three scenes in 'forward' chronology after the marriage break-up, covering relations between Emma and Jerry and Jerry and Robert, before it moves into reverse chronology, although with another 'forward' scene after Emma's confession to Robert in Venice.
15 In *Double Indemnity* (1944), directed by Billy Wilder from a screenplay he co-wrote with Raymond Chandler from a James Cain story, the deceived lover dictates his story as a confession while already mortally wounded.
16 *Double Indemnity* was re-cast in extended flashback form during scripting; and Wilder went on to use an 'impossible' version of the voice-over/flashback form in *Sunset Boulevard* (1950), which is narrated by its dead protagonist.
17 *An Experiment with Time* (1927) by J.W. Dunne was a best-seller which promoted the idea of 'precognition' in an apparently scientific manner. Dunne, an aircraft

designer, proposed on the basis of his own dream diaries that anticipating future events was possible, arguing that time was, literally, a fourth dimension. On Dunne's place in English 'time culture', see Christie (2000: 27–8).
18 It may be significant that the narrative of *Irreversible* take place over 24 hours, recalling the unity of classical Greek drama, from which the theory of *katharsis* was derived by Aristotle.
19 On the cinema's 'impression of reality', see especially Metz (1974), Chs. 6 and 7, pp. 101–19.
20 See 'The location of cultural experience' in Winnicott (1971: Ch. 7).

References

Amis, M. (1991) *Time's Arrow, or The Nature of the Offence*. London: Vintage, 2003.
André, J. and André, M. (1987) *Une Saison Lumière à Montpellier*. Perpignan: Institut Jean Vigo.
Christie, I. (1994) *The Last Machine: Early Cinema and the Birth of the Modern World*. London: BBC/British Film Institute.
Christie, I. (2000) *A Matter of Life and Death*. London: BFI Classics.
Dunne, J.W. (1927) *An Experiment with Time*. London: Faber, 1946.
Eisenstein, S. (1995) *Beyond the Stars: the Memoirs of Sergei Eisenstein*, ed. Richard Taylor, trans. William Powell. London: BFI Publishing/Seagull Books.
Freud, S. (1913) Totem and taboo, in *Standard Edition*, Vol. XIII. London: Hogarth Press, 1953.
Freud, S. (1919) 'The "uncanny" ', in *Standard Edition*, Vol. XVII. London: Hogarth Press, 1955.
Hammond, P. (1981) 'Georges, this is Charles', *Afterimage* (UK), Spring, 8–9: 39–48.
Harding, C. and Popple, S. (eds) (1996) *In the Kingdom of the Shadows: a Companion to Early Cinema*. London: Cygnus Arts.
Metz, C. (1974) *The Imaginary Signifier: Psychoanalysis and the Cinema*. Bloomington, IN: Indiana University Press, 1992.
Shklovsky, V. (1925) *The Theory of Prose*, trans. Benjamin Sher. Normal, IL: Dalkey Archive Press, 1990.
Trotter, D. (2005) Virginia Woolf and Cinema, *Film Studies: An International Review*, Summer, 6: 13–26.
Winnicott, D.W. (1971) *Playing and Reality*. Harmondsworth: Penguin, 1980.
Woolf, V. (1926) The Cinema, in V. Woolf (ed. Rachel Bowlby) *The Crowded Dance of Modern Life: Selected Essays*, Vol. 2. Harmondsworth: Penguin, 1993.

Films index

All About My Mother (Pedro Almodóvar, 1999) 66, 69
Anne and Muriel (François Truffaut, 1971) 166n1
L'Année dernière à Marienbad (Alain Resnais, 1961) 172–3

Bad Education (Pedro Almodóvar, 2004) 72
Le Ballet Mécanique (Fernand Léger and Dudley Murphy, 1924) 171
Battleship Potemkin (Sergei Eisenstein, 1925) 93, 95, 170
A Beautiful Mind (Ron Howard, 2001) 7
Belleville Rendez-Vous (The Triplets of Belleville) (Sylvain Chômet 2003) 132–44
Betrayal (David Jones, 1983) 173–4
The Blood of a Poet (Jean Cocteau, 1930) 170–1, 172
Broken Wings (Nir Bergman, 2002) 35–6

Caché (Michael Haneke, 2005) 178–9, *178*
Carnal Knowledge (Mike Nichols, 1971) 47
Un Chien Andalou (Luis Buñuel, 1928) xviii–xix, 3, 92–101, 172
Come and See (Elem Klimov, 1985) 173–4
Comment j'ai tué mon père (Anne Fontaine, 2001) 2, 6–18
Crash (David Cronenberg, 1996) 58, 98
Cries and Whispers (Ingmar Bergman, 1972) 2, 160–6

The Dark Mirror (Robert Siodmak, 1946) 166n2
Dead Man (Christian Petzold, 2001) 57

The Demolition of a Wall (Louis Lumière, 1896) 168, 179n2
The Diary of Anne Frank (George Stevens, 1959) 79
Donne Senza Nome (Géza Radványi, 1949) 79
Double Indemnity (Billy Wilder, 1944) 175, 180n15, n16

The Embalmer (Matteo Garrone, 2002) 47
Entr'acte (René Clair, 1924) 171
Eternal Sunshine of the Spotless Mind (Michel Gondry, 2004) 180n13

The Fall of the Romanov Dynasty (Esther Shub, 1927) 110
Fateless (Lajos Koltai, 2005) 85–8, 90n5
Father (István Szabó, 1966) 81–3
Fight Club (David Fincher, 1999) 7
First Love (Matteo Garrone, 2004) 3, 46–55
5 x 2 (François Ozon, 2004) 174–5, *176*
The Flight of the Eagle (Jan Troell, 1982) xix, 119–31
Free Fall (Péter Forgács, 1996) 83–5
Funny Games (Michael Haneke, 1997) 178

Ghosts (Christian Petzold, 2005) 57
The Great Dictator (Charlie Chaplin, 1940) 106

Hannah and Her Sisters (Woody Allen, 1986) 166n2
Hiroshima mon amour (Alain Resnais, 1959) 172–3
Hungarian Passport (Sandra Kogut, 2003) 90n4

Films index

Inner Security (Christian Petzold, 2000) 57
The Inquisitive Boots (Cecil Hepworth, 1905) 171
Irréversible (Gaspar Noé, 2002) 176–8, *177*, 181n18

Jabberwocky (Jan Svankmajer, 1971) 102–4, 106, 107
Japonaiserie (Gaston Velle, 1904) 169

Kapó (Gillo Pontecorvo, 1960) 79
Kino Eye (Dziga Vertov, 1925) 169

The Last Stop (Wanda Jakubowska, 1948) 79–80
Late Marriage (Dover Kosashvili, 2001) 35
Live Flesh (Pedro Almodóvar, 1997) 66
Long Is the Road (Herbert Fredersdorf and Marek Goldstein, 1948) 75

Man With a Movie Camera (Dziga Vertov, 1929) 89, 93, 97, 169–70, 180n7
Memento (Christopher Nolan, 2000) 14, 180n13
Mother Dao – the Turtle-like (Vincent Monnikendam, 1999) xx, 3, 109–18

Night and Fog (Alain Resnais, 1956) 79, 110

October (Sergei Eisenstein, 1928) 93, 170
Oedipus Rex (Pier Paolo Pasolini, 1967) 94
One Flew Over the Cuckoo's Nest (Milos Forman, 1975) 31
Or (Mon Tresor) (Keren Yedaya, 2004) xviii, 2, 35–45
Un'ora sola ti vorrei (Alina Marazzi, 2002) 21–34
Orphée (Jean Cocteau, 1950) 172
Our Children (Shimen Dzigan and Shaul Goskind, 1948) 74–5

Per Sempre (Alina Marazzi, 2005) 34
The Piano Teacher (Michael Haneke, 2001) 166n4, 178
Private Hungary (Péter Forgács, 1989–2005) 76, 83, 90n4
Punch and Judy (Jan Svankmajer, 1966) 102–3, 104–7

The Raftsmen (Judit Elek, 1989) 90n4
Rain Man (Barry Levinson, 1988) 166n2
Rocco and His Brothers (Luchino Visconti, 1960) 166n2

Scenes on Every Floor (Pathé, 1904) 171
Scenes from a Marriage (Ingmar Bergman, 1973) 175
Schindler's List (Steven Spielberg, 1993) 79, 90n2
Secrets of a Soul (Georg Wilhelm Pabst, 1926) 95
Shackleton's Legendary Antarctic Adventure (George Butler, 2000) 120
The Shadow of a Doubt (Alfred Hitchcock, 1943) 166n2
Shoah (Claude Lanzmann, 1985) 90n2
Somewhere in Europe (Géza Radványi, 1947) 77–9, 82
Sophie's Choice (Alan Pakula, 1982) 79
The Strike (Sergei Eisenstein, 1925) 170
Sunset Boulevard (Billy Wilder, 1950) 180n16
Sunshine (István Szabó, 1999) 82, 83, 90n4
Sweet Sixteen (Ken Loach, 2002) 36
The Swimming Pool (François Ozon, 2003) xix, 7, 145–8, 153–8

Talk to Her (Pedro Almodóvar, 2002) xix, 3, 65–72
Le Testament d'Orphée (Jean Cocteau, 1960) 172
That Obscure Object of Desire (Luis Buñuel, 1977) 100, 101n2
Train Arriving at the Station (Louis and Auguste Lumière, 1895) 168–9

Under the Sand (François Ozon, 2000) xix, 145–53, 158

Vertigo (Alfred Hitchcock, 1958) 61, 62–3

Wolfsburg (Christian Petzold, 2003) xix, 2, 56–64
Women on the Verge of a Nervous Breakdown (Pedro Almodóvar, 1988) 66

Index

Note: *italic* page numbers denote references to photographs.

abandonment 32, 141
Abraham, N. 13–15, 16
'afterwardsness' 117
ageing process 134, 135, 142, 147, 148–9
Alkabetz, Ronit 35, *40*, *43*
Allen, Woody 161, 166n2
Almodóvar, Pedro xix, 3, 66, 69, 71, 72
ambivalence 5
Amis, Martin 174, 180n10, n11
analysts xix–xx, 9, 46–7, 56; guilt 63; listening 65, 66
Andersson, Harriet 161, *163*
Andrée, August Salomon 119–20, 121–7, 128–9
animation 132–3, 136, 138
Anna O 44n8, 65, 70
anorexia 48, 49, 51, 52–3, 54
Anthelme, Robert 87
anti-heroes 77
anxiety: anorexia 52, 53; separation 51
après-coup xx, 54n1
art 106
Artaud, A. 94
associations 10
Atria, Benni 30
Auschwitz 74, 75, 79–80, 82–3, 86–8, 110
autobiographical narratives 76, 81, 86, 89
avant-garde 92, 110, 169, 171

Bach, S. 148, 150
bad object 38
Balázs, Béla 78, 79
Ballestra, Silvia 25
Barthes, Roland 93, 117

Bausch, Pina 68
Becker, Israel 75
Bellucci, Monica 176, *177*
Berardinelli, J. 161
Bergman, Ingmar 2, 161, 162, 164
Bergman, Nir 35–6
Berling, Charles 6, *15*
Berman, Emanuel xviii, 2, 35–45
Bettelheim, Bruno 148
body 47–8, 49, 50, 51–3
Bollas, Christopher 13, 19n8
Bouquet, Michel 7, *12*
Bowlby, John 1
Brancusi, Constantin 170
Breuer, Joseph 44n8, 65
Bruno, Giuliana 98–9
Buñuel, Luis xix, 3, 92, 95–6, 100, 172
Burr, Ty 7

Cámara, Javier 66, *67*, *68*, *71*
camera movement 37, 44n2
carnal knowledge 47
Carroll, Lewis 102
cars 58
Casar, Amira 11, *12*
Cassel, Vincent 176, *177*
castration xviii, xix, 96, 126
Catacchio, Antonello 26
Centre of Psychoanalysis, Milan 25, 31
Cescon, Michela 48–9, *48*, *53*
Chaplin, Charlie 106
Chasseguet-Smirgel, J. 50, 156
Chekhov, Anton 161
Chômet, Sylvain 132, 136

Index

Christie, Ian xx, 3, 168–81
cinematographic images 28
city cinema 92
Clair, René 171
Cocteau, Jean 170–2
Colarusso, C.A. 140
collective trauma 114
colonialism 110–13, 114, 115, 116
coma victims 66–72
communication: coma victims 68; Holocaust films 78; listening 65, 66; non-verbal 138–9
compilation films 109–18
Costantini, Maria Vittoria 3, 46–55
creativity 153, 156, 157
Cremer, Bruno 149
Crespi, Alberto 27
Czechoslovakia 76

Dali, Salvador 92, 172
Dance, Charles 154
Dante Alighieri 148
Dawson, Tom 7
De Mijolla, Alain 54n1
death 69, 71, 89–90; denial of 138, 148, 150, 151, 152; *The Flight of the Eagle* 126, 127, 128; midlife contemplation of 147; sexuality association with 164; *see also* loss
death instinct 127
découpage 96, 98, 100
'deep structures' xviii
defence mechanism 5
'deferred action' 116–17
Delbo, Charlotte 87
depression 32–3
depressive position 58
Derrida, Jacques 18, 20n14
desirability 145–6
destructiveness 58, 62, 63, 147, 153, 157
Diamond, Diana xix, 3, 145–59
discontinuity editing 97
dissociation 39
dreams 5, 8–9, 10; *Belleville Rendez-Vous* 133, 134, 136, 139; *Un Chien Andalou* 172; Svankmajer 102, 108
Dunne, J.W. 180n17
Dutch East Indies 3, 110–11, 116

Ebert, Roger 7
ego: failure in synthetic function 123; fantasy 9; incorporation 14; introjection 16; melancholia 13; splitting 148, 150, 152; *see also* self
ego ideal 14, 37, 52

Eisenstein, Sergei 44n6, 80, 92–3, 95, 170, 180n8
Elek, Judit 90n4
Eluard, Paul 105–6
emotions 46, 47
empathy 58, 64
Erewhon 28
Erikson, E. 137
Eros 48
eroticism 157, 164–5
expressionism 92
Ezouz, Sari 37, 43, 44n4

Fairbairn, W.R.D. 38
fairy tales 148
'false self' 32
fantasy 7, 8–9, 10, 16, 17; dominant cultural 130; idealized 142, 150; narcissistic 120, 121–8; parental reunion 139, 141; perverse 50, 156; regenerative 143; rescue 36, 71; return to mother's womb 70; sadomasochistic 140; single body 51–2; *see also* phantasy
Feldman, Shoshana 80
femininity 133
feminism 43, 44n8
Ferzetti, Fabio 27
fetishism 50, 154; Buñuel 100; cars 58; lace 92, 93, 97–8; Svankmajer 106
film shots 152–3
flashbacks 28, 66, 164, 174, 180n16
Flores, Rosario 66, *68*
Fontaine, Anne 2, 6–8, 14–15, 16, 17–18
Forgás, Péter 76, 83–5, 90n4
Fraenkel, Knut 120, 122, 124, 125, 126, 127
Fredersdorf, Herbert 75
free associations 65, 66, 84, 102
Freiss, Stéphane 175, *176*
Freud, Anna 160
Freud, Sigmund: analyst's state of listening 66; Anna O 44n8, 65; body 47; dreams 108, 134; gifted individuals 156; magic and omnipotence 178; Marx tension with 92; melancholia 13; mourning 4, 9–10, 12, 17, 18; *Nachtraglichkeit* xx, 116; Svankmajer 102; trauma 114; *see also* psychoanalysis
Friedlander, Saul 74
Fürmann, Benno *59*

Gabbard, Glen O. xvii–xxi
Garrone, Matteo 3, 47–8, 53
gaze xviii, xix, 145, 146; admiring 122, 123,

186

Index

124; colonial power 115; maternal 23, 125; midlife issues 147
Goisis, Pietro Roberto 2, 21–34
Goldstein, Marek 75
Golinelli, Paola 46–55
Grandinetti, Mario 66, *68*
grandiosity 3, 120, 123, 125
grandparenthood 135, 137–8
Gróo, Diana 76, 90n4
Guillon, Stephane 7
guilt: Holocaust victims 89; masochism 51; orphans 141; survivor 38; *Wolfsburg* 58, 59, 60–1, 62, 63–4

Hamlet 6, 10–11, 13, 19n3, n4, 5, n9, n11
Haneke, Michael 166n4, 178
Hartmann, Geoffrey 74
hate 147, 157
Helenowek Colony 75
helplessness 114–15
Hepworth, Cecil 170
hermeneutics 117
history 110, 113–14, 115, 117, 118
Hitchcock, Alfred 61, 62, 166n2
Hitler, Adolf 82, 86, 173, 174
Hodge, Patricia 174
Hoepli, Ulrico 21
Holocaust 3, 73–91
home movies: Holocaust 84; *Un'ora sola ti vorrei* 21–34
homoeroticism 70, 124, 155
Hungary 74, 76, 78–9, 81, 82, 83–5, 86

idealization 142, 150, 152, 157
identification: analysts 47; Holocaust victims 89; melancholia 13; with mother 26–7, 33, 41; *see also* projective identification
identity, Jewish 73, 74, 76, 82
imagination 86, 106
imagined characters 7
imago 17
immortality 125, 129, 149
incorporation 13–14, 16, 18
indigenous people 111–13, 115, 117
individuation 141
intercontextuality 57, 63
internalization 38, 141, 142
intimacy 50–1
introjection 13, 14, 16, 18
Irons, Jeremy 174
Isaacs, Susan 9
Ivgi, Dana 35–6, *37, 40, 43*

Jakubowska, Wanda 79, 80

Jancsó, Miklós 90n4
Jaques, Eliot 147
Jews 73–7, 79, 82, 83–5, 86–8, 89
Jones, David 174–5
Jones, E. 19n4, n5, n9

Kertész, Imre 85, 86, 88
keyhole device 171
Kézdi-Kovacs, Zsolt 82
Khan, Masud 50, 51
kineticism 138
Kingsley, Ben 175
Klein, Melanie 58
Kleinian theory 58, 63
Klimov, Elem 173
Kline, T. Jefferson 2, 6–20
Kogut, Sandra 90n4
Koltai, Lajos 90n5
Kosashvili, Dover 35
Kristeva, Julia 15, 19n12
Kulb, Karl-George 75

Lacan, Jacques xviii, 117–18
LaCapra, Dominick 15, 17, 18
lace 92–4, 97–8, 99–100
Laing, R.D. 11
Langer, Lawrence L. 74
Lanzmann, Claude 90n2
Laplanche, Jean 116–17
Léger, Fernand 171
Levi, Primo 87
Levinson, Barry 166n2
Leyda, Jay 110
libido 9, 13
Lichtenstein, D. 69
Liebman, Stuart 80
loneliness 32, 120
loss xvii, 1–4, 157; absent fathers 81–2; of child 164; denial of 148, 149, 150–1; developmental processes 133, 134–5, 136–7; Holocaust 89–90; incorporation 13–14, 16; indigenous people 111–12; midlife 147, 148, 149; of mother 22, 26–7, 33, 164; multiple 70–1; *see also* death; mourning
love 17, 70, 122, 125, 147, 157
Lumière brothers 4, 168

McDougall, J. 51
Makk, Károly 78
Marazzi, Alina 2, 21–3, 24–5, 26–9, 30–1, 33–4
Mareuil, Simone *95*
Máriassy, Felix 78

Index

Marx, Karl 92
masculinity 133, 140
masochism 51, 165
masturbation 145, 150
Matuszewski, Boleslaw 109
Meisel, Edmund 170
melancholia 13, 14, 18; developmental processes 133; murderous 17
memory 30, 33, 47; compilation films 110; 'deferred action' 116–17; Holocaust 74, 76, 83, 89; memorials 77–8
Metz, Christian xviii
'mid-mourning' 18, 20n14
midlife xix, 127, 145–59
Miller, J. Hillis 11, 19n6
mise-en-abyme 98, 100
mise-en-scène 94
Mitchel, Elvis 7
Mitchell, J. 160–1
Monastyrsjki, Boros 80
Monnikendam, Vincent 110–11
montage 44n6, 98, 111
Morricone, Ennio 86
mother: body of 47; death of 21–2, 26–7; maternal gaze 23, 125; maternal inaccessibility 32; *Or* 36–43; single body fantasy 51; *see also* parents
mother-infant bond 47, 140, 141
mourning xvii, 4, 8, 9–10, 18; departed parents 12; developmental processes 133, 134–5; failed 148, 150, 152, 153; Holocaust 83; incorporation 14; midlife 147; pathological 150; substitution of lost object 17; *see also* loss
Mulvey, Laura xviii, xx, 3, 13, 109–18
Murphy, Dudley 170
music 29–30, 84, 125, 138
mutilation 94–6

Nachtraglichkeit xx, 3, 116, 117
narcissism: *The Flight of the Eagle* xix, 120, 121–8, 129, 130; idealized fantasy 142, 150; melancholia 13; primary needs 140
Nature 107–8
neo-realism 78, 79
neurosis 156
Nichols, Mike 47
Noé, Gaspar 175–6
Nolot, Jacques 149
non-verbal communication 138–9
nostalgia 27, 34
nudity 37

object-perspective 56

Oedipal complex 13, 14, 160
Oedipal conflict 5, 17; maternal inaccessibility 32; orphans 141; unresolved 155–6, 162
omnipotence 121, 176, 179
orality 140
the Other 56, 60, 61, 62, 63
Ozon, François 3, 145–50, 152–3, 154–8, 174, 175

Pabst, Georg Wilhelm 95
Pakula, Alan J. 79
Pappenheim, Bertha 44n8
parents: internalization of bad aspects 38; loss of 134, 136–7; *see also* mother
Pasolini, Pier Paolo 94
Pathé 170
persecutory object 52, 53, 54
perversion: failed mourning 148, 150, 152; *First Love* 50, 51; *Swimming Pool* 154, 155–6, 157, 158; *Talk to Her* 69
Pető, György 84
Petzold, Christian xix, 2, 57, 62, 63
phallic images 121–2, 123
phantasy 9, 13; *see also* fantasy
photographic images 114, 128–9
Picabia, Francis 171
Pinter, Harold 174, 175
Plato 4
playfulness 179
Plenker, F.P. 58, 63
Poland 75–6
politics 92, 110
Pontalis, Jean-Baptiste 116–17
Pontecorvo, Gillo 79
Portuges, Catherine 3, 73–91
power 115–16
powerlessness 50, 115, 128, 129
primal scene xviii, 94, 96, 100, 155, 156
primary process 10
projective identification 135
prostitution 35, 38–9, 40–3, 44n4, n5, n7, n8
psychiatric illness 21, 31–3
psycho-drama 95
psychoanalysis xvii, xviii, 46–7, 54, 65, 162–3; avant-garde filmmaking 92; Central European 83; compilation films 110, 116; cult behaviour 108; history comparison 113–14; Holocaust films 78, 80; inner/outer reality 60; key themes 5; Kleinian 58, 63; Marazzi on 30–1; methodological parallels with cinema 33, 66, 84; prostitution 44n5; reverse motion

Index

179; siblings 160; suture concept 94, 96; *see also* analysts; Freud, Sigmund
psychosis 9
Pygmalion 11, 19n6, 147

'quasi-person' concept xix, 56, 57

Racalbuto, A. 47
Raczymow, Henri 88
Radványi, Géza 79
Rampling, Charlotte xix, 146–7, *146*, 149, 152, 153, *155*
rape 69, 176–7
realism 78, 169, 179
reality testing 10
Régnier, Natacha 6, *15*
Reik, Theodor 66
reparation 58, 60, 61, 62–3, 64, 157
representation 46
repression 14, 17, 60, 61, 134–5, 156
Resnais, Alain 79, 110, 172, 173
resurrection 71–2
reverse motion xx, 168–9, 170, 172, 173–4, 178–9
reverse narration 174–8, 179
Ricciardi, Alicia 9–10, 20n14
Rossi, Elena 28
Rothberg, Michael 80
Russian Revolution 170

Sabbadini, Andrea xvii, xix, xx, 1–5, 65–72, 160–6
Sacks, Oliver 70
sadism 13, 51, 52, 115
sadomasochism 140, 154
Sagnier, Ludivine *146*, 154
St. Augustine 168
Santner, Erik 18, 19n12
satire 105
Schiffer, Pál 82
Schneider, Gerda 79
Schneider, Gerhard xix–xx, 56
Second World War 3, 73–91, 173–4
self: bad parts 60, 63; death of the 121; 'false' 32; ideal 142, 150; narcissistic dilemma 126, 127–8; splitting 50; subjective 89; *see also* ego
self-analysis 33, 56, 66
self-hate 40
self-referentiality 114
separation 38, 50, 121, 137; anxiety 51; failure of mourning 150; narcissistic dilemma 126
sexuality 102, 141; cars 58; death association

with 164; *The Flight of the Eagle* 122; *Or* 39, 41, 42; *Swimming Pool* 155, 156
Shakespeare, William 1, 6
shame 14, 89, 150
Shine, C. 148
Shklovsky, Viktor 170, 180n9
Shub, Esther 110, 111
siblings 160–6
Silverman, K. 101n1
Silverstone, J. 161
Simon, J. 129
Siodmak, Robert 166n2
Sklarew, Bruce 162
slow motion 171, 172
social coldness 57, 58, 63, 64
Sorrentini, Barbara 30
sounds 30, 140
speech 111
Spielberg, Steven 79, 90n2
splitting 38, 50, 54, 148, 150, 152
Stalin, Josef 82
Stein, Alexander 2, 132–44
Steiner, J. 150–1
Sterne, Lawrence 170, 180n9
Stevens, George 79
Stevenson, Robert Louis 174, 180n12
Stoppard, Tom xviii
Strindberg, Nils 120, 124, 126–7, 128
subject-perspective 56
subjectivity 73, 76, 77, 85, 89
suicide 21, 26, 71
Suleiman, Susan 88
Sundman, Per Olof 129
superego 52, 63, 121
surrealism 92, 102, 103, 105–6, 133
survivor guilt 38
suture 94, 96, 98
Svankmajer, Jan 102–8
Sylwan, Kari 161, *162*
Szabó, István 81, 82–3, 90n4
Szemzö, Tibor 84

tableaux 104, 171
Taylor Robinson, Helen 3, 102–8
Tedeschi, Valeria Bruni 175, *176*
therapeutic relationship 66
therapy 31
Thulin, Ingrid 161, *162*
time xx, 3, 28, 34, 168–81; *Belleville Rendez-Vous* 133, 135, 136, 138, 139–40; compilation films 109–10, 114, 116; *The Flight of the Eagle* 122; metaphors 117–18
Torok, M. 13–15, 16

189

Index

totems 106, 107
transference 84, 89
trauma: cinematic recreation of xvii; colonization 112, 113, 114, 115; compilation films 110; Holocaust 74, 80, 83, 87, 88; lace 97, 98; primary object loss 134; psychoanalytic theory of 116; time confusion 117
traumatism 100
Trevisan, Vitaliano *48*, 49, *53*
Tristram Shandy 170, 180n9
Troell, Jan xix, 119, 128, 129
Truffaut, François 26, 166n2

Ullmann, Liv 161, *162*, 164
unconscious 102, 110, 118

Veloso, Caetano 68
Vermeer, Jan 3, 97, 98–9, 100
Vertov, Dziga 89, 92–3, 169–70, 180n7
Visconti, Luchino 166n2
voyeurism xviii–xix, 29, 44n2, 98, 177; power relations 115; *Swimming Pool* 148, 154, 155, 156

Watling, Leonor 66, *67*, *68*
Webber, Andrew xviii–xix, 3, 92–101
Weinstein, Lissa xix, 3, 119–31
Wiesel, Elie 80
Wigoder, Shimshon xviii, 2, 35–45
Wilder, Billy 180n15, n16
Williams, Linda 96
window scenes 92–3, 97
Winnicott, D.W. 179
Wolff, E. 123
women xviii, 133, 147
Woolf, Virginia 151, 169
Wurmser, Leon 61

Yedeya, Keren 35, 43, 44n4
Young-Breuhl, E. 150

Zimetbaum, Mala 80
Zwiebel, Ralf xix–xx, 2, 56–64